INFORMIX® Press

OPTIMIZING INFORMIX APPLICATIONS

Robert D. Schneider

For book and bookstore information

http://www.prenhall.com
gopher to gopher.prenhall.com

PRENTICE HALL P T R UPPER SADDLE RIVER, NJ 07458

Library of Congress Cataloging-in-Publication Data

Schneider, Robert D.
Optimizing INFORMIX applications / Robert D. Schneider
p. cm.
Includes index.
ISBN 0–13–149238–1
1. Relational databases. 2. Informix-SQL. 3. INFORMIX-4GL
(Computer program language) I. Title.
QA76.9.D3S297 1995
005.75'65—dc20
95–3656
CIP

Prentice-Hall, Inc.
A Simon & Schuster Company
Upper Saddle River, NJ 07458

Informix Press
Informix Software, Inc.
4100 Bohannon Drive
Menlo Park, CA 94025

Cover design: *Jeannette Jacobs*
Composition: *Mary Strunk, Kent Dannehl*
Acquisitions editor: *Mark L. Taub*
Manufacturing manager: *Alexis R. Heydt*

Manager, Informix Press: *Todd Katz*

The publisher offers discounts on this book when ordered in bulk quantities. For more information, contact: Corporate Sales Department, Prentice Hall PTR, One Lake Street, Upper Saddle River, NJ 07458
Phone: 800-382-3419, Fax: 201-236-7141, e-mail: corpsales@prenhall.com

Printed in the United States of America
10 9 8 7 6 5 4 3 2 1

ISBN 0–13–149238-1

Prentice-Hall International (UK) Limited, *London*
Prentice-Hall of Australia Pty. Limited, *Sydney*
Prentice-Hall Canada Inc., *Toronto*
Prentice-Hall Hispanoamericana, S.A., *Mexico*
Prentice-Hall of India Private Limited, *New Delhi*
Prentice-Hall of Japan, Inc., *Tokyo*
Simon & Schuster Asia Pte. Ltd., *Singapore*
Editora Prentice-Hall do Brasil, Ltda., *Rio de Janeiro*

Contents

Dedication

In memory of my father, Jerome P. Schneider, Esq.

Acknowledgements

The author is deeply grateful to the following people for their invaluable assistance in producing this book: Stewart Robinson and Tom Houston for technical and content review; Mary Strunk and Kent Dannehl for composition; Joanne Eglash for copy editing; Jane Bonnell for production; Mark Taub for project management; Lynn Z. Schneider for organization and encouragement; and Nicole Sierra Schneider for general inspiration.

Chapter 1
About This Book

INTENDED AUDIENCE

Informix tools and engines let you quickly build powerful and reliable database applications. This alone is often not enough; users also demand high performance. It takes skill and experience to produce such high-quality systems, but many Information Systems (IS) professionals don't have the time to learn the intricacies of Informix products. *Optimizing Informix Applications* gives you the insight you need to produce the fast database applications your users want.

Optimizing Informix Applications is a tool for application developers, database administrators, systems analysts, and system administrators who are interested in designing, developing, maintaining, and administering efficient applications that use Informix database engines and tools.

To get the most out of this book, programmers and analysts should be comfortable with:

- Basic Structured Query Language (SQL).
- A procedural programming language, such as C, COBOL, or 4GL.

Database administrators should understand:

- Relational database design concepts.
- Intermediate or advanced SQL.
- Informix engine architecture.

System administrators should understand:

- Informix engine architecture.
- The UNIX operating system at an intermediate level.

BENEFITS OF USING THIS BOOK

Optimizing Informix Applications provides you with these benefits:

- **Enhanced productivity.** It's hard for a user to be productive if a typical query takes three minutes to return data. End-of-week reports that take 36 hours to run generally don't lead to a more robust bottom line, either. In this book, we cite dozens of specific changes you can make to your applications and systems to upgrade your organization's productivity.
- **Increased application reliability.** Generally, an inefficient application is an unreliable application. At the very least, slow systems are perceived as being less reliable than fast systems. When you increase a system's speed, you will improve its reliability.

- **Reduced hardware expenditures.** Few organizations can afford to continually upgrade their hardware environments to get better performance. Therefore, they expect their IS staff to do more with less. You can use the suggestions in this book to squeeze extra speed out of your existing hardware.
- **Simpler applications**. In many cases, the simplest solution is the fastest solution. You will find many tips in this book to help you increase a system's speed while reducing its complexity.
- **More satisfied users.** In the past, most users were mainly concerned with whether a system worked; performance wasn't a major consideration. Today's users are more sophisticated than ever, and view system speed as the crucial element. Many organizations have learned this painful lesson the hard way, when users don't approve a slow system, no matter how well-designed.

How to Use This Book

This book is divided into five major sections:

1. **Introduction.** In this chapter, we discuss how you can best use this book, as well as how to set up the most effective optimization test environment.
2. **Creating a Well-Designed Database.** Your entire application relies on an efficient database design. In this chapter, we review some of the most important facets of a good database design.
3. **Optimizing Application Code.** This chapter describes how to write efficient database application code, using a variety of programming languages.
4. **Tuning the Database Engine.** Even the most efficient application can be sluggish if the underlying database engine is tuned incorrectly. In this chapter, we review many techniques you can use to make your database engine run as rapidly as possible.
5. **Case Studies.** This chapter contains five case studies. Each case study features several interrelated problems.

You don't need to read this book from cover to cover. To get the most benefit from our suggestions, review only those sections that apply to your particular situation. For example, if you are running a distributed ESQL/C application that uses the OnLine engine, you really don't need to spend much time reading the sections about 4GL or Informix-SE. However, there are several sections that deserve your attention, regardless of your situation. These include:

- **Setting Up an Optimization Test Environment.** It is a big mistake to rush in and start making performance enhancement changes to your system without first observing a few very important details. This section covers these details.

- **General Tips.** This section contains numerous suggestions that can help you develop better, faster applications, no matter what engine or tools you use.
- **Relational Database Design Concepts.** A good database design is the foundation of a system that performs well. This section teaches you how to implement the relational model when you design a database. It also covers specific situations where the relational model is not appropriate.
- **Indexing Strategies.** The wrong indexing strategy can wreck an otherwise perfect database design. We list some straightforward indexing techniques you can use to dramatically raise your system's throughput.
- **SQL Tips.** Without SQL, you can't access data. In this section, we cite several ideas you can incorporate to improve your SQL statements.
- **Case Studies.** This chapter contains a number of multi-faceted case studies. Spend some time reviewing them: chances are, you may already have experienced some of the problems we illustrate.

How to Use the Examples

You'll find numerous examples in each chapter, which we have made as clear and concise as possible. This will help you implement our suggestions quickly. Because this book is intended as a reference, the examples in one chapter do not rely on another. This will help you concentrate on specific problems and solutions. Keep in mind that while the examples in this book may not exactly match your database design, application software, and/or engine configuration, you can still apply them to your specific problems.

Setting Up an Optimization Test Environment

When faced with a sluggishly performing application, or an engine that appears out of tune, most administrators and programmers are eager to roll up their sleeves, and begin the optimizing process. Unfortunately, there are a number of potentially tiresome, yet very important steps that you must first take before you begin the "real work" of tuning. If you don't set up a stable, accurate test environment, you face the very real risk of making inaccurate judgments about the root cause(s) of your system's current woeful performance. You might then use these incorrect assumptions as the base of an entire action plan, only to later learn that your original hypotheses were wrong.

In this section, we address these important issues. We've divided the section into three major parts. The first deals with the agenda you should cover before you even begin your testing efforts. This includes ensuring that the right hardware, operating system, database, and application software are in place. In addition, we discuss some organizational issues that you should address immediately at the start of the optimization.

Next, we spell out some methods that you can use to help point the way while your testing is going on. While the most successful system testers and tuners rely heavily on their test plan to guide them during this process, they also choose the right blend of discipline and creativity when following up on new, promising performance leads.

Finally, we illustrate how you can translate the knowledge that you gained during testing process into real performance improvements.

While this section is primarily designed for people tuning existing systems and applications, you can still apply these suggestions if you're doing new development. In fact, one way to help guarantee a production system that meets your standards is to treat good performance as one of the most important development deliverables.

Steps to follow before testing

HARDWARE CONSIDERATIONS

Your hardware environment really consists of a number of different components, each of which plays a meaningful role in your overall performance picture. Let's illustrate each of these components in more detail:

- **CPU.** Ideally, both your production and test environment have similar CPU speeds and capacities. If not, you'll always have to wonder which numbers you should believe: those from the production system, or those from the test system. The same problem often arises at multi-processor sites, where the production machine may have 12 CPUs, while the test machine has one. This really becomes a problem if you're tuning the OnLine engine, especially if you're using OnLine 6.00 or newer.
- **Memory.** It's crucial that your test platform have the same amount of memory as your production system. Slow-running applications can experience a "miracle cure" when you add a few megabytes of memory to the hardware. If your test and production systems have vastly different memory configurations, be careful before you draw conclusions from your research.
- **Disk drives.** If your production system uses older, slower disk drives, and your test system has the speed benefits of the newest generation data storage devices, you're bound to come to some erroneous conclusions about each machine's capacity and response. If you're attempting to test your OnLine engine's response, try to match the production machine's disk configuration when you set up your test machine. Disk sizing and layout can have a big impact on engine throughput; you'll get more realistic results if you're working with a real-life disk profile.
- **Connections (local and network).** If your production application uses a distributed database or works in a client/server environment, it's important that you configure your testing platform to accurately reflect these connections.

Network and client/server overhead can be substantial; if you omit these factors from your testing, you might not get completely accurate performance information.

Ideally, your test system and production system are carbon copies of each other. In reality, however, most administrators and developers are lucky even to have a test machine; few organizations can afford to have a production caliber machine sitting idle. If this is the case in your organization, try to use the production machine for your tests whenever possible. This may mean that you only have access to the equipment after hours, or on weekends. See the "Operational considerations" section of this chapter for more information about gaining access to the production system for testing.

SOFTWARE CONSIDERATIONS

Once you've set up a testing system, your next challenge is to obtain the right software and correctly configure it. In this section, we divide the software into the following elements:

- **Operating system.** It's important that your optimizing platform have the same operating system configuration as your production system. Slight differences in UNIX kernel parameters can cause wide disparities in performance; these differences might skew your findings. If you don't know how to check your kernel parameters, ask your system administrator to check them for you. If possible, try to work with identical kernel parameters.
- **Database and tools.** Try to ensure that you've installed the same versions of your production system's database server and tools in your test environment. This is especially important if you're examining a client/server system, using the I-STAR or I-NET connectivity products. Even if you don't use any client/server features, remember that Informix continually enhances the query optimizer. You can expect your performance statistics to vary, depending on which version of the database engine you're using.
- **Application.** One way to guarantee an unpleasant optimizing experience is to work with different versions of your application on the development, production, and test machines. Sometimes, a one-line difference in a program can have a tremendous influence on performance. Insist on testing the same version of application software that the users are complaining about. Otherwise, you may (rightly) come to the conclusion that there is no performance problem: when you ran your version of the application, it performed perfectly.

DATA CONSIDERATIONS

After you have set up your hardware and software environment, the next topic to consider is the data that you plan to use during your testing. Ideally, your test database should exactly match the database that's currently in development or production. This means having the same number of tables, indexes, views, stored procedures, and triggers under the testing environment as you do on the production environment.

One common mistake that administrators and developers make when setting up a test database is using an undersized data set. If you don't make your test database big enough, it's possible that you might get an incorrect picture of true system performance. Even the most poorly written query may perform well on a tiny database, whether or not the underlying database design is good.

If possible, use an exact copy of your production database on your test platform. The easiest way to obtain a full copy of a database is to use the 'dbexport' command on the production system, followed by the 'dbimport' command on the test system. If your production database is too large, or if your test system doesn't have enough storage space, it's still important that you create a test database with the same number of tables, indexes, views, and stored procedures. You can use the 'dbschema' utility on the production database to obtain the SQL necessary to create a duplicate test database. If you're testing a query that only works with two moderate-sized tables from your production database, you only need to copy the contents of those two tables from the production system to the test system.

Once you've set up your testing database, and filled it with the correct amount of data, don't forget to run UPDATE STATISTICS with the same options that you chose for your production database.

SETTING UP A TEST PLAN

It's not absolutely essential that you write a test plan prior to beginning your experiments. However, a well-designed test plan can make your tasks much easier by providing a clear sense of direction. This is especially important if you have a multi-person test team. Without a plan, team members might duplicate each other's work, and potentially damage the integrity of your test results. You can also use your test plan to form the basis of your summary report once you finish your examinations.

You don't need to spend an inordinate amount of time on your plan; it should simply define, at a high level, which procedures you expect to follow when conducting your evaluations, along with any assistance you might need from other users or developers.

For example, look at the following set of entries from a sample test plan:

Example 1.1 Test Plan:

```
...
...
...
Test #:          17
Date:            03/09/95
Start time:      08:00
```

Finish time:	11:00
Platform:	Production
Action:	Experiment with adding/altering indexes on the call_tracking table.
Special needs:	May need to briefly lock tables when adding/altering indexes.
Team members:	Nicole - Primary Jed - Assist Li - Assist
Test status:	<unfinished>
Test results:	<unfinished>

Test #:	18
Date:	03/09/95
Start time:	12:15
Finish time:	16:30
Platform:	Production
Action:	Raise number of shared memory buffers to test OnLine engine performance. Monitor engine statistics for balance of day.
Special needs:	Need to restart OnLine - will result in approx. 2 minutes database downtime.
Team members:	Lynn - Primary Karl - Assist
Test status:	<unfinished>
Test results:	<unfinished>

Test #:	19
Date:	03/10/95
Start time:	08:00
Finish time:	17:30
Platform:	Development
Action	Alter cc01288.ec, cc03432.ec programs to use dirty read isolation levels instead of current cursor stability isolation. Monitor application response times before & after modification.
Special needs:	None
Team members:	Miguel - Primary Lynn - Assist
Test status:	<unfinished>
Test results:	<unfinished>

Test #:	20
Date:	03/11/95
Start time:	08:00
Finish time:	17:30
Platform:	Production

Action:	If test #19 improves performance, move the cc01288 and cc03432 programs into production.
Special needs:	Need user input regarding response times.
Team members:	Miguel - Primary Meyer - Assist Sandra - Assist
Test status:	<unfinished>
Test results:	<unfinished>

...
...
...

You could even store your test plan in the database, and then use SQL to create helpful queries.

Operational considerations

After you've finished setting up your hardware, software, and database, and have designed a good test plan, you face perhaps your biggest challenge: obtaining operational support for your tuning efforts.

Operational issues are often the most frustrating part of optimizing an application. Management may be unwilling to allow you full or partial access to the resources that you need. Users are often reluctant to help isolate a performance problem, even though they have the most to gain from any discoveries that you make. The designers and/or developers of the application may be nervous about what your investigation might uncover.

Unfortunately, you can only get a true picture of what is really happening on the system by requesting cooperation from management, users, and developers. Before you begin your experiments, you have every right to ask for each of the following:

- **System availability**. If you don't have a dedicated test platform, you'll have to run your experiments on the production system. This probably means you'll be working some late nights or weekends, but it's better than having no system at all. If management is reluctant to grant access to you, point out that you'll be able to solve their performance problems much faster if you can work on the platform where the response delays are occurring.
- **User input and support.** You should try to make your tuning experiments as scientific as possible. If users are complaining about response time, it's reasonable for you to ask them to cite specific examples. It's even better if you can sit by their side as they work. You will have a much better chance to diagnose a problem if you observe it while it happens, instead of hearing about it three days later. Once you've investigated and (hopefully) corrected the problem, you still need feedback and assistance from your user community. Otherwise, you may never truly know if your enhancements helped.

- **IS staff support.** Unless you're the only person in the IS department, chances are you'll need to work with your peers when optimizing new or existing applications. If you're an administrator, you need good rapport with the programmers and analysts who designed the system. If you're a programmer or an analyst, you need the cooperation of the database administrator. Unfortunately, a large proportion of tuning exercises become mired in politics and finger-pointing. Therefore, whatever your job responsibility, it's important that you conduct your investigation and present your suggestions with sensitivity and tact. (Almost) no one sets out to design a deliberately slow application or database. In addition, a well-designed application can slow down over time under the weight of increased volume and altered requirements. Remember that there are many ways to solve design challenges; the decisions that your peers made during the design process may have been, at that time, the right ones to meet the requirements. Few people find non-constructive criticism enjoyable; keep this in mind as you proceed with your work.

Steps to follow during testing

DISCIPLINE VERSUS CREATIVITY

What should you do if, during testing, you discover a completely new and potentially exciting path that you feel bears further investigation? Do you abandon your carefully thought-out tuning strategies? Do you merely write down your idea and get back to the original plan? What if you realize that your plan doesn't really meet your needs?

The most practical answer to all of the above questions is to remain flexible while you conduct your tuning exercises. Don't be afraid to yield to your creative impulses; sometimes the most promising optimizing leads appear out of nowhere. You should never allow an idea to escape because you were too busy to write it down.

On the other hand, don't discard your testing plan just because it's now partially obsolete. Instead, why not incorporate your new ideas into the existing plan? For example, using the example from earlier in this chapter, suppose that you've just run test 19:

Example 1.2

Test #:	19
Date:	03/10/95
Start time:	08:00
Finish time:	17:30
Platform:	Development

Action:	Alter cc01288.ec, cc03432.ec programs to use dirty read isolation levels instead of current cursor stability isolation. Monitor application response times before & after modification.
Special needs	None
Team members:	Miguel - Primary Lynn - Assist
Test status:	COMPLETED
Test results:	Yielded no performance gain, but we discovered an indexing problem. See test 19.1.

You learned that the problem with the two ESQL/C programs wasn't the isolation levels, as you had originally thought. Instead, you realized that each program used an ORDER BY clause in several SELECT statements. By reviewing the output from SET EXPLAIN, you discovered that there was no index on the columns listed in the ORDER BY clause. Once you added an index, each program ran in one-fifth of its original time. How can you record this information? One way is to add a new test that reflects the results of your additional test:

Example 1.3

Test #:	19.1
Date:	03/10/95
Start time:	08:00
Finish time:	17:30
Platform:	Development
Action:	Place a composite index on the territory_number and zip_code fields in the 'leads' table. Test impact on cc01288 and cc03432 programs. See test 19 for original plan.
Special needs:	None
Team members:	Miguel - Primary Lynn - Assist
Test status:	COMPLETED
Test results:	cc01288 and cc03432 both ran much faster.

This approach lets you follow your creative ideas, without straying from a disciplined methodology.

Steps to follow after testing

FORMAL ASSESSMENT

Once you've finished your testing and (hopefully) confirmed your hypotheses, it's time to formally document your findings. Unfortunately, this is true even if you learn that every one of your hypotheses was completely wrong. It's important that you commit your conclusions to paper for several reasons:

- **Better communication.** If you enlisted the support of other people during the optimization process, it's only fair that you provide them with the results of your examination. You could do this verbally, but you'll reduce the potential for confusion and misunderstanding by writing the results. If your recommendations include database, engine configuration, or application modifications, you definitely need to put them in writing, if you expect anyone to take them seriously and implement the changes. Even if you didn't need the help of any users or developers, or don't recommend any alterations, chances are that your management will want to know what you learned.
- **Future testing.** Unless this round of testing solved every performance issue that you faced, chances are that you'll need to re-test and re-tune your applications and environment at some point in the future. In fact, even if you eliminated every problem, it's still a good idea to periodically monitor your system's response. You'll find written documentation of earlier test plans and results to be a very useful tool when faced with subsequent assessments.
- **Assisting new personnel.** Current turnover rates virtually guarantee that you'll need to explain your testing methodologies and procedures to a new hire at some point in the future. By documenting your findings now, you can help reduce the amount of time that you'll be obligated to spend during future orientations, as well as increasing the accuracy of your presentations.

DETERMINING THE NEXT STEP

Even if you feel that you've located every performance bottleneck, it's important not to rush in and immediately make widespread changes after you finish your tuning experiments. Instead, consider applying one change at a time. After you apply each modification, run some simple performance tests to see what effect your change had on throughput.

For example, suppose that you learn, through your experiments, that your system is hampered by three major performance impediments:

1. Not enough shared memory buffers
2. Unnecessarily high levels of isolation
3. Insufficient indexing

How should you proceed in this case? Generally, it's a good idea to implement the simplest alterations first. It's also wise to make one change at a time. By only modifying one variable each time, you stand a better chance of learning which variations had the most impact.

Regardless of which alteration you implement, always remember to keep a copy of the original code, database structure, or engine configuration. In the above example, the shared memory buffers problem is easiest to address: it requires no code or database modifications, and you need only briefly bring OnLine down for the new buffers parameter to take effect. Once you raise the number of shared memory buffers, your next step should be to monitor performance to see what effect your change had. Try to make your evaluations as scientifically as possible, but don't be afraid to go back to your users and get their opinions as well.

Once you've obtained some updated throughput statistics, your next step is to evaluate whether or not your enhancement was helpful. If it wasn't, or if the improvements weren't substantial enough, return the system to its original state. If it was, leave it in place, and move on to the next modification.

Continue following this cycle until you've investigated each performance enhancement. When you have finished, you should have a better performing system.

Chapter 2
Creating a Well-Designed Database

INTRODUCTION

Whether you are designing a new system from scratch, or maintaining one that has been in production for years, your database design is one area that should receive special attention. In this chapter, we cover several topics that fall under the heading of database design.

In the first section, we examine a number of items that interest database designers and systems analysts during the design process. These include:

- Data normalization, along with the three normal forms.
- Situations where full normalization may not be appropriate.
- Constraints and referential integrity.

A good indexing strategy can help even the most badly designed database perform acceptably; a bad indexing strategy can ruin the response of even the most efficient database design. With that in mind, our next section reviews all facets of indexing, from determining if your existing indexes are sufficient through specific situations that require index modification.

The OnLine engine supports several additional features that aren't present in SE, such as the BLOB and VARCHAR data types. The next section discusses these added capabilities, along with the differences between OnLine row IDs and SE row IDs.

Finally, we'll look at the Informix optimizer. This includes the mechanisms the optimizer uses to process queries. We'll also learn how to tell what the optimizer is doing, and how we can "help" it reach the right conclusions. Beginning with OnLine and SE, version 6.0 and newer, the optimizer is even more configurable than before, so we'll spend some time learning about these new enhancements.

RELATIONAL DATABASE DESIGN CONCEPTS

Your database design is the most important factor in determining the kind of performance you can expect from your application. Many applications that benefit from well-written programs and well-thought-out procedures still collapse under the weight of a bad relational database design. On the other hand, a good database design doesn't always guarantee good system performance, and a bad database design doesn't always ensure poor performance. Even with those caveats in mind, you should still strive to design your databases as efficiently as possible.

A full exploration of relational database design would take up an entire book. In fact, there are many excellent books on this topic. In this chapter, we take a more streamlined approach to this subject, focusing on normalization and the three normal forms. We'll also discuss situations where you should back away from full normalization. Finally, we'll explore constraints, and how they can help simplify and speed up your applications.

If you want more information on normalization in particular, see James Martin's *Managing the Database Environment.*

Normalization

Normalization, as defined by James Martin, is actually a set of criteria that can be used as a guideline in designing a relational database. In this section, we discuss each of the three normal forms. We'll see some examples of designs that violate the three normal forms, along with ways to modify them so that they conform.

FIRST NORMAL FORM

The first normal form states that a table's structure cannot contain any repeating data fields. We can best illustrate this with an example. Suppose you are developing a system to track job applicants. During the design phase, you learn that your users want to store two reference phone numbers for each candidate:

Table 2.1 Candidates

candidate_id	reference_1	reference_2
1144	916 555-2933	714-555-0900
1145	408 555-9550	602-555-8310

This design violates the first normal form, because the phone numbers repeat. This can cause problems, especially if during production, your users want to track yet another reference phone number. To do this, you must add a new column and then rebuild the Candidates table. You run the risk of "breaking" existing programs, since they may fail when confronted with a new table layout.

A better design would look like this:

Table 2.2 Candidates

candidate_id	...
1144	...
1145	...

Table 2.3 Candidates_ref

candidate_id	ref_sequence	ref_phone
1144	1	916 555-2933
1144	2	714 555-0900
1145	1	408 555-9550
1145	2	602 555-8310

Now, your users can add as many reference phone numbers as they like without jeopardizing your database design or application code. This new design also conforms to the first normal form, since the records don't contain any repeating data.

SECOND NORMAL FORM

The second normal form refers to rows where each column is functionally dependent on the primary key. Let's look at an example that violates the second normal form:

In this example, you are maintaining a property management maintenance system. One of your tables stores profile information for individual properties:

Table 2.4 property_profile

lot_id	address	city
1766	1313 Mockingbird Lane	Paterson
1767	2454 Legion Street	Pattybelle Junction
1768	540 E. 23rd Street	Lynnville
.	.	.
.	.	.

Another table stores data about maintenance procedures:

Table 2.5 maint_procedures

procedure_id	procedure_cost
102	70.99
103	21.00
104	502.54
.	.
.	.

You use a third table to track service calls for your properties:

Table 2.6 service_calls

lot_id	procedure_id	address	description	date_of_work
1767	103	2454 Legion Street	Tree trimming	11/15/94
1767	11	2454 Legion Street	Winterize	12/01/94
955	7	707 Condador Rd	Furnace repair	12/03/94
.	.	.	.	.
.	.	.	.	.

You identify the primary key on the "service_calls" table as a combination of the "lot_id" and "procedure_id" columns.

Can you see the problem with this design? The "service_calls" table has at least two columns that are not fully functionally dependent on the primary key. These columns are the "address" and "description" fields. Clearly, the address of a property generally doesn't change between service calls. The description of a particular task also usually remains the same, regardless of where you perform the task.

To alleviate this situation, you would move the "description" column from the "service_calls" table into the "maint_procedures" table. The "address" column in the "service_calls" table already exists in the "property_profile" table, so you need only to remove it from "service_calls".

The updated tables now conform to the second normal form, and look like this:

Table 2.7 maint_procedures

procedure_id	procedure_cost	description
102	70.99	Gutter cleanout
103	21.00	Tree trimming
104	502.54	Weather-strip
.	.	.
.	.	.

Table 2.8 service_calls

lot_id	procedure_id	date_of_work
1767	103	11/15/94
1767	11	12/01/94
955	7	12/03/94
.	.	.
.	.	.

THIRD NORMAL FORM

The third normal form refers to records that both conform to the second normal form and do not have any transitive dependencies. A transitive dependence exists when a table contains a particular column that is not a key, but still defines other columns. Let's look at this in more detail:

Suppose that you are designing a system to track test grades. One of your tables looks like this:

Table 2.9 test_scores

student_id	class_id	date_of_test	grade	cumulative_avg
3549	CIS091	10/17/94	84	81
8021	MGT100	10/17/94	72	77
1944	CIS091	10/17/94	93	90
.	.	.	.	.
.	.	.	.	.

The primary key for this table is the combination of the "student_id", "class_id", and "date_of_test" columns. The "cumulative_avg" column entry represents the student's average for all courses. This column is transitively dependent on the "student_id" column, and therefore violates the third normal form. You should move this column out of the "test_scores" table, and into a table that holds student profile information:

Table 2.10 student_profile

student_id	last_name	first_name	cumulative_avg
1944	Migdal	Sylvia	90
3549	Berson	Mary	81
8021	LaFong	Carl	77
.	.	.	.
.	.	.	.

Table 2.11 test_scores

student_id	class_id	date_of_test	grade
3549	CIS091	10/17/94	84
8021	MGT100	10/17/94	72
1944	CIS091	10/17/94	93
.	.	.	.
.	.	.	.

This change benefits you in at least two ways:

- **Reduced space requirements.** Before, you had to store a student's cumulative average after every test. By moving the column into the "student_profile" table, you only store the information once.
- **Reduced application complexity.** Before the change, if you wanted to change a student's cumulative average, you had to update all rows in the "test_scores" table. After the change, you only need to update a cumulative average in one place.

When not to normalize

Even though you should always try to satisfy each of the three normal forms, there are times when you may need to "bend" the rules somewhat. In this section, we'll discuss two situations that may require special handling. These situations are:

1. Storing calculated values in the database.
2. Separating historical information into other tables.

CALCULATED VALUES

Normally, a well-designed relational database doesn't store any calculated data such as sums, averages, and maximum and minimum values. Instead, these figures are calculated at runtime, usually by running through the underlying detail data.

There are cases, however, where it may be simpler, faster, and wiser to store a calculated value instead of generating it at runtime. For example, assume that you are developing a frequent-flyer application. Two of your tables are designed as follows:

Table 2.12 passenger

passenger_id	passenger_first	passenger_last
ETA17094	Dale	Cooper
.	.	.
OLT09334	Leo	Weiser
.	.	.
ZOR00934	Jean	Shepherd
.	.	.
.	.	.

Table 2.13 flights

passenger_id	flight_num	flight_date	miles_credited
OLD09334	11	1994-11-08	2490
.	.	.	.
ZOR00934	1794	1994-11-09	753
.	.	.	.
.	.	.	.

As you size the database, you realize that the "flights" table will grow very rapidly, eventually reaching a size of several million rows. This presents a potential problem, because customers will be calling your reservations center, wanting to know how many miles they have in their accounts. The customers expect to get instant answers, yet it may take several seconds for your lookup program to run through the "flights" table and add up all the individual mileage numbers. Fortunately, there is another way to provide this information more rapidly.

This involves storing the sum information with the main records:

Table 2.14 passenger

passenger_id	passenger_first	passenger_last	passenger_miles
ETA17094	Dale	Cooper	18095
.	.	.	
OLT09334	Leo	Weiser	7609
.	.	.	
ZOR00934	Jean	Shepherd	753
.	.	.	

To keep the miles count current, you update the totals each night by running a batch program. This change provides you with at least two benefits:

- **Instant access to mileage totals.** Now, when a customer calls in, your telephone representatives can determine the mileage total as soon as they look up the customer's account.
- **Better load balancing.** By running the batch update program at night, you off load heavy system processing to a time of day when it has less impact on interactive users.

Chances are, in your own applications, there are places where this type of change may help you as well.

HISTORICAL INFORMATION

Suppose you are maintaining a system to track credit card purchases. Customers call in, generally wanting to discuss charges on their most recent statements. Occasionally, however, they want to investigate charges from several months ago. Your largest table in this application is laid out as follows:

Table 2.15 transactions

trans_id	customer_id	date_of_purchase	amount
1093932	4765-095-393	1994-09-01	144.44
.	.	.	.
1204955	5099-144-091	1994-09-12	56.09
	.	.	.
.			
.	.	.	.

As you would expect in this type of application, the "transactions" table quickly grows to many millions of rows. Locating all detail rows for a particular customer account takes several seconds. In fact, both customers and account service representatives are beginning to complain about the response time. How can you improve this situation?

Since customers usually only want to discuss the most recent month's transaction information, you could break up this table into thirteen subtables, for example:

Table 2.16 curr_transactions

trans_id	customer_id	date_of_purchase	amount
1093932	4765-095-393	1994-09-01	144.44
.	.	.	.
1204955	5099-144-091	1994-09-12	56.09
.	.	.	.
1250444	3303-554-995	1994-09-30	1655.32

Table 2.17 prev1_trans

trans_id	customer_id	date_of_purchase	amount.
993932	7077-665-992	1994-08-01	75.00
.	.	.	.
.	.	.	.
1093900	4455-676-432	1994-08-31	753.11
.	.	.	.
.	.	.	.
.	.	.	.

Table 2.18 prev12_trans

trans_id	customer_id	date_of_purchase	amount
556709	1122-587-009	1993-09-01	4.22
.	.	.	.
.	.	.	.
659321	3390-102-168	1993-09-30	90.33

At the end of each month, you run a batch job to delete (or save on tape) the oldest information from the "prev12_trans" table. You then move the data from each table "back" one table (e.g., "prev11_trans" data into "prev12_trans", "prev10_trans" into "prev11_trans", etc.)

Your lookup programs should run much faster now, since they only process one-twelfth of the data that they used to. You don't need to hard-code table names into your application: you locate current data in the "curr_transactions" table, one-month-old data in "prev1_trans", etc.

Constraints

Simply expressed, constraints are conditions that you place on tables and/or columns in your database. In this section, we'll discuss several constraints, including:

- Primary key constraints
- Foreign key constraints
- Unique constraints
- Check constraints

We'll also examine how defining default values for columns can reduce your application's complexity and workload.

Two system tables exist to service constraints and referential integrity. These tables are "sysconstraints" and "sysreferences". Before beginning our discussion, let's look at how these tables are structured:

Table 2.19 sysconstraints

column name	**type**	**purpose**
constrid	serial	Identifier assigned by system.
constrname	char(18)	Name of the constraint. Assigned by the user or the system.
owner	char(8)	The user id of the constraint's owner
tabid	integer	The table identifier (corresponds to the "systables" table)
constrtype	char(1)	The type of constraint:
		C : check constraint
		P : primary key
		R : referential
		U : unique
idxname	char(18)	The system-generated index name

Adding a constraint also creates an entry in the "sysindexes" table, unless there is already an appropriate index in place.

Table 2.20 sysreferences

column name	**type**	**purpose**
constrid	serial	Identifier assigned by system.
primary	integer	The constraint id for the primary key.
ptabid	integer	The table id where the primary key is located.
updrule	char(1)	Not used at this time.
delrule	char(1)	Not used at this time.
machtype	char(1)	Not used at this time.
pendant	char(1)	Not used at this time.

PRIMARY KEY CONSTRAINT

Primary key constraints define a column or columns as the primary identifier of rows within the table. This means that there can be no duplicates between rows within this column or columns. Each of your tables should have a primary key defined. You can define primary key constraints in one of two ways:

- Implicitly, by creating a unique index on the column or columns.
- Explicitly, by using the PRIMARY KEY syntax. This method is especially important if you are defining a parent-child relationship. Note that another name for "parent-child" relationships is "master-detail" relationships.

As an example of explicitly defining a primary key constraint, let's use a table from a time and attendance application. In the "employee_detail" table, you plan to store timecard information. During your analysis, you determine that the combination of the employee number and date of work will be enough to uniquely identify each row. You decide that the system should never allow two records with the same employee number and date of work in the table. You can define this when you create the table:

```
CREATE TABLE EMPLOYEE_DETAIL
(
    EMPLOYEE_NUM    INTEGER,
    DATE_OF_WORK    DATETIME YEAR TO DAY,
    HOURS_WORKED    INTERVAL HOUR TO MINUTE,
    PRIMARY KEY (EMPLOYEE_NUM, DATE_OF_WORK)
);
```

Defining the "employee_num" and "date_of_work" columns as the primary key generates a unique index for these combined columns:

Index name	Owner	Type	Cluster	Columns
112_3	db_user	unique	No	employee_num
				date_of_work

It also places an entry in the "sysconstraints" table:

constrid	3
constrname	u112_3
owner	db_user
tabid	112
constrtype	P
idxname	112_3

If you wanted to implicitly make these two columns the primary key, you need only to create a unique index on the two columns:

```
CREATE UNIQUE INDEX EMP_DTL1 ON EMPLOYEE_DETAIL
    (EMPLOYEE_NUM, DATE_OF_WORK);
```

Remember that you can't use both methods; you must decide whether to explicitly or implicitly define your primary key. If you try to create an index on the columns defined as the primary key, the database server returns an error, stating that the columns are already indexed:

350: Index already exists on column
108: ISAM error: key already exists

FOREIGN KEY CONSTRAINT

Foreign key constraints define relationships among tables. Typically, these are known as "parent-child" or "master-detail" relationships. Using our example from above, let's say that each employee has a profile record which holds information about the employee's name, address, etc.:

```
CREATE TABLE EMPLOYEE_HEADER
(
        EMPLOYEE_NUM    INTEGER,
        EMPLOYEE_FIRST CHAR(10),
        EMPLOYEE_LAST   CHAR(20),
        PRIMARY KEY (EMPLOYEE_NUM)
);
```

The "employee_detail" table holds time card information. An employee can have only one "employee_header" record, but can have many "employee_detail" records. This is a classic "parent-child" relationship, where the "employee_header" table is the parent, and the "employee_detail" table is the child.

You can define a foreign key in the "employee_detail" table which helps you avoid having child records without corresponding parent records. Remember that you must also define a primary key constraint for the parent record.

For example, suppose that you first define a primary key for the "employee_header" table, and then define a foreign key for the "employee_detail" table. If you attempt to add an employee's time stamp data without first creating an "employee_header" record, your application receives an error from the database server:

691: Missing key in referenced table for referential constraint...

111: ISAM error: no record found.

You'll also receive an error if you try to delete a parent without first deleting all affected children:

692: Key value for constraint (db_user.u115_7) is still being referenced.

The SQL to define a foreign key looks like this:

```
CREATE TABLE EMPLOYEE_DETAIL
(
    EMPLOYEE_NUM    INTEGER,
    DATE_OF_WORK    DATETIME YEAR TO DAY,
    HOURS_WORKED    INTERVAL HOUR TO MINUTE,
    PRIMARY KEY (EMPLOYEE_NUM, DATE_OF_WORK),
    FOREIGN KEY (EMPLOYEE_NUM) REFERENCES
                 EMPLOYEE_HEADER(EMPLOYEE_NUM)
);
```

The indexes that these SQL statements create are:

Table 2.21 employee_header:

Index name	Owner	Type	Cluster	Columns
115_7	db_user	unique	No	employee_num

Table 2.22 employee_detail:

Index name	Owner	Type	Cluster	Columns
116_8	db_user	unique	No	employee_num
				date_of_work
116_9	db_user	dupls	No	employee_num

The entries in the "sysconstraints" table are:

constrid	7
constrname	u115_7
owner	db_user
tabid	115
constrtype	P
idxname	115_7
constrid	8
constrname	u116_8
owner	db_user
tabid	116
constrtype	P
idxname	116_8

constrid	9
constrname	r116_9
owner	db_user
tabid	116
constrtype	R
idxname	116_9

UNIQUE CONSTRAINT

Let's say that you have another column in the "employee_header" table that is unique, but you don't want to use it as a primary key. You can set up a unique constraint instead.

If you defined a unique constraint during table creation, your SQL would look like this:

```
CREATE TABLE EMPLOYEE_HEADER
(
    EMPLOYEE_NUM   INTEGER,
    EMPLOYEE_FIRST CHAR(10),
    EMPLOYEE_LAST  CHAR(20),
    EMPLOYEE_SSN   CHAR(9),
    UNIQUE (EMPLOYEE_SSN)
);
```

This automatically places a unique index on the "employee_num" column:

Index name	Owner	Type	Cluster	Columns
110_2	db_user	unique	No	employee_ssn

It also places an entry in the "sysconstraints" table:

constrid	2
constrname	u110_2
owner	db_user
tabid	110
constrtype	U
idxname	110_2

Since you didn't provide a name for the constraint, the engine generated one for you.

One final word regarding constraints: If you want to remove a constraint, you must drop the constraint, rather than simply deleting the index. You use the ALTER TABLE statement to drop constraints:

```
ALTER TABLE <table name>
DROP CONSTRAINT <constraint name>
```

If you want to alter an existing constraint, it's best to first drop it, and then re-create it.

CHECK CONSTRAINT

Suppose you want to prevent application programs or users from entering dates outside of a specified boundary. By using a check constraint, you can safeguard your database from these types of data errors. Using our payroll example, we place a check constraint on the "date_of_work" column:

```
CREATE TABLE EMPLOYEE_DETAIL
(
    EMPLOYEE_NUM     INTEGER,
    DATE_OF_WORK     DATETIME YEAR TO DAY,
    HOURS_WORKED     INTERVAL HOUR TO MINUTE,
    PRIMARY KEY (EMPLOYEE_NUM, DATE_OF_WORK),
    FOREIGN KEY (EMPLOYEE_NUM) REFERENCES
                  EMPLOYEE_HEADER(EMPLOYEE_NUM),
```

```
        CHECK (DATE_OF_WORK BETWEEN "1994-01-01" AND
                                    "1994-12-31")
);
```

This places entries into both the "sysconstraints" and "sysreferences" tables:

Table 2.23 sysconstraints:

constrid	15
constrname	c120_15
owner	db_user
tabid	120
constrtype	C
idxname	

Table 2.24 sysreferences:

constrid	primary	ptabid	updrule	delrule	matchtype	pendant
14	12	119	R	R	N	N

DEFAULT VALUES

Informix OnLine and SE, versions 5.0 and newer, let an administrator define default values when creating or modifying a table. These default values are stored in the "sysdefaults" system table:

Table 2.25 sysdefaults

column name	type	purpose
tabid	integer	The table's id - corresponds to the "systables" table.
colno	smallint	The column's id - corresponds to the "syscolumns"
		table.
type	char(1)	The default type:
		C : Current
		L : Literal default
		N : Null
		S : Database server name
		T : Today
		U : User identifier
default	char(256)	If the type is (L)iteral, this is the actual value to use.

Let's look at an example of a personnel application. As part of the system, you maintain a table to store salary adjustments:

Table 2.26 salary_adjust

employee_id	adjust_date	adjust_amount
1109	07/19/94	4.250
445	07/19/94	5.250
1380	07/19/94	3.000
.	.	.
.	.	.

You can simplify your application code and improve performance by instructing the database engine to use default values for certain columns if they are not provided by the user. In this case, you learn from your users that they want to use today's date as a default, as well as an adjustment amount of 3 percent. The SQL to create the table would look like this:

```
CREATE TABLE SALARY_ADJUST
(
    EMPLOYEE_ID    INTEGER,
    ADJUST_DATE    DATE DEFAULT TODAY,
    ADJUST_AMOUNT DECIMAL(5,3)  DEFAULT 3.000
);
```

If your users expect to use these values most of the time, you can reduce the size and complexity of your application. For these cases, your insertion logic would look like this:

```
INSERT INTO SALARY_ADJUST (EMPLOYEE_ID)
VALUES (nnnn);
```

where "nnnn" is an employee id supplied at runtime.

The two biggest benefits of default values are increased data integrity and reduced traffic between the front-end process and the database server. This traffic reduction is especially important in client-server configurations, where the client and server may be separated by long distances.

INDEXING STRATEGIES

Introduction

With the exception of correctly defined primary and foreign keys, there is no right or wrong way to index a database. Different applications have different data access profiles. An indexing strategy that works for one application may not work for another.

For example, some applications require instantaneous access to data, using numerous search columns and sort combinations. Other systems are more rigidly defined, with only a few possible search columns and sort combinations. While the Informix query optimizer can choose the most efficient query plan even if the underlying data changes, your users may request completely new queries and reports: what satisfied them in January may not suffice in October. Therefore, it is up to each administrator and analyst to continually analyze their index strategy, and make modifications as necessary.

Ideally, you analyze your database and generate your indexes before bringing your application into production. However, if you miss something before you go into production, don't worry. It is very easy to put the proper indexes in place on a production system, because adding, altering, or dropping indexes generally does not require you to alter existing source code. Furthermore, Informix engines version 5.00 and later utilize fast indexing, which makes adding indexes at a later date much faster than in previous versions. If you're using Informix OnLine version 7.00 or newer, index construction is even faster, since that version of OnLine can build indexes in parallel.

This chapter addresses some of the methods you can use to create effective indexes, or make existing indexes more efficient.

FAST INDEXING

Fast indexing is the process that Informix engines use to rapidly generate indexes. Briefly, this is how fast indexing works:

1. The engine sorts the data to be indexed, using the key that makes up the new index.
2. The keys, along with the row IDs of the rows, are written to temporary storage. This storage resides in the directory pointed to by DBTEMP. If DBTEMP is not set, then the temporary storage is written to the /tmp directory. For parallel processor machines, the engine uses the PSORTTEMP environment variable to determine where to place temporary files.

   If you're using OnLine version 6.00 or newer, you can set DBSPACETEMP at the environment or ONCONFIG file level. This tells the engine to store these temporary sort files in the listed dbspaces.

OnLine 6.00 and newer follows this sequence to determine where to write these sort files:

1) PSORTTEMP.
2) The DBSPACETEMP environment variable.
3) The DBSPACETEMP ONCONFIG file variable
4) The /tmp directory.

For more information about setting up temporary storage dbspaces, see the "OnLine tips" section.

3. The engine creates the index by retrieving the key values and row IDs from the temporary storage.

This process results in less disk access and B+ tree manipulation. Fast indexing is only used for tables that are sufficiently large to warrant it (generally more than 500 rows or more than 30 pages).

If you do not want your system to use fast indexing, set the NOSORTINDEX environment variable.

SET EXPLAIN

Whether your application is in production, or is still in the development phase, the easiest way to determine which indexes are being accessed is to use the SET EXPLAIN ON command. This command tells the Informix optimizer to write all query plans to the sqexplain.out file, located in your current directory.

You can use the results of this file to examine the queries, as well as the query plans that the optimizer produces. Each query plan provides valuable information, including:

1. The original query.
2. The indexes that were used to satisfy the query.
3. Any temporary tables that were created.

Remember to comment out or remove the SET EXPLAIN ON command from your source code after you have performed your analysis, because the sqexplain.out file can grow very rapidly. This command also slightly slows the application.

For additional information about using SET EXPLAIN, see the "Understanding the Informix optimizer" section.

UPDATE STATISTICS

One of the most important jobs that an Informix database administrator performs is to regularly run the UPDATE STATISTICS statement. For a detailed description of what this crucial statement does, see the "Understanding the Informix Optimizer" section.

REBUILDING INDEXES

As an administrator, you may have used other databases that required you to periodically rebuild your indexes. Earlier versions of Informix also benefited from regular index rebuilds, but this is no longer necessary in versions 5.0 and later. However, there are some points to consider with both Informix OnLine and Informix-SE.

The OnLine engine automatically reclaims index pages once they become empty. The pages are freed, although they still belong to their original extent. These pages can then be filled with index, data, or BLOB (Binary Large Object) values. If you feel that your extents are too fragmented, or you want to allocate these pages to other extents, see the "OnLine tips" section for more detail about extent management.

Informix-SE also reclaims index space within the .idx file. However, if you have a large table (and consequently, a large .idx file), and you delete many rows from the table, neither the .dat nor the .idx files become smaller. If the deleted rows are eventually replaced with new data, this is not a problem. If, on the other hand, you do not believe that the table will ever be as large as it once was, you can still free some of the disk space as follows:

1. Using SQL via isql, dbaccess, or a program, alter the table by adding a new column:
   ```
   ALTER TABLE table_name ADD (TMP CHAR(1))
   ```
   Informix copies the contents of the table into new UNIX files. You must have enough disk space for two copies of the table (old and new). This added disk requirement is only temporary, since the old copy of the table is removed as soon as the new copy is complete.
2. Using SQL via isql, dbaccess, or a program, remove the temporary column:
   ```
   ALTER TABLE table_name DROP (TMP)
   ```
   Informix again copies the table into new storage. This time, the table is identical to your original table, except it now uses less UNIX file system disk space.

Primary keys

Each table should have an index on the primary key. The Informix engines automatically perform this task for you if you use the following syntax:

```
CREATE TABLE ABC
(
    COLUMN1 INTEGER PRIMARY KEY,
    COLUMN2 CHAR(10),
         .       .
         .       .
)
```

For tables that have composite primary keys, use this syntax:

```
CREATE TABLE CDE
 (
   COLUMN1 INTEGER,
   COLUMN2 CHAR(10),
   COLUMN3 SMALLINT,
   PRIMARY KEY (COLUMN1, COLUMN2)
)
```

If you have an earlier version of the Informix engines (before version 5.00) or do not wish to use this syntax, you should still create a unique index on the column or columns that make up your primary key. This significantly speeds access to the table by allowing the engine to make only one read to determine if a particular row exists. In addition, sorting the table on the primary key (to create a report, for example) is much faster.

Filter columns

If you frequently search a table based on a particular value in a column, you should place an index on that column. This is especially true in cases where the table has many rows and the values within the column are diverse (e.g., not highly duplicated). Let's use an example from a point-of-sale system. Assume that this table has two million rows, 40,000 different stock numbers, and 5,000 different store numbers:

Table 2.27 pos_detail

sku_no	store_no	date	amount
5409	636	11/01/94	1.55
112	636	11/01/94	32.00
.	.	.	.
.	.	.	.
.	.	.	.
1154	709	11/02/94	93.99
5903	709	11/03/94	5.87
.	.	.	.
.	.	.	.

Users continually wish to retrieve information with the following query:

```
SELECT * FROM POS_DETAIL
WHERE STORE_NO = (number entered by user)
AND   SKU_NO   = (number entered by user)
```

If there are no indexes on the filter columns, this query requires a sequential scan of the table. In this case, you would benefit by creating the following index:

```
CREATE INDEX POS_DETAIL_IX1
   ON POS_DETAIL (STORE_NO, SKU_NO)
```

The engine should now be able to process the previous query much more rapidly. The only exception to this rule would be if the engine is already using another index on the table to satisfy a join or another filter. Remember that the optimizer can generally only use one index at a time when searching a table. Since the previous query doesn't have another filter condition or a join to another table, the new index should help.

Join columns

Wherever possible, you should create indexes on both sides of a frequently used join relationship. Let's use the following example from a sales prospecting system. Assume that we wish to join between the "prospects" and "sales_staff" tables, to produce a report showing the link between salespeople and prospects:

Table 2.28 prospects

prospect_num	region	sales_id
3654	W	taylor
6092	E	svale
496	S	lynn
1003	W	robs
7123	W	lafong
32	E	rejak
.	.	.
.	.	.

Table 2.29 sales_staff

sales_id	first_name	last_name
robs	Robert	Simon
lynn	Lynn	Zlotnick
taylor	Douglas	Taylor
lafong	Carl	Lafong
rejak	Bill	Rejak
svale	Steve	Vale
.	.	.
.	.	.

In this case, assume that the report is first reading the "sales_staff" table (to get the first and last names and sales_id of each salesperson), and then reading the "prospects" table (to get information about each salesperson's potential customers). If there is no index on prospects.sales_id, the engine is forced to sequentially read all rows in the "prospects" table to find matches based on prospects.sales_id.

In the absence of indexes on join columns, the optimizer may take advantage of sort-merge joins or autoindexing to speed up the query. For more information about the various techniques that the optimizer uses to retrieve information, see the "Understanding the Informix optimizer" section. Despite these sophisticated alternative join methods, you should always investigate the performance impact of placing indexes on join columns.

Unique versus non-unique

A unique index guarantees that there will be only one row with a particular column value within a table. This enables the Informix engine to rapidly locate and retrieve the row. Additionally, a unique index on a column prevents users from entering duplicate values and possibly damaging the integrity of the database through applications or direct data entry.

If you have an Informix engine version 5.0 or later, using the PRIMARY KEY syntax in the CREATE TABLE statement automatically generates a unique index.

Character versus numeric

If you have an indexed character column that is composed solely of numeric information, you should consider changing the column's data type to either a smallint (if no value will exceed 32,767) or to an integer. A smallint requires two bytes of storage, while an integer needs four bytes, so this helps save space and speeds processing.

For example, assume that you have a column that has been defined as a char(10), and holds only numeric values that range between 0 and 10,000. By defining the column as a char(10), you use ten bytes of storage for this column in each row and index. By changing the data type of the column to a smallint (since no value exceeds 32,767), you only use two bytes of storage within each row and index. This is a substantial saving of space, especially when multiplied by the number of rows in a large table.

In terms of indexing, if the column is defined as a char(10), the Informix engine needs to read all ten bytes when traversing the index tree, versus only two bytes if the column is changed to a smallint. Joins are also much faster between integer columns than between character columns.

Composite index issues

There are probably many times that you want to retrieve or sort information from a table based on more than one column. Let's use the following table from a sales prospecting system as an example:

Table 2.30 prospects

prospect_num	region	area_code
3654	W	602
6092	E	516
496	S	713
1003	W	415
7123	W	415
32	E	212
.	.	.
.	.	.

You estimate that there are 100,000 distinct prospect numbers, 300 area codes, and four regions in this table. Your system contains a number of screens and reports that are designed to present information from this table. Some of the more commonly used reports present information sorted by prospect number within area code, within region. If the table is small, it may not be necessary to create a composite index with these columns. If, on the other hand, the table is large and the data must be sorted by these values frequently, you should consider creating the following index:

```
CREATE INDEX prospects_ix1 ON
   PROSPECTS(REGION, AREA_CODE, PROSPECT_NUM);
```

This lets you sort by those three columns. In addition, the optimizer can use the index for queries that sort by area_code within region, as well as queries that sort only by region. The drawback to this particular index is that the root position (region) is highly duplicate. This yields a shallow B+ tree, which is not the most efficient index structure. If you only need to search on these three columns (instead of sorting on them), try creating this index instead:

```
CREATE INDEX prospects_ix2 ON
   PROSPECTS (PROSPECT_NUM, AREA_CODE, REGION);
```

In contrast to the "prospects_ix1" index, "prospects_ix2" has a far more unique root position, because there are many thousands of prospect numbers, as opposed to only four regions. The optimizer should also be able to choose between these two indexes, depending on what kind of data retrieval request you submit. Remember that unlike sorting, searching a table using an index doesn't require you to work from left to right, as long as you search on all parts of the composite index. This means that the optimizer would be able use the prospects_ix2 index to locate data as long as you searched on "region", "area_code", and "prospect_num":

```
SELECT *
FROM   PROSPECTS
WHERE  REGION = "E"
AND    AREA_CODE = 415
AND    PROSPECT_NUM = 1234;
```

--- or ---

```
SELECT *
FROM   PROSPECTS
WHERE  PROSPECT_NUM = 1234
AND    REGION = "E"
AND    AREA_CODE = 415;
```

--- or ---

```
SELECT *
FROM   PROSPECTS
WHERE  AREA_CODE = 415
AND    PROSPECT_NUM = 1234
AND    REGION = "E";
```

And so on, for all other possible combinations of these three columns.

Avoiding highly duplicate indexes

A highly duplicate index is one where there are a limited number of unique values contained in the index. For example, if you place an index on a column that contains no more than two or three values, you have a highly duplicate index.

It is worse to have a highly duplicate index on a column than not have one at all. This is because the engine must perform a great deal of work to process the index.

For example, assume you have the following table that tracks maintenance contracts for customers:

Table 2.31 contracts

client_num	purchased
409	Y
1954	Y
78	N
3	Y
1044	N
12	Y
.	.
.	.

If you place an index on the "purchased" column, you will only have two possible values: (Y)es or (N)o. When you add a new row into this table, the engine must go all the way to the end of index to write the new value. Deleting, querying, or sorting based on the index also causes the engine excess work. This adds a great deal of unnecessary I/O operations to your system, and can actually degrade performance. It also doesn't make much sense to ask the database engine to use an index to find such heavily duplicated data, since it's probably faster and simpler for the engine to go directly to the data and read it sequentially.

In those cases where you must sort or search on a highly duplicate value, combine the column in question with a more unique column to make up a composite index. In the previous example, the correct composite index would be:

```
CREATE INDEX contracts_ix1 ON
   CONTRACTS(CLIENT_NUM, PURCHASED);
```

The "client_num" column is much more unique than the "purchased" column. Combining these two columns yields a more unique and efficient index. You can now use this index to search for and sort by "client_num", all clients who have purchased a service contract. Don't forget that to use a composite index in filtering or sorting data, you must always start from the left and work to the right.

Clustered indexes

When it comes to access, all tables within an application are not created equally. Some tables are updated hundreds or thousands of times an hour, while others are updated only in batch mode at night. Some tables are updated very infrequently, if at all. For those tables that are not updated frequently, you may want to consider clustered indexing. Clustering a table on an index means that the table is written to disk in the physical order of the index. For example, assume that the following table has several thousand rows, is relatively static, and is used primarily for lookup purposes in an outboard motor maker's inventory application:

Table 2.32 parts

part_num	part_description	part_cost
22905	4-blade propeller	165.03
3467	engine cowling	205.44
910	interior gasket	.58
1093	drive shaft	443.00
.	.	.
.	.	.
.	.	.
.	.	.
22906	3-blade propeller	145.99
911	lower unit gasket	3.00
.	.	.
.	.	.

As you can see, the data within this table is stored in a random order, with closely related items separated by non-related items. For example, parts 22905 and 22906 are both propellers. In certain types of queries and reports, it is likely that when fetching information on one, the user will want to fetch data on the other. By placing a clustered index on the "part_num" column, the Informix engine physically rewrites the table as follows:

```
CREATE CLUSTER INDEX PARTS_IX1 ON PARTS(PART_NUM);
```

Table 2.33 parts

part_num	part_description	part_cost
910	interior gasket	.58
911	lower unit gasket	3.00
1093	drive shaft	443.00
3467	engine cowling	205.44
.	.	.
.	.	.
.	.	.
.	.	.
22905	4-blade propeller	165.03
22906	3-blade propeller	145.99
.	.	.
.	.	.

This yields faster performance for those screens and reports that access blocks of information by the "part_num".

The Informix database engine allows only one clustered index per table; if you attempt to add a second, you will receive an error.

If, after creating the clustered index, you substantially modify the data within the table, you can "refresh" the clustered index as follows:

```
ALTER INDEX index_name TO CLUSTER;
```

You can also use this syntax to change a non-clustered index to a clustered index.

The engine re-creates the clustering by first copying the original table into a new table and then dropping the original table. Therefore, you must have enough space for two copies of the table at one time. This can be a problem for sites that do not have enough disk space. As an alternative you could:

1. Unload the table to a flat file, sorted by the column(s) that you wish to cluster by.
2. Drop the table.
3. Re-create the table with the clustered index in place.
4. Reload the sorted data that you unloaded.

You can even place composite indexes on tables that change frequently; the only drawback is that you'll need to "refresh" the clustered index more frequently than if the table rarely changed.

Sort columns

Sorting is one of the areas where indexing is most helpful. Reports and lookup screens typically use sorting as a way to organize and present data. If no indexes are in place to handle the sort, the Informix engine creates a temporary table. For reports that run through large quantities of data, these temporary tables can be enormous, requiring large amounts of processing and storage. Fortunately, Informix database engines version 6.00 and newer employ faster and more sophisticated sorting techniques, which reduce the amount of time necessary to create temporary tables. See the "Understanding the Informix optimizer" section for more information about how the optimizer processes data. Remember that no matter what version of Informix engines you use, these temporary tables still can consume large amounts of disk space.

The easiest way to determine if your system is making excessive use of temporary tables is to monitor the results of the SET EXPLAIN command. If you find that many queries are creating temporary tables to handle sorting, consider placing indexes on the columns that are used in the ORDER BY. Keep in mind that the optimizer may still need to create a temporary table if the optimizer is already using the index to resolve a join or filter condition. See the "SQL tips" section for more information about efficient sorting.

Finally, try not to create excessive numbers of indexes. Over-indexing a table can be worse than under-indexing a table. See the "Excess Indexing" section that follows for more detail.

Excess indexing

It is possible to have too much of a good thing. Some database administrators, in an effort to anticipate every possible sort and search combination, create indexes on practically every column in every table. Obviously, this is an extreme example. Nevertheless, there are cases where you can have too many indexes, such as when programmers create "test" indexes on tables and forget to drop them later.

Having too many indexes hurts your system in many ways:

- Every time you perform an insert or delete, the indexes and the data need to be modified.
- When you update an indexed column, the Informix engine updates all affected indexes. This can have the added undesirable effect of causing the engine to restructure the B+ trees. You, as an administrator, would have no way of knowing if and when this would occur.
- Excess indexes consume more disk space, and disk space is usually at a premium in most organizations.

The best way to know if you have too many indexes is to test your application with the SET EXPLAIN command. Try to simulate a typical work day. When you are finished, remember to remove the SET EXPLAIN from your application, and then review the sqexplain.out file. You should be able to quickly determine which of your indexes are being used. You can then remove any indexes which are not commonly referenced.

There are times when you need excess indexes to handle specific, easily identifiable tasks, such as an end-of-month processing suite. In these cases, you can simply create the indexes immediately before they are needed, and drop them as soon as you finish.

Index fill factor

If you're using OnLine version 6.00 or newer, you can specify how full your index nodes should be when OnLine creates an index. To understand this concept, let's first review how indexes are structured.

When you add an index, OnLine creates a B+ tree. B+ trees are composed of one or more levels of nodes. Each node is made up of key values and pointers, and is the size of a disk page.

If the B+ tree is only one level deep, the pointers point to actual rows. For multi-level B+ trees, only the lowest level (level 0) nodes point to data rows; higher level nodes point to lower level nodes.

As index nodes fill up, the engine splits them into two nodes, which are then both half full. The engine can then add more key values into these two half-full index pages.

You can use the oncheck utility, with the -pT option, to determine the fullness for each index in your database.

As an administrator, your goal is to control the number of node splits, because they impact system performance in these ways:

- **Locked pages.** The splitting pages are locked until the split has finished. While this locking is very brief and transparent to user processes (for example, you don't need to write code to handle it), it still has the potential to delay system throughput.
- **Additional disk space.** Less filled index nodes mean more index pages. This consumes more disk space, which may be at a premium.
- **Lower cache rate.** The more pages it takes to contain an index, the less likely it is that OnLine will be able to cache all these pages in shared memory. Shared memory caching is one of OnLine's biggest performance benefits, so a large, sparsely-filled index can reduce OnLine's overall throughput.

Fortunately, you can customize each index's fullness, in the following ways:

- By setting the FILLFACTOR value in the ONCONFIG file. This sets a global fill factor for all indexes within all databases in the OnLine instance.
- By using the FILLFACTOR clause in the CREATE INDEX statement.

If you don't use either of these methods, the default fill factor is 90 percent. Let's look at an example to learn more about how to correctly set this important parameter.

Suppose that you're developing an application to register students for training classes. Four of your most important tables have these layouts:

Table 2.34 students

student_id	student_last	student_first	student_zip ...
.	.	.	.
11012	Dial	Samuel	94070
11013	Skinner	Robert	11710
11014	Escare	Alexis	10017
.	.	.	.

Table 2.34 has two indexes: one on "student_id", and one on "student_last".

Table 2.35 training_centers

center_id	address	phone
.	.	.
17	234 Wilshire Blvd	213 555-3939
18	1425 Manhattan St	602 555-8813
.	.	.

Table 2.35 has one index on "center_id".

Table 2.36 zip_codes

zip_code	city_name
00001	Augusta
00002	Bangor
.	.

Table 2.36 has two indexes: one on "zip_code" and one on "city_name".

Table 2.37 nearest_center

zip_code	center_id
.	.
20112	11
20113	11
.	.

Table 2.37 has one index on "zip_code".

Your application follows these steps to register a student:

1. When a prospective student calls in, the service representative asks for the student's zip code.
2. If the student doesn't know the zip code, the service representative asks for the city instead.
3. If the student's zip code is known, the service representative uses it to locate the nearest training center by searching the "nearest_center" table.
4. If only the student's city is known, the service representative first reads the "zip_codes" table to find the corresponding zip code, then locates the nearest training center by searching the "nearest_center" table.
5. If the student has never registered before, the service representative adds a record into the "students" table.

With this in mind, how should you set the fill factor for each index? Generally, if you know that a table isn't likely to grow, set the fill factor higher. In the above example, the table that is least likely to grow is "zip_codes". For this table, you could use a fill factor of 100 percent:

```
CREATE INDEX ZC1 ON ZIP_CODES(ZIP_CODE)FILLFACTOR 100;
CREATE INDEX ZC2 ON ZIP_CODES(CITY_NAME)FILLFACTOR 100;
```

A fill factor of 100 means that OnLine attempts to completely fill in all space in each index node.

The "training_centers" and "nearest_center" tables may grow somewhat, but should never experience extreme numbers of inserts. With that in mind, you can accept the default fill factor of 90 percent, which means that you don't need to specify any fill factor in your CREATE INDEX statement. Remember that OnLine uses 90 percent as a default if you don't have another number specified in your ONCONFIG file.

The "students" table is most likely to grow, since you're adding new students every day. For this table, use a lower fill factor when creating indexes:

```
CREATE INDEX ST1 ON STUDENTS(STUDENT_ID)FILLFACTOR 50;
CREATE INDEX ST2 ON STUDENTS(STUDENT_LAST)FILLFACTOR 50;
```

When OnLine creates these indexes, it leaves each index node only half full. This uses up more disk space, and lowers the cache rate, but it also leaves room for growth.

Finally, remember that the fill factor isn't maintained indefinitely; it only applies when the index is created. This is a good argument for periodically analyzing index node fullness, and rebuilding indexes where appropriate.

Index location

Before OnLine 7.00, your indexes were stored in the same dbspace as your data. You can still use this storage method in OnLine 7.00 and newer, but you can also use these methods to distribute your indexes:

- **Index fragmentation.** You can tell OnLine to divide an index among several dbspaces, using one of several distribution algorithms. For more information about these fragmentation algorithms, see the "OnLine tips"section.
- **Single, separate dbspace.** You can specify a dbspace for OnLine to store an index as follows:

  ```
  CREATE INDEX IDX1 ON ABC(COL1,...) IN INDEX_DBSPACE;
  ```

  Remember that if you don't specify a separate dbspace, the IDX1 index is stored in the same dbspace as the ABC table. Also, if the ABC table is fragmented, and you don't name a separate dbspace, OnLine fragments the index as well.

Disk access is often the most time-consuming component of returning information from a query. Therefore, distributing indexes among several disk drives can have a dramatic effect on data access throughput, especially on multi-processor machines.

DIFFERENCES IN DATABASE DESIGN BETWEEN ONLINE AND SE

Introduction

Many sites now use both Informix engines: OnLine and Informix-SE. Generally, an efficiently-designed database works well with either engine. However, there are certain data types present in OnLine that merit special attention. These include Binary Large Objects (BLOBs), and variable length character fields (VARCHARs).

This section explores the optimal way to use these data types, as well as how row IDs differ between OnLine and SE, and the benefits and dangers of using row IDs in your application.

Finally, we discuss the implications of using these features if you are running both OnLine and SE.

BLOBs

BLOBs let you store additional types of information in your database. These can include text, music, images, and even program executables. BLOBs are available in the OnLine engine, but not in SE.

In this section, we will explore the database design implications of BLOBs. For information on optimizing BLOB disk storage, as well as writing efficient BLOB-handling software, see the "OnLine Tips" section.

There are two types of BLOBs that you can use: TEXT and BYTE. Use the TEXT data type to store groupings of printable character information, such as letters and other documents. Use the BYTE data type to store any type of information; the limit is two gigabytes of information within a single BLOB instance.

BLOB RESTRICTIONS

The BLOB data types have certain SQL restrictions:
SQL math or boolean operations. You cannot perform engine-level calculations, either math or boolean, on a BLOB.

- **ORDER BY/GROUP BY.** You cannot sort based on the values contained within BLOB fields.
- **UNIQUE.** You cannot ask the engine to determine if a value in a BLOB field is unique.
- **Indexing.** You cannot include a BLOB in an index, whether it is composite or single.
- **Substrings.** You cannot search on a substring within a BLOB.

BLOB EXAMPLES

Let's explore some design scenarios where we might consider using one of these data types:

Case 1

In this case, assume that you are designing a problem-tracking system. The users communicate with customers via electronic and surface mail, as well as fax. In the near future, you also expect that customers will communicate using voice mail. Your users want to keep copies of all correspondence; for the purpose of our example, assume that any correspondence (except voice mail) can be represented in plain ASCII.

You expect that you will never need to search through the actual contents of this correspondence. Instead, you plan to maintain other fields that will contain information about the correspondence. Users will use these fields to locate particular rows.

This is a good candidate for a BLOB data type. The question remains: which type of BLOB should you use? If you only plan to store ASCII information, a TEXT BLOB would most likely suffice. However, suppose you know that the users will eventually store voice mail in the database. This cannot be easily represented using the ASCII character set, so you would decide in favor of the BYTE BLOB data type:

```
CREATE TABLE CUST_CORRESPOND
(
    CUST_NO          INTEGER,
    MAIL_TYPE        CHAR(1),
    MAIL_DATE        DATE,
    MAIL_CONTENTS    BYTE
);
```

Case 2

In this case, assume that you are creating a system to log customer comments about a product or service that your organization provides. You will receive comments in one of two ways:

- Written on customer response surveys that you have sent out to your customers. These are then keyed into the system by customer service personnel.
- Directly typed in by customer service personnel during phone calls with your customers.

Your users want to be able to search through the actual comments, looking for particular strings, such as "furious," "delighted," "lawsuit," "grateful," etc.

This would be a good candidate for the TEXT data type, but there is one problem: you cannot perform substring searches on a BLOB field. This means that you would have to FETCH each BLOB into a variable, and then parse the data to locate any strings. This would be time-consuming and unnecessarily complex.

As an alternative, you could create a table using the standard CHAR data type:

```
CREATE TABLE CUST_COMMENTS
(
    CUST_NO              INTEGER,
    SEQ_NO               INTEGER,
    COMMENT_DATA         CHAR(80)
);
```

Each line of customer comments would receive a row in this table. You could then search through the "comment_data" column to find any matches to your keywords.

If your "cust_comments" table gets large, however, query times could become quite slow. You might consider making one entry per keyword in the following table whenever you insert or update a row in "cust_comments":

```
CREATE TABLE KEYWORD_LOCATIONS
(
   KEYWORD          CHAR(10),
   CUST_NO          INTEGER,
   SEQ_NO           INTEGER,
   PRIMARY KEY (KEYWORD, CUST_NO, SEQ_NO)
);
```

When users want to find all rows containing a keyword, this table acts as an index into the "cust_comments" table.

VARCHAR

The CHAR data type stores characters as fixed length strings. This means that if you define a field to be 80 bytes in length, but you only fill 10 of those bytes with data, the engine fills in the remaining 70 bytes with spaces. In a small database, or on a system with excess storage capacity, this is not a problem. If, on the other hand, you have a large database or limited disk space, you should consider using the VARCHAR data type.

VARCHAR is a variable length character field. It is available only with Informix OnLine. You define a field with this type as VARCHAR(a,b). The first number inside the parentheses is the maximum length that the field will be. Remember that OnLine does not permit a VARCHAR field to be longer than 255 bytes. The second number is the minimum amount of space for OnLine to store in the field. This can be between zero and the actual length of the field.

In addition to the actual data stored in field, OnLine attaches a one-byte length field to the column. If you want to see how OnLine actually stores a VARCHAR, run "tbcheck -pp" for the database, table, and page/rowid that you want to examine.

For example, the following simple table contains only one VARCHAR field with a maximum length of 30 bytes, with a minimum length of five bytes. There are three rows in this table.

Using the tbcheck utility to dump the contents of the data page produces a hexadecimal interpretation of the data, as well as the ASCII translation:

```
addr    stamp  nslots  flag  type  frptr  frcnt  next  prev
100d5f 3442    3        1     DATA  46     1986   0     0
              slot ptr   len   flg
              1    24    6     0
              2    30    8     0
              3    38    8     0
```

```
slot   1:
    0:  5 68 65 6c 6c 6f                                      .hello.........
slot   2:
    0:  7 74 65 73 74 20 20 20                                 test   ........
slot   3:
    0:  7 74 65 73 74 20 20 20                                 .test   .......
```

COST OF USING VARCHARS

Although VARCHARs are very beneficial in terms of data storage, they also have some extra costs. These costs include:

- **Extra storage space.** For each VARCHAR, OnLine adds one extra byte. This is used to store the actual length of the VARCHAR data.
- **Slower data retrieval.** You might encounter slower data retrieval if OnLine is forced to split a row among several pages. This can occur when a VARCHAR field is updated with a new value that is substantially larger than the original. If the updated row cannot fit on the page, OnLine leaves a four-byte forwarding pointer, moves the entire row to another page, and frees up the row's original space on the first page. If the row is too big to fit on a single page, OnLine divides the row among several other pages.

  One way that you can help minimize this overhead is to allocate enough default space for the VARCHAR. You can do this by determining how many bytes the majority of the values stored in the field require. You then define the field with that number as a minimum.

  For example, if you are defining a field that will be a VARCHAR with a maximum of 100 bytes, and you know that 80 percent of the rows will have at least 50 bytes in this field, you can define it as VARCHAR(100,50). OnLine will allocate at least 50 bytes for each row. Only 20 percent of your rows will exceed this; many of them still may not present a storage problem.

In addition to the costs mentioned above, there are some programming issues regarding the way that your host variables work with VARCHARs. For more information on this topic, see the "Optimizing Application Code" section.

VARCHAR EXAMPLES

Let's examine two different cases where you should consider using the VARCHAR data type:

Case 1

In this case, you are designing a table to hold contact information for a sales tracking system:

```
CREATE TABLE CONTACTS
(
   CONTACT_NUMBER   INTEGER,
      .      .      .      .
   COMPANY          CHAR(50),
   TITLE            CHAR(50),
      .      .      .      .
);
```

During your analysis, you learned that this table will hold hundreds of thousands of rows. You also anticipate that storage will be scarce.

In addition, you know that the data in both the "title" and "company" fields will have widely varying lengths; some contacts may not even have information in these fields. You do feel confident, however, that the majority of rows in this table will have at least ten bytes of storage in both fields. Since you want to conserve disk space wherever possible, this table is a good candidate for the VARCHAR data type:

```
CREATE TABLE CONTACTS
(
   CONTACT_NUMBER   INTEGER,
      .      .      .      .
   COMPANY          VARCHAR(50,10),
   TITLE            VARCHAR(50,10),
      .      .      .      .
);
```

Case 2

In this case, you are designing a table to hold shipping information:

```
CREATE TABLE SHIPMENTS
(
   ORDER_NUMBER          INTEGER,
      .      .      .      .
   PACK_INSTRUCTIONS     CHAR(200),
      .      .      .      .
   EXPECTED_SHIP_DATE    DATE
);
```

During your design analysis, you learned that the table will never hold more than 10,000 rows at one time. You also learned that certain shipments are much more complex than others. These shipments will often fill the entire 200 bytes of "pack_instructions", and some users requested up to 1000 bytes of storage for this field.

In this case, making "pack_instructions" a VARCHAR does not solve what is essentially a design problem. Instead, you should rethink your original design and allow the users of the system to enter as much information into the "pack_instructions" field as they need to:

```
CREATE TABLE SHIPMENTS
(
    ORDER_NUMBER           INTEGER,
      .       .       .      .
    EXPECTED_SHIP_DATE     DATE
);

CREATE TABLE PACK_INFO
(
    ORDER_NUMBER           INTEGER,
    SEQUENCE_NUMBER        SMALLINT,
    PACK_INSTRUCTIONS      CHAR(80)
);
```

In summary, consider using the VARCHAR data type when you have some or all of the following conditions:

- A very large table.
- Limited storage space.
- A character field within a reasonable range (generally, a minimum of 20 bytes, and never more than 255 bytes)
- A field that should remain with the table, (e.g., not be separated into a separate table).

Rowid

In both OnLine and SE, a rowid is a four-byte integer field that uniquely identifies the location of a data row.

In OnLine, the rowid is a hidden, pseudo column. It is a combination of the page number and the location in the slot table of the row. If a row is spread among more than one table, the rowid refers to the first page that contains the row.

If the table has indexes, OnLine stores the row IDs for the table on the index pages. If no indexes exist for the table, OnLine may read the actual data sequentially from the table, or construct a temporary table and then index the newly created temporary table.

In SE, the rowid is simply a sequential number that refers to the row's position within a table. SE row IDs always begin with one, and proceed upward.

DANGERS OF USING ROWID AS A PRIMARY KEY

You should avoid using a rowid as a table's primary key for these reasons:

- **Possibility of erroneous updates/deletes.** Regardless of the engine that you are using, it is dangerous to rely on row IDs as a primary key in your application, because once a row is deleted, its rowid is available for new rows to use.

  Let's explore a situation that could easily happen if you rely on row IDs as your primary key:

  A batch program is running through a large table, performing a series of calculations, and then updating each row as it is processed. The batch program is using the rowid as the primary key (e.g., the "WHERE rowid = `` clause in the UPDATE statement).

  At the same time, an interactive user has retrieved a row from the same table, and then deleted it. The user then adds a new, unrelated row into the table. It is very possible that the newly inserted row will receive the same rowid as the just-deleted row.

  If the batch program then attempts to update the old, deleted row based solely on the rowid it has stored in a program variable, it will update the newly inserted row instead.

  Compounding this problem will be the difficulty in determining what went wrong. This usually happens days or even weeks later, when a user finally notices something amiss with the new row.

- **Relation between rowid and data.** Row IDs, by their very nature, have absolutely no relation to the contents of their rows. Primary keys, on the other hand, are usually a value that have real-world significance, such as customer ids, account numbers, etc.
- **Non-standard.** If you want your table design to comply with ANSI standards, you should assign primary keys instead of relying on row Ids. Note that the Microsoft ODBC standard also does not support rowids.

It is much easier on programmers, database administrators, and users if you simply design (and then use) a meaningful, unique primary key for each table in your database.

Row IDs do have their place in SELECT statements and self-join conditions, but you should avoid relying on them as unique primary keys.

As an example, suppose that you have the following table:

Table 2.38 pos_detail

sku_no	store_no	sale_date	amount
5409	636	11/01/94	1.55
112	636	11/01/94	32.00
.	.	.	.
.	.	.	.
1154	709	11/02/94	93.99
5903	709	11/03/94	5.87
.	.	.	.
.	.	.	.
5409	636	11/01/94	1.55

The primary key consists of sku_no, store_no, and sale_date, but you created the table without the PRIMARY KEY syntax or a unique index on these columns.

You suspect that an update program may have duplicated some data in the table. You can use row IDs to help locate any duplicate entries:

```
SELECT X.ROWID, X.SKU_NO, X.STORE_NO, X.SALE_DATE
FROM POS_DETAIL X, POS_DETAIL Y
WHERE X.SKU_NO     = Y.SKU_NO
AND   X.STORE_NO   = Y.STORE_NO
AND   X.SALE_DATE  = Y.SALE_DATE
AND   X.ROWID     != Y.ROWID
```

By scanning the table twice, this query will return all rows that have the same values in the three-column primary key, but different row IDs.

Note: To avoid this kind of duplication, use the PRIMARY KEY syntax when you create your tables:

```
CREATE TABLE POS_DETAIL
  (
   SKU_NO INTEGER,
   STORE_NO INTEGER,
   SALE_DATE DATE,
   AMOUNT MONEY (10,2),
```

```
      .        .         .
      .        .         .
    PRIMARY KEY (SKU_NO, STORE_NO, SALE_DATE)
);
```

ROW IDS AND FRAGMENTATION

Beginning with OnLine 7.00, Informix introduced data fragmentation as another tool that you can use to speed up your queries. We discuss fragmentation in much greater detail in the "OnLine tips" section. In terms of the relationship between row IDs and fragmentation, note that one of the side-effects of fragmentation is that OnLine no longer uses row IDs on fragmented tables. This means that if your application expects to find row IDs, it will fail when reading a fragmented table.

While the best strategy is to minimize your use of row IDs, if you absolutely must use row IDs on fragmented tables, you can create the table as follows:

```
CREATE TABLE ABC
(
    .   .   .
.   .   .
) WITH ROWIDS;
```

You can also add row IDs to an existing fragmented table as follows:

```
ALTER TABLE ABC ... ADD ROWIDS;
```

In addition, you can create a rowid column when fragmenting an existing table as follows:

```
ALTER FRAGMENT ON TABLE ABC INIT WITH ROWIDS ... ;
```

You would only use the WITH ROWIDS or ADD ROWIDS clauses if the table was fragmented; using either clause on a non-fragmented table returns an error.

OnLine follows these steps when you add a rowid to a fragmented table:

1. The row IDs 4 byte integer value is added to each row.
2. The newly-created row IDs are indexed.
3. The "sysfragments" system table is updated to reflect the newly-created rowid on this table.

Again, remember that row IDs and fragmented tables are only an issue if you're using OnLine 7.00 or newer. It's always a good idea, however, to lessen your reliance on row IDs regardless of the engine you're using.

UNDERSTANDING THE INFORMIX OPTIMIZER

Introduction

As an administrator or developer, it's a good idea to understand some basic concepts about the Informix optimizer. In this section, we explain what an optimizer is, along with how it works.

Next, we describe how to instruct the optimizer to show us its query plans, via the SET EXPLAIN command. We suggest ways to use this helpful command in both development and production environments, as well as how to interpret its output.

The optimizer is completely dependent on the intelligence supplied by the UPDATE STATISTICS command. The next section details this crucial command, including what it does, when you should run it, and what options you can provide. As part of this section, we also explore what data distribution is, why it's used, and how to use UPDATE STATISTICS to generate a good sample.

Finally, we discuss how you can design your programs to work more efficiently with the optimizer, including when to use the SET OPTIMIZATION command. For those of you porting an application from another database product to Informix, we also point out the differences between runtime optimization and compile-time optimization, and their effect on performance.

What is an optimizer?

Data normalization is one of the most important advantages that relational databases provide over older data models. When you design a normalized database, your goal is to house separate data entities in separate tables. For example, in our sample appliance servicing database, we store employee profile information in the "employees" table, and service call data in the "service_calls" table. If a user wants to see the name of an employee who worked on a particular case, we need to retrieve information from both tables, and somehow combine and present this data. Not only do we want to retrieve and present this data, we also want to acquire it as efficiently as possible. This is where the optimizer enters the scene. The optimizer's job is to determine the best course of action to get us what we want.

Optimizer features and algorithms

When you request information from the database, the optimizer must decide on the best path to follow to locate and return your data. It does this by generating query plans for all possible ways to access the information. A query plan is simply the series of steps that the optimizer will take when it finds and retrieves data to satisfy a query. Each query plan answers a number of important questions, including:

- Which index(es) should it use? The database engine uses indexes for a number of different purposes, including:

– **Filtering.** When you request that the database provide you with a subset of all data, the engine filters the information to satisfy your request. For example, in the following query, we're asking the engine to filter using the "EMPLOYEE_LAST" column, and only return those rows with a value of "Sierra":

```
SELECT * FROM EMPLOYEES
WHERE EMPLOYEE_LAST = "Sierra"
```

The optimizer also determines how selective each filter is. Selective refers to how unique the filter is; more unique filters generally mean fewer reads. For example, if you were filtering on a column that held equal amounts of only two values, such as "Y" and "N", you wouldn't have a very selective filter. On the other hand, a unique customer id is extremely selective; the engine only needs to perform one read to satisfy your request.

– **Sorting.** When you use GROUP BY or ORDER BY in your query, the optimizer attempts to satisfy your sorting request with an index. If it can't, then it creates a temporary table.

As part of each query plan, the optimizer includes the index(es) that it expects to use. Different query plans often use different indexes; it's the optimizer's job to choose the best plan.

- How should it join tables? If you're joining the "employees" and "service_calls" tables, for example, the optimizer decides whether to read "employees" first, and then "service_calls", or whether to read "service_calls" first, and then "employees". As part of generating each query plan, the optimizer also chooses between two joining techniques:

– **Sort-merge join.** If the optimizer chooses this approach, the engine reads each table in the join, using the index on the joined column(s) to sort and quickly locate matching rows.

When the engine finishes processing the individual tables, it merges the resulting sets, and returns the joined rows to the requesting process. One way that you can help the optimizer choose this rapid method is to index the columns in your joins. For more information about indexing join columns, see the "Indexing strategies" section.

– **Nested loop join.** If the optimizer chooses this course, it chooses one of the tables to be the primary, or outer, table. Any other tables are designated as inner tables. The engine then follows these steps to retrieve information:

1. Read a row from the outermost table.
2. Build up a key to use for reading the next inner table.

3. Read the inner table, using the key from step 2. If there is an index on this key for this table, use it. If there isn't, either build an index, or read the table sequentially.

The engine repeats steps 2 and 3 for each table in the join, using the products of the previous steps 2 and 3 to create the join key. So, if you were joining a total of three tables, the engine performs steps 2 and 3 twice, once for the first inner table, and again for the second inner table.

Even though the sort-merge join technique generally is faster than the nested-loop tactic, there are cases where the nested-loop join has an advantage. The optimizer generates query plans using both methods, and then uses the cost of each plan to determine which method to use.

After generating each query plan, the optimizer assigns a relative cost to the plan. What do we mean by cost? Cost is not an absolute number: it doesn't reflect a number of seconds or CPU cycles. The optimizer assigns a cost to a query plan using this formula:

1. Estimate the amount of disk I/O that it needs to perform to satisfy the query, using all available statistics. These include information such as number of rows in the tables, index profiles, etc. If you're not running UPDATE STATISTICS frequently enough, the optimizer might easily miscalculate this component of the equation.
2. Estimate the amount of CPU work necessary to process the query.
3. Assign a weight coefficient to the CPU part of the cost. Since CPU time is much faster than I/O time, the optimizer uses a fractional coefficient to convert CPU time to the same unit of measurement as I/O time.
4. Combine the I/O and weighted CPU cost to produce the full cost.

After it finishes generating all possible plans, and calculating their costs, it chooses the fastest query plan. The engine then uses this query plan to locate and return data.

As an administrator or developer, you don't have much control over which query plan the optimizer chooses. You also can't force the optimizer to use sort-merge or nested-loop joins. However, you can design your database, indexes, and queries to speed up data retrieval response.

Optimizer diagnostics

How can you determine what the optimizer is doing? How can you tell if your database and index changes are making things better? How can you track problem programs or queries? You can find the answer to all these questions by using the SET EXPLAIN command.

SET EXPLAIN tells you a number of very important facts, including:

- Which query plan has the optimizer chosen?
- What is the estimated cost of the selected query plan?

- How many rows does the optimizer expect to return?
- Which indexes does the optimizer plan to use?
- What filters will the optimizer use?
- Will the engine need to create any temporary tables?

Let's learn more about this useful utility.

Before we begin discussing some examples, let's first describe the database that we'll be using in the following pages. We designed this database to track service calls for an appliance manufacturer.

```
CREATE TABLE EMPLOYEES
(
   EMPLOYEE_ID       SERIAL PRIMARY KEY,
   EMPLOYEE_FIRST    CHAR(15),
   EMPLOYEE_LAST     CHAR(20),
   EMPLOYEE_CITY     CHAR(20),
   EMPLOYEE_STATE    CHAR(2),
   DATE_OF_HIRE      DATE
) ;

CREATE INDEX EMPLOYEES_1 ON EMPLOYEES(EMPLOYEE_LAST);
CREATE INDEX EMPLOYEES_2 ON EMPLOYEES(EMPLOYEE_CITY);

CREATE TABLE APPLIANCES
(
   APPLIANCE_ID        SERIAL PRIMARY KEY,
   APPLIANCE_MANUF     CHAR(20),
   APPLIANCE_DESCRIP CHAR(60),
   APPLIANCE_COST      DECIMAL(7,2),
   APPLIANCE_RETAIL    DECIMAL(7,2)
) ;

CREATE INDEX APPLIANCES_1 ON
    APPLIANCES(APPLIANCE_DESCRIP);
CREATE INDEX APPLIANCES_2 ON
    APPLIANCES(APPLIANCE_MANUF);
CREATE INDEX APPLIANCES_3 ON
    APPLIANCES(APPLIANCE_COST);


CREATE TABLE SERVICE_CALLS
(
   SERVICE_ID          SERIAL PRIMARY KEY,
```

```
    SERVICE_EMP        INTEGER REFERENCES EMPLOYEES,
    SERVICE_DATE       DATE,
    SERVICE_APP        INTEGER REFERENCES SERVICE_CALLS,
    SERVICE_COST       DECIMAL(5,2)
) ;


CREATE TABLE PROBLEM_DESCRIP
(
    PROBLEM_ID         SERIAL PRIMARY KEY,
    PROBLEM_SERVICE    INTEGER REFERENCES SERVICE_CALLS,
    PROBLEM_SEQUENCE   SMALLINT,
    PROBLEM_TEXT       CHAR(80)
) ;

CREATE INDEX PROB_DESCRIP1 ON
    PROBLEM_DESCRIP(PROBLEM_SERVICE, PROBLEM_SEQUENCE);


CREATE TABLE COMPLAINTS
(
    COMPLAINT_ID    SERIAL PRIMARY KEY,
    COMPLAINT_TEXT CHAR(80),
    COMPLAINT_APP   INTEGER
);
```

USING SET EXPLAIN IN A DEVELOPMENT ENVIRONMENT

If you're developing an application, you should try to run SET EXPLAIN on every SQL statement that reads or modifies data. This is the best way to guarantee that your new application should perform well. The simplest and fastest way to profile your queries is to separate them into standalone scripts. Then, run SET EXPLAIN against these scripts. This is much less time-consuming than writing your application, and then testing the SQL by running the actual program. For example, look at this section of an ESQL/COBOL program:

```
PROCEDURE DIVISION.
    .       .       .
    .       .       .

PERFORM A2000-CREATE-CURSOR.
PERFORM E6500-GET-EMPLOYEE-DATA.
PERFORM S7500-GET-SERVICE-DATA.
```

```
    .       .       .
    .       .       .

A2000-CREATE-CURSOR.
    EXEC SQL.
       DECLARE SVC-CUR CURSOR FOR
       SELECT SERVICE_DATE,
              SERVICE_APP,
              SERVICE_COST
         FROM SERVICE_CALLS
        WHERE SERVICE_CALLS.SERVICE_EMP =
            :WS-SERVICE-EMP
     ORDER BY SERVICE_DATE, SERVICE_COST
    END EXEC.

E6500-GET-EMPLOYEE-DATA.
    EXEC SQL.
       SELECT EMPLOYEE_FIRST,
              EMPLOYEE_LAST
         INTO :WS-EMP-FIRST,
              :WS-EMP-LAST
         FROM EMPLOYEES
        WHERE EMPLOYEES.EMPLOYEE_NUM = :WS-EMP-NUM
    END EXEC.

S7500-GET-SERVICE-DATA.
    MOVE WS-EMP-NUM TO WS-SERVICE-EMP.
    EXEC SQL.
       OPEN SVC-CUR
    END SQL.

    EXEC SQL
       FETCH SVC-CUR INTO :WS-SERVICE-DATE,
                          :WS-SERVICE-APPLIANCE,
                          :WS-SERVICE-COST
    END EXEC.
    .       .       .
    .       .       .
```

You could wait until you've compiled the program before you begin performance testing. If you follow that approach, however, it might be difficult to determine which SQL statement is causing the most delays. You can get a better picture of your program's true performance peaks and valleys by building and testing each SQL statement individually. It's best if you can test the SQL against as realistic a database as possible. Sometimes, even an inefficient SQL runs well against an unrealistically small database; therefore you might get a false sense of security if your data set is too small. Another common mistake that developers make when building test databases is to use too narrow a variety of data. This might affect the optimizer's choice of indexes, and thereby skew your testing.

Regardless of your application development methodology, before you begin full-scale system testing, you should feel confident that you've written the best SQL you possibly can. This helps to reduce the number of "surprises" that you encounter during testing and production.

USING SET EXPLAIN IN A PRODUCTION ENVIRONMENT

Even if you're maintaining an already existing application, it's never too late to run SET EXPLAIN for your SQL. If you suspect that a particular program or routine is having performance difficulties, try recompiling your program with a SET EXPLAIN ON command at the start of the program. Then, run the program again, and examine the sqexplain.out file. Remember to remove or comment out the SET EXPLAIN command after you finish testing; the sqexplain.out file can get very large in a very short amount of time.

Once you've identified the problem SQL, try placing it into its own, separate script. Experiment with it until you get better performance. This may require you to make database or index changes; you might want to run your tests against a non-production database. Keep in mind that your sample database should be close to the same size and distribution of your production database; you'll get more realistic results that way. This approach is much faster and simpler than endlessly recompiling and testing your program executables.

Let's look at some sample SET EXPLAIN output to understand what the optimizer reports.

INTERPRETING RESULTS FROM SET EXPLAIN

In our first example, we're running a simple SELECT against the EMPLOYEES table, looking for any employees who have the last name "Robinson":

```
QUERY:
------
SELECT * FROM EMPLOYEES
WHERE EMPLOYEE_LAST = "Robinson"

Estimated Cost: 12
Estimated # of Rows Returned: 10

1) db_user.employees: INDEX PATH
```

```
   (1) Index Keys: employee_last employee_first
       Lower Index Filter:
  db_user.employees.employee_last = 'Robinson'
```

Since the "employee_last" column is indexed, the optimizer uses the index to quickly find the correct rows. "Lower Index Filter" means that the database server starts searching the index with a search criteria of "Robinson". Note that the optimizer actually chooses the index containing both the "employee_last" and the "employee_first" column, even though the search is on the first column. Remember that composite indexes are always evaluated from left to right. This means that if we were searching on "employee_first" instead, the optimizer wouldn't be able to use the index. For more information about using composite indexes, see "Composite indexing issues" in the "Indexing strategies" section of this chapter.

Before we move on to our next query, let's discuss how you should interpret the "Estimated Cost" and "Estimated # of Rows Returned" information. Recall from the "Optimizer features and algorithms" section of this chapter that the optimizer generates a cost for each query plan. It then chooses the fastest (e.g., lowest cost) query plan to do the actual work. This figure is only meaningful when compared with the cost of other query plans.

The estimated number of rows returned is the optimizer's best estimate, given available information, of how many rows you can expect your query to locate. You can generally disregard this information when testing various queries; your main goal should be to design your database and queries to run as quickly as possible.

In our next query, we're looking for any appliance that costs between $750 and $1,000:

```
QUERY:
------
SELECT * FROM APPLIANCES WHERE APPLIANCE_COST BETWEEN
     750 AND 1000

Estimated Cost: 1
Estimated # of Rows Returned: 1

1) db_user.appliances: INDEX PATH

    (1) Index Keys: appliance_cost
        Lower Index Filter:
   db_user.appliances.appliance_cost >= 750
        Upper Index Filter:
   db_user.appliances.appliance_cost <= 1000
```

The optimizer uses the index on "applicance_cost" to find the rows that satisfy our query. It uses the "Lower Index Filter" to begin searching the index for values greater than or equal to 750, and it uses the "Upper Index Filter" to exclude any values greater than or equal to 1,000.

The next query produces a weekly appliance repair status report:

```
QUERY:
------
SELECT APPLIANCE_DESCRIP,
       EMPLOYEE_LAST,
       EMPLOYEE_FIRST,
       SERVICE_DATE,
       SERVICE_COST
FROM   APPLIANCES, EMPLOYEES, SERVICE_CALLS
WHERE  APPLIANCES.APPLIANCE_ID =
    SERVICE_CALLS.SERVICE_APP
AND    SERVICE_CALLS.SERVICE_EMP =
    EMPLOYEES.EMPLOYEE_ID
AND    SERVICE_CALLS.SERVICE_DATE BETWEEN
    "11/13/1994" AND
       "11/20/1994"

Estimated Cost: 7
Estimated # of Rows Returned: 3

1) db_user.service_calls: SEQUENTIAL SCAN

   Filters: (db_user.service_calls.service_
    date >= '11/13/1994' AND
            db_user.service_calls.service_
    date <= '11/20/1994')

2) db_user.employees: INDEX PATH

   (1) Index Keys: employee_num
       Lower Index Filter:
    db_user.employees.employee_id =
    db_user.service_calls.service_emp

3) db_user.appliances: INDEX PATH

   (1) Index Keys: appliance_id
       Lower Index Filter:
```

```
    db_user.appliances.appliance_id =
    db_user.service_calls.service_app
```

The optimizer decided that the most efficient way to process this query was to first read the "service_calls" table sequentially, looking for rows that meet the "service_date" criteria. Next, it joins the resulting set to the "employees" table, and then joins the results to the "appliances" tables. The optimizer can use indexes to speed access to both of the subsequent tables.

If you believe that your application would frequently run this query, you could improve the query's speed by placing an index on the "service_date" column in the "service_calls" table. The optimizer could then quickly locate rows using the new index, instead of reading every row in what could be a large table. However, remember that the optimizer can only use one index per table during the query, so adding a new index might not help in all cases. Review the "Indexing Strategies" section to learn more about the engine works with indexes.

In the next query, we examine what happens if you sort by columns from more than one table:

```
QUERY:
------
SELECT APPLIANCE_DESCRIP,
       SERVICE_ID,
       SERVICE_DATE,
       PROBLEM_SEQUENCE,
       PROBLEM_TEXT
FROM   APPLIANCES A, SERVICE_CALLS S, PROBLEM_DESCRIP P
WHERE  A.APPLIANCE_ID  = S.SERVICE_APP
AND    S.SERVICE_ID    = P.PROBLEM_SERVICE
ORDER BY S.SERVICE_ID, P.PROBLEM_SEQUENCE

Estimated Cost: 17
Estimated # of Rows Returned: 12
Temporary Files Required For: Order By

1) db_user.p: SEQUENTIAL SCAN

2) db_user.s: INDEX PATH

    (1) Index Keys: service_id
       Lower Index Filter: db_user.s.service_id =
                                db_user.p.problem_service
```

```
3) db_user.a: INDEX PATH

    (1) Index Keys: appliance_num
       Lower Index Filter: db_user.a.appliance_num =
                                db_user.s.service_app
```

The optimizer can't sort on columns from more than one table, even if those columns are indexed. Instead, it creates a temporary table for the resulting data set. In the above example, you could rewrite the query so that you sort on the "service_id" column from the "problem_descrip" table, instead of from the "service_calls" table. "problem_service" is the corresponding column to "service_id" in the "problem_descrip'table.

The next query illustrates how the optimizer utilizes the "sort-merge" join:

```
QUERY:
------
SELECT APPLIANCE_MANUF,
       APPLIANCE_DESCRIP,
       COMPLAINT_TEXT
FROM   APPLIANCES A,
       COMPLAINTS C
WHERE  A.APPLIANCE_ID = C.COMPLAINT_APP

Estimated Cost: 11
Estimated # of Rows Returned: 10

1) db_user.a: SEQUENTIAL SCAN

SORT SCAN: db_user.a.appliance_id

2) db_user.c: SEQUENTIAL SCAN

SORT SCAN: db_user.c.complaint_app

MERGE JOIN
    Merge Filters: db_user.c.complaint_app =
    db_user.a.appliance_id
```

Since there aren't any indexes for the optimizer to use to process this query, it first reads through both tables. It then sorts the information, and merges the results during the join operation.

In the "SQL tips" section of Chapter 3, we point out how ascending indexes don't help you if you're requesting a descending sort. The following queries demonstrate what the optimizer produces for both an ascending sort and a descending sort.

```
QUERY:
------
SELECT *
FROM   SERVICE_CALLS
ORDER BY SERVICE_COST

Estimated Cost: 12
Estimated # of Rows Returned: 10

1) db_user.service_calls: INDEX PATH

   (1) Index Keys: service_cost
```

Since there is an index on "service_cost", the optimizer uses it to sort the resulting data set. On the other hand, look what happens if we request a descending sort:

```
QUERY:
------
SELECT *
FROM   SERVICE_CALLS
ORDER BY SERVICE_COST DESC

Estimated Cost: 25
Estimated # of Rows Returned: 10
Temporary Files Required For: Order By

1) db_user.service_calls: SEQUENTIAL SCAN
```

Since the database engine can't use the "service_cost" index, it creates a temporary table to hold the results.

Next, let's look at how SET EXPLAIN reports on a subquery. In this case, we're running a query to return all column names for the "service_calls" table.

```
QUERY:
------
SELECT TABNAME, COLNAME
FROM   SYSTABLES A, SYSCOLUMNS B
WHERE  B.TABID IN
(SELECT TABID
```

```
 FROM   SYSTABLES
 WHERE  TABNAME = "service_calls")
AND A.TABID = B.TABID

Estimated Cost: 33
Estimated # of Rows Returned: 55

    1) db_user.b: INDEX PATH

        (1) Index Keys: tabid colno
            Lower Index Filter: db_user.b.tabid =
    ANY <subquery>

    2) db_user.a: INDEX PATH
         (1) Index Keys: tabid
            Lower Index Filter: db_user.a.tabid =
    db_user.b.tabid

    Subquery:
    ---------
    Estimated Cost: 11
    Estimated # of Rows Returned: 9

    1) informix.systables: INDEX PATH

         (1) Index Keys: tabname owner
            Lower Index Filter:
     informix.systables.tabname = 'service_calls'
```

Our subquery first returns the "tabid" for the table that has a "tabname" equal to "service_calls". The optimizer chooses the index on "tabname" to quickly locate the "tabid" value. Next, the optimizer uses the results from the subquery to drive the search on the "syscolumns" table. Finally, it joins the results to the "systables" table, using the "tabid" column as a key.

In the "Optimizing SQL" section, we discussed how you can get better performance by using the UNION option. The following example demonstrates this concept. In this case, we want information from the "employees" table that satisfies one of two conditions:

```
QUERY:
------
SELECT *
FROM   EMPLOYEES E
```

```
WHERE  (E.EMPLOYEE_LAST = "Lafong" AND
    E.EMPLOYEE_CITY = "Philadelphia")
OR     (E.EMPLOYEE_LAST = "Hasenfeffer")

Estimated Cost: 2
Estimated # of Rows Returned: 10

1) db_user.e: SEQUENTIAL SCAN

  Filters: ((db_user.e.employee_last = 'Lafong' AND
           db_user.e.employee_city = 'Philadelphia' )
           OR db_user.e.employee_last = 'Hasenfeffer' )
```

Even though both the "employee_last" and "employee_city" columns are indexed, the optimizer decided that it would be faster to sequentially scan the "employees" table. By using a UNION clause to separate the OR conditions, we can "force" the optimizer to use the appropriate indexes:

```
QUERY:
------
SELECT *
FROM   EMPLOYEES E
WHERE  E.EMPLOYEE_LAST = "Lafong" AND
    E.EMPLOYEE_CITY = "Philadelphia"

UNION

SELECT *
FROM   EMPLOYEES E
WHERE  E.EMPLOYEE_LAST = "Hasenfeffer"

Estimated Cost: 15
Estimated # of Rows Returned: 6

1) db_user.e: INDEX PATH

    Filters: db_user.e.employee_last = 'Lafong'

   (1) Index Keys: employee_city
       Lower Index Filter:
          db_user.e.employee_city = 'Philadelphia'
```

```
Union Query:
------------

1) db_user.e: INDEX PATH

    (1) Index Keys: employee_last employee_first
        Lower Index Filter:
           db_user.e.employee_last = 'Hasenfeffer'
```

UPDATE STATISTICS

The optimizer can only make good data access decisions if it has reliable information about the current state of the database. UPDATE STATISTICS is the command that provides this information to the optimizer.

WHAT DOES UPDATE STATISTICS DO?

The UPDATE STATISTICS command instructs the database server to answer the following questions for each table:

- How many rows does the table currently have?
- How many pages of data does the table currently use?
- What is the data distribution for a column(s) within the table? See the "Data distribution" section later in this chapter for more information about this option.
- What is the second smallest value for each column?
- What is the second largest value for each column?

For each index within the table, UPDATE STATISTICS also answers these questions:

- How many unique keys are there in the index?
- How close is the actual physical order of the table to the order of the index? (This is known as clustering.)
- How many unique keys are there in the index?
- How many levels does the btree occupy?
- How many level 0 nodes are there?

In addition, you can run UPDATE STATISTICS to refresh your stored procedure query plans. Recall that pre-optimization is one of the major benefits of stored procedures; UPDATE STATISTICS can improve your stored procedure performance by re-examining and re-optimizing procedures.

WHEN SHOULD YOU RUN UPDATE STATISTICS?

UPDATE STATISTICS collects data that plays a crucial role in query optimization. Consequently, it's important that you run this command often enough. On the other hand, if you run UPDATE STATISTICS too often, you can degrade your system's performance, and possibly inconvenience users as well. Like many other tuning issues, your goal should be to achieve a balance: run UPDATE STATISTICS often enough to provide the optimizer with accurate information, but only when necessary. Fortunately, you can run this command in a wide variety of ways. You can run UPDATE STATISTICS for:

- The entire database (all columns within all tables)
- One table in the database (all columns)
- One column within one table
- All stored procedures
- One particular stored procedure

Use the following "do and don't" guidelines to help achieve the right balance:

- Do run UPDATE STATISTICS at least once for every table in your database. Remember that these statistics aren't automatically updated; you must run the command at least once to gather this vital information.
- Don't repeatedly run UPDATE STATISTICS for static tables. If a table doesn't change, there's no need for you to go to the effort of continually running UPDATE STATISTICS for it. In fact, this suggestion holds true for tables that change infrequently, as well.

  For example, suppose that you're maintaining a billing system. One of your largest tables holds account history information, and you update it via a batch program once a month. In this case, you don't need to run UPDATE STATISTICS nightly, or even weekly for this table. Instead, run the command only after you make your major changes.
- Do create automated jobs to run UPDATE STATISTICS when the system isn't very busy. It's easy to forget to run this important command; executing it via an automated process ensures that you'll run it regularly. This is essential for tables that frequently change; if the optimizer doesn't have an accurate picture of what the table looks like, it could choose the wrong query plan.
- Don't run UPDATE STATISTICS during peak processing time. This command briefly locks the system table entries for each data table that it updates. This might cause concurrence problems with other application programs that are running at the same time, especially if those programs create or modify indexes. However, if you use the SET LOCK MODE TO WAIT option, your programs should be able to gracefully handle a row that is briefly locked.

- Do be careful when you request the MEDIUM/HIGH (version 6.00 and newer) options. These powerful options come at a price: it might take a long time for the optimizer to finish processing all the rows that it needs to read to satisfy a MEDIUM/HIGH request. Therefore, try to schedule these requests to run when your system isn't too busy.
- Don't forget to use the HIGH option to generate accurate data distributions for indexed columns. For more information about this option, see the "UPDATE STATISTICS and data distribution" section of this chapter.
- Do run UPDATE STATISTICS for temporary tables that you plan to use heavily. For example, if you build and index a large temporary table within your application, you can instruct the optimizer to perform all UPDATE STATISTICS tasks for the temporary table.

WHAT OPTIONS CAN YOU USE WITH UPDATE STATISTICS?

Data distribution

With each new release, Informix has refined the optimizer's capability and intelligence. Beginning with version 6.00, the optimizer generates data distribution information to help it choose the best query plan. Let's examine this topic in more detail, especially as it relates to performance.

You can think of data distribution as a survey of a column's actual values. When creating a data distribution, the optimizer scans the column being surveyed, and evenly distributes the retrieved values into a number of containers. These aren't true containers; they're closer to logical groupings of information. Any heavily duplicated values get placed into their own containers.

After the optimizer has finished assigning data to containers, it analyzes the data within each container to determine certain information, including:

- Number of distinct values in the container.
- The largest value within the container.

Once the optimizer finishes scrutinizing the containers, it's ready to create a data distribution profile. This profile includes:

- The biggest and smallest value for the column.
- The number of values that each container held.
- The last container size, since it might be smaller than the rest of the containers.

After the optimizer completes this last task, it records the information in the "sysdistrib" system table, which looks like this:

Table 2.39 'sysdistrib" system

Column name	Data type	Explanation
tabid	integer	Table number for the surveyed table.
colno	smallint	Column number for the surveyed table.
sequence	integer	Ordinality (for multiple entries).
constructed	date	Creation date of this distribution.
mode	char(1)	(H)igh, (M)edium, or (L)ow.
resolution	float	Distribution's resolution.
confidence	float	Distribution's confidence.
encdat	char(256)	Distribution's histogram, encoded.

Before we proceed any further, let's define what we mean by "confidence" and "resolution".

Confidence refers to the reliability of your data sample, and is only a factor when you use UPDATE STATISTICS MEDIUM. We'll explain the different levels of UPDATE STATISTICS a little later. Confidence ranges between .80 and .99, with a default of .95. The optimizer uses this value when it decides how many rows to evaluate at data distribution creation time. If you specify a low confidence value of .80, for example, this tells the optimizer that you're not interested in a very high level of data distribution confidence. With this in mind, the optimizer then samples fewer rows than it would if you had specified a confidence level of .99.

Resolution is a number that tells the optimizer how many containers to create when generating the distribution. You request this number when you run UPDATE STATISTICS. We'll examine exactly how you specify it a little later. Resolution is expressed as a percentage, and can be between .005 and 10. If you request 10, the optimizer puts 10 percent of your data into each container, thereby creating 10 containers. If you specify two, the optimizer creates 50 containers, each holding two percent of your data. The optimizer gets a better picture of your data when it has more containers to work with. However, you can go too far, and cause the optimizer to work unnecessarily hard if you create too many containers (by using a very low resolution). Try experimenting with this value to learn the best resolution for a particular column.

UPDATE STATISTICS and data distribution

You can now choose one of three possible modes (low, medium, or high) when you run UPDATE STATISTICS. Let's look at what happens when you select each of these modes, especially as it relates to data distribution:

1. **Low** This is the least investigative mode; it doesn't generate any data distribution at all. It's also the default mode, and is the mode that earlier

versions of the optimizer used. When you use this mode, the optimizer reads all rows from the data table, but only updates rows in the "systables", "syscolumns", and "sysindexes" tables; the optimizer doesn't produce a data distribution map for the table.

2. **Medium** Like the "low" mode, this method also reads all the rows in the table. The optimizer uses a random subset of these rows to build the data distribution. The "confidence" parameter partially influences the amount of time that UPDATE STATISTICS MEDIUM takes; see the examples of data distribution later in this chapter for more information about "confidence". Generally, you can run UPDATE STATISTICS MEDIUM for any column that's not at the start of an index. For columns that are at the start of an index, run UPDATE STATISTICS HIGH, and use whatever resolution you feel is appropriate.
3. **High** This is the most inquisitive of the three UPDATE STATISTICS modes. It's also the most time consuming. It reads and evaluates all rows in the table to create a data distribution. It's a good idea to use this option for any columns that are at the start of an index; the optimizer can use the index to gather the statistics quickly.

While there's no way for you to directly determine how much time that this command takes, you can exercise some control by modifying the "resolution" parameter. For more information about this parameter, see the previous section.

Data distribution examples

You can use the "dbschema" utility to examine the optimizer's distribution. For example, suppose that you're maintaining an accounts receivable system. One of your larger tables is the "accounts" table, which holds profile information for your customers. One important column in this table is the "account_balance" column. Let's look at what the optimizer produces for two different UPDATE STATISTICS requests.

For the first request, we ran this UPDATE STATISTICS command:

```
UPDATE STATISTICS MEDIUM
      FOR TABLE ACCOUNTS(ACCOUNT_BALANCE)
    RESOLUTION 7 .99
```

These parameters instruct the optimizer to put seven percent of the data into each container. In addition, the confidence factor of .99 means that the optimizer samples a large percentage of the values when creating the distribution.

After you run the UPDATE STATISTICS command, use "dbschema -d ar_database -hd accounts" to produce this output:

```
Distribution for db_user.accounts.account_balance

Constructed on 01/30/95

Medium Mode, 7.000000 Resolution, 0.990000 Confidence


--- DISTRIBUTION ---

       (                                  3.00)
   1: ( 3401,    3309,                  570.00)
   2: ( 3401,    3401,                 1071.00)
   3: ( 3401,    3309,                 1701.00)
   4: ( 3401,    3401,                 2223.00)
   5: ( 3401,    3309,                 2655.00)
   6: ( 3401,    3217,                 3045.00)
   7: ( 3401,    3309,                 3527.00)
   8: ( 3401,    3309,                 4040.00)
   9: ( 3401,    3401,                 4640.00)
  10: ( 3401,    3401,                 5845.00)
  11: ( 3401,    3309,                 7103.00)
  12: ( 3401,    3309,                 8678.00)
  13: ( 3401,    3401,                12595.00)
  14: ( 3401,    3401,                19397.00)
  15: ( 2390,    2390,                50529.00)
```

Since we requested a seven percent resolution, the optimizer created 15 containers. How do you interpret this information? The first column is the number of values held in the container. In this case, the optimizer set up fifteen containers, and stored 3401 values in each of the first fourteen. The fifteenth container held 2390 rows. The second column is the number of distinct values in the container. For example, of container eight's 3401 values, 3309 are distinct. Finally, the third column is the high value found in the container. For container seven, the high value was 3527.

Next, we ran this UPDATE STATISTICS command:

```
UPDATE STATISTICS HIGH
FOR TABLE ACCOUNTS(ACCOUNT_BALANCE) RESOLUTION 5
```

This instructed the optimizer to create enough containers so that each held five percent of our data. Since we chose the HIGH option, the optimizer read all the rows in the table; there was no need to specify a confidence level. The output looked like this:

```
Distribution for db_user.accounts.account_balance

Constructed on 01/30/95

High Mode, 5.000000 Resolution


--- DISTRIBUTION ---

      (                                3.00)
   1: ( 2500,    396,                410.00)
   2: ( 2500,    349,                768.00)
   3: ( 2500,    350,               1126.00)
   4: ( 2500,    348,               1482.00)
   5: ( 2500,    350,               1842.00)
   6: ( 2500,    351,               2198.00)
   7: ( 2500,    349,               2556.00)
   8: ( 2500,    350,               2911.00)
   9: ( 2500,    351,               3269.00)
  10: ( 2500,    347,               3626.00)
  11: ( 2500,    366,               4001.00)
  12: ( 2500,    439,               4457.00)
  13: ( 2500,    550,               5032.00)
  14: ( 2500,    699,               5783.00)
  15: ( 2500,    899,               6792.00)
  16: ( 2500,   1132,               8206.00)
  17: ( 2500,   1429,              10406.00)
  18: ( 2500,   1594,              14359.00)
  19: ( 2500,   1847,              22755.00)
  20: ( 2495,   2368,              50529.00)
```

Another way that you could use this information would be to import it into a spreadsheet, and then create data distribution reports and graphs.

Programming considerations

SET OPTIMIZATION

As a programmer, you can control the level of optimization that the database server performs. This can be very helpful in certain situations. Normally, the optimization level is HIGH. This means that the optimizer evaluates all possible query plans and chooses the one that should yield the best performance. However, this may actually hamper response, especially if you're joining many tables, using very complex views, or running against small sets of data.

If you request that the optimization level be set to LOW, the optimizer uses a simpler, faster procedure to choose a query plan. In most cases, this query plan won't be as efficient as the plan that a HIGH level chooses. However, if you're having a difficult time with a particular query, try experimenting with both levels of optimization. You might find one of the cases where a LOW optimization actually returns data more rapidly.

Note that one additional factor that you must take into consideration is the size of your database. If you're testing queries against a small subset of data, or against data that doesn't have a realistic distribution, the optimizer may choose one path during development, and another path during production. Furthermore, SET OPTIMIZATION LOW might work well against the small database, but result in poor productivity when faced with a more truthful data profile. The best time to use SET OPTIMIZATION LOW is when you feel that the optimizer's cost of evaluating permutations far outweighs the cost of the actual data access. This occurs chiefly during very complex queries executed against small data sets.

Just as you can use different isolation levels (with OnLine) within the same program, you can also change your optimization level inside one program as often as you need. Let's look at an example, using 4GL and the appliance repair database from earlier in this chapter:

```
DECLARE EMPLOYEE_CUR CURSOR FOR
   SELECT EMPLOYEE_NUM.
          EMPLOYEE_LAST,
          EMPLOYEE_FIRST,
            EMPLOYEE_HIRE
     FROM EMPLOYEES
    WHERE EMPLOYEE_HIRE < "01/01/1990"

OPEN EMPLOYEE_CUR

    .         .         .         .
    .         .         .         .

SET OPTIMIZATION LOW

DECLARE WORK_CUR CURSOR FOR
   SELECT APPLIANCE_NUM,
          APPLIANCE_DESC,
          SERVICE_DATE,
```

```
            SERVICE_EMP,
            PROBLEM_TEXT
      FROM  APPLIANCES A,
            SERVICE_CALLS S,
            PROBLEM_DESCRIP P
     WHERE  A.APPLIANCE_NUM = S.SERVICE_APP
       AND  S.SERVICE_ID = P.PROBLEM_SERVICE

OPEN WORK_CUR

    .         .         .         .
    .         .         .         .

SET OPTIMIZATION HIGH
```

Realistically, however, your query should be much more complex than the one listed above before you issue a SET OPTIMIZATION LOW command.

DYNAMIC OPTIMIZATION VERSUS COMPILE-TIME OPTIMIZATION

Unless you PREPARE your statements, or use stored procedures, the optimizer re-evaluates your SQL at runtime. This is very different than some other database products, which only optimize SQL at compile-time. If you port a previously-written application to Informix, you might notice some performance degradation, especially if you'd previously grouped all your SQL together.

For example, suppose that you repeatedly call the following routine:

```
void declare_cursors()
{
   EXEC SQL
      DECLARE E_CURSOR CURSOR FOR SELECT *
        FROM EMPLOYEES
   END EXEC;

   EXEC SQL
      DECLARE A_CURSOR CURSOR FOR SELECT *
        FROM APPLIANCES
   END EXEC;

   EXEC SQL
      DECLARE S_CURSOR CURSOR FOR SELECT *
        FROM SERVICE_CALLS
   END EXEC;
}
```

For database products that optimize when you compile your programs, the above function doesn't cause any unnecessary work, regardless of how many times you call it, since the SQL was optimized when the program was bound.

However, if you port your application to Informix, each time you DECLARE a cursor, the SQL gets re-optimized. This would make repeated calls to the above routine very expensive. How can you prevent this extra optimizer work? There are a number of ways:

- Only call the "declare_cursors" routine once, when you start the program. This approach requires the least amount of changes to your existing application.
- Use a global or static variable to prevent re-declaring the same cursor:

```
static int e_cur, a_cur, s_cur = 0;

void declare_cursors()
{
   if !(e_cur)
   {
      EXEC SQL
         DECLARE E_CURSOR CURSOR FOR
           SELECT * FROM EMPLOYEES
      END EXEC;
      e_cur++;
   }

   if !(a_cur)
   {
      EXEC SQL
         DECLARE A_CURSOR CURSOR FOR
           SELECT * FROM APPLIANCES
      END EXEC;
      a_cur++;
   }

   if !(s_cur)
   {
      EXEC SQL
         DECLARE S_CURSOR CURSOR FOR
           SELECT * FROM SERVICE_CALLS
      END EXEC;
      s_cur++;
   }
}
```

- Use PREPARE to pre-optimize your SQL. For more information about the benefits of PREPARE, see the "General tips" section.

Chapter 3
Optimizing Application Code

INTRODUCTION

In this chapter, we explore how much impact your application code has on system performance.

Since Structured Query Language (SQL) is the primary means of communicating with an Informix database, we devote the first section to a discussion about optimizing your application's SQL code. This includes tips on retrieving information from the database by using joins, substring searches, unions, views, and subqueries. We also examine how to best use (and avoid) temporary tables and math inside your SQL statements. This includes some new SQL math functions found in Informix 6.00. Finally, we explore several sorting issues, including composite indexes, ascending and descending indexes, and controlling sort memory usage.

Our next section deals with general programming topics, regardless of what programming language you use to build your applications. These topics include efficient memory utilization, transactions, concurrency, reducing pipe traffic, and error checking, along with special cursor issues and locking. We also explore a number of techniques that you can use to load data in bulk.

Since so many programmers use INFORMIX-4GL to build powerful, robust applications, we dedicate a separate section to specific 4GL topics, such as forms, reports, and compilation hints. Since there may be situations when you should "jump out" of 4GL to C, we also cite examples of these types of cases.

There are a number of ways to improve ESQL/C performance. These topics form the basis of the next section, and include memory management, built-in functions, dynamic SQL, compilation hints, and process control.

Informix engines version 5.00 and newer provide stored procedure support. In the next section of this chapter, we examine how you can use stored procedures to improve performance, especially in the areas of client/server and security. Since Informix engines 5.01 and newer enable you to use triggers, we also discuss how triggers can help with data replication and audit trails. If you're using Informix 6.00, you can also take advantage of cascading deletes to speed up and simplify your programs.

Closing out this chapter is a detailed discussion of how to program efficient applications for distributed systems and client/server environments.

SQL TIPS

With the exception of your database design, your SQL statements have the most impact on system performance. Consequently, it is a good idea to carefully examine your SQL during development as well as during production.

In this section, we focus on some of the most common areas for SQL performance improvement. Data types can affect performance, so we'll explore the costs of non-numeric versus numeric joins and filters, as well as character substring searches. Temporary tables can have a big effect on performance too, so we'll learn where and when to use them. Views, embedded SQL math, subqueries, and unions are all helpful features, but each of them has a cost that you should consider. To conclude, we'll discuss the implications of sorting.

If your system is in production and you have a large volume of data, consider creating a small scale test case before you implement any of the SQL changes suggested in this chapter. This would involve the following steps:

1. Create copies of the existing table(s) schema.
2. Populate these tables with a manageable amount of data.
3. Turn on SET EXPLAIN.
4. Test the new query/sort.
5. Adjust the query and/or database design to improve the query plan.

You should modify your production environment only if you are convinced that your change improves performance.

Numeric versus non-numeric joins and filters

When you build a table through the ISQL or DBACCESS utilities, the default data type for each column is CHAR. A surprising number of developers and DBAs simply accept this default data type for columns that really only contain numeric information. This can decrease performance on filters and join conditions, as well as increase storage requirements. For example, assume that you have an application that tracks pieces of equipment that are stored at several different sites:

Table 3.1 Inventory_header

part_number	part_desc .....
78	Monochrome ASCII terminal
143	Monochrome 3270 terminal
.	.
.	.
11058	Filing cabinet

Table 3.2 Inventory_detail

location	part_number	part_count....
Phoenix	78	0
Detroit	78	25
New York	78	148
.	.	.
.	.	.
Tampa	11058	17
Boston	11058	62

During your design, you note that the "part_number" is a number that is always between 1 and 12000. However, when you create the tables through DBACCESS, you define the fields as a CHAR(20), and you place an index on these columns in each table.

A commonly used report in your application prints a listing of the count of inventory items at all locations:

```
SELECT B.LOCATION,   A.PART_NUMBER,
       A.PART_DESC, B.PART_COUNT
FROM   INVENTORY_HEADER A, INVENTORY_DETAIL B
WHERE  A.PART_NUMBER = B.PART_NUMBER
ORDER BY B.LOCATION, A.PART_NUMBER
```

If the "part_number" columns in both tables is defined as CHAR(20), the join operation requires the optimizer to compare the values in each table byte-by-byte, up to 20 times per row.

Since you know from your research that the "part_number" column is always numeric, and always between 1 and 12000, you should redefine the column in both tables as SMALLINT. This aids your application in several ways:

- Since SMALLINTs are stored in only two bytes, you save a significant amount of CPU work during join operations or filter conditions, especially if there are many rows to process.
- You save 18 bytes per row per table (assuming that it was previously defined as CHAR(20)).
- You save 18 bytes per row per table for all indexes that use this column.

Ideally, as part of your initial systems analysis, you determine which fields should be stored as SMALLINT or INTEGER. If, on the other hand, you have a production system, you should consider examining the data in CHAR columns to see if there are any candidates for data conversion. Pay special attention to join columns; many times you find a CHAR field being joined to an INTEGER or SMALLINT.

Substring searches

Searching through indexed character data is inherently easier when your search criteria starts in the leftmost position and moves to the right, than when your search criteria begins elsewhere in the data. For example, imagine that you were handed an enormous phone book, and told to locate two types of information:

- All last names in the phone book that start with the letter "L".
- All entries in the phone book that have "L" as the third letter in the last name.

The first request would be far easier to produce, since the phone book is already "indexed" (by last name, first name). You would simply turn to the section of the book that starts with "L", and then begin reading off the names, until you found the first entry where the last name began with "M". This type of processing is analogous to running the following SQL statement:

```
QUERY:
------
SELECT * FROM NAMES WHERE LAST_NAME = "L*"

Estimated Cost: 2
Estimated # of Rows Returned: 1

1) db_user.names: INDEX PATH

    (1) Index Keys: last_name
        Lower Index Filter:
            db_user.names.last_ name = 'L*'
```

If there is an index on the "last_name" column in the "names" table, the optimizer uses it to help process the above query.

The second request is harder to process, for both machines and humans. If you had the phone book in front of you, you would need to read the first three letters of every entry, from cover to cover. You would mark off all records where the third letter was "L". This type of processing is analogous to running the following SQL statement.

```
QUERY:
------
SELECT * FROM NAMES WHERE LAST_NAME[3] = "L"

Estimated Cost: 2
Estimated # of Rows Returned: 1
1) db_user.names: SEQUENTIAL SCAN

      Filters: db_user.names.last_name[3,3] = 'l'
```

Even though there is an index on "last_name", the optimizer is unable to use it. To satisfy your request, the optimizer is forced to operate sequentially, on what could be an enormous table. This definitely hurts performance.

If you find that there are cases where you need to sort on a non-initial substring, consider revising your database design. For example, assume that you are working with a table like this:

Table 3.3 Contracts

client_num	sign_date ....
E1203T	11/15/94
S0054D	11/17/94
C0078D	04/24/94
W0003M	02/14/94
E0144T	05/17/94
C0012M	09/03/94
.	.
.	.

This table tracks the status of contracts signed with clients, and has many thousands of rows. The "client_num" field is indexed, and is composed as shown in Figure 3.1 below:

Figure 3.1

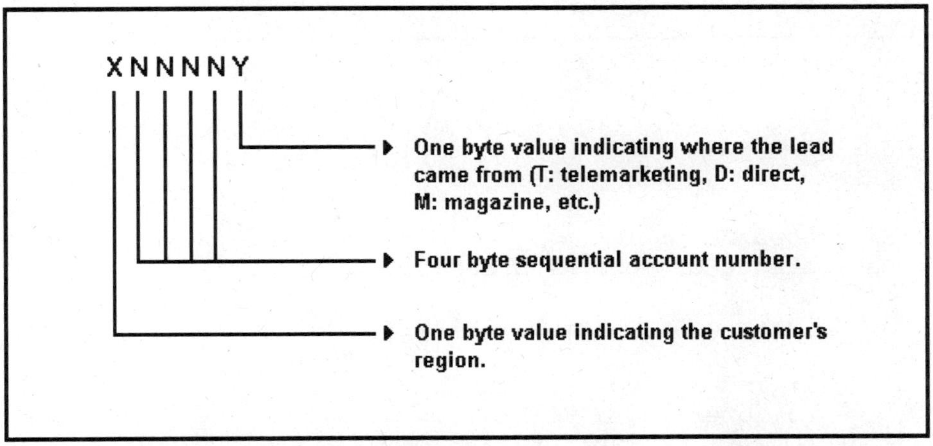

At some point, a user requests a report that only retrieves information based on the account number, which is the middle four bytes of the client_num:

```
QUERY:
------
SELECT * FROM CONTRACTS
WHERE CLIENT_NUM[2,5] BETWEEN "0025" AND "0100"

Estimated Cost: 2
Estimated # of Rows Returned: 1

1) db_user.contracts: SEQUENTIAL SCAN

    Filters: (db_user.contracts.client_num[2,5]
     >= '0025'
            AND db_user.contracts.client_num[2,5]
     <= '0100' )
```

On a large table, this type of query results in very slow performance. It would be better to redesign the table, and separate the account number into its own field. As an additional benefit, you could now change the "account_num" data type to SMALLINT, which yields better performance on joins and conserves disk storage as well:

Table 3.4 Contracts

region_code	**account_num**	**lead_source**	**sign_date ....**
E	1203	T	11/15/94
S	54	D	11/15/94
C	78	D	04/24/94
W	3	M	02/14/94
E	144	T	05/17/94
C	12	M	09/03/94

```
QUERY:
------
SELECT * FROM CONTRACTS
WHERE ACCOUNT_NUM BETWEEN 25 AND 100

Estimated Cost: 1
Estimated # of Rows Returned: 1

1) db_user.contracts: INDEX PATH

    (1) Index Keys: account_num
        Lower Index Filter:
    db_user.contracts.account_num >= 25
        Upper Index Filter:
    db_user.contracts.account_num <= 100
```

There are also cases where you search for information by using the LIKE and MATCHES keywords. Again, watch for cases where you do not use initial strings. Run SET EXPLAIN if you are not sure whether you are using indexes.

Temporary tables

Temporary tables are a double-edged sword: they can be very helpful when used properly; they can also greatly diminish your application's performance.

These tables are created in one of two ways:

1. Implicitly: by the Informix engine
2. Explicitly: by the application program or query

Let's explore both types of temporary table, as well as situations where they can either help you or hurt you.

IMPLICIT TEMPORARY TABLES

The engine creates implicit temporary tables when you request any of the following:

1. Sort of information on non-indexed columns
2. Scroll cursor
3. DISTINCT or UNIQUE

For more information about scroll cursors and their use of temporary tables, refer to the "General tips" section.

One of the worst types of implicit temporary tables is created when a user or application requests an enormous set of data, sorted by a non-indexed column(s). See the "Sorting" section of this chapter.

Even a small number of temporary tables can have a big impact if dozens, hundreds, or even thousands of users are concurrently creating these "small tables". You might find that eliminating even one temporary table per application substantially improves throughput and response time.

Implicit temporary tables hurt performance in at least four ways:

1. Their CPU usage slows down the application that creates them.
2. Their disk usage slows down the application that creates them.
3. They devour CPU time that could probably be spent on other applications.
4. They consume disk space that other applications may legitimately need.

Fortunately, you can control the location of this disk space by setting the DBTEMPSPACE environment variable. We discuss DBTEMPSPACE a little later in this chapter, when we review temporary table placement.

It's clearly in your best interest to hunt down and eliminate as many implicit temporary tables as you can.

Explicit temporary tables

You create explicit temporary tables voluntarily, through your application, by using one of the two following statements:

```
SELECT (column list) from (table) INTO TEMP (temp name)
```

- or -

```
CREATE TEMP TABLE (temp name) ( column list )
```

There are certain types of situations where you can improve performance by creating and using a relatively small temporary table as a subset of a much larger table.

For example, assume that you have a transaction table that contains 40 million rows, and spans four months. Suppose that you need to run a series of reports for only one day's data. By analyzing your query plan and application code, you realize that your program makes multiple passes of the transaction file to retrieve roughly only 1/160th (one day out of four months) of the data. This is a case where you would benefit from creating a temporary table and populating it with the (relatively) small subset of data. You could then create any necessary indexes on the temporary table, and begin your multiple pass process.

If you're using the OnLine engine, version 7.00 or later, you can use table fragmentation to achieve the same performance results without having to generate a temporary table. See the "OnLine tips" section for more detail about this feature.

IMPROVING TEMPORARY TABLE PERFORMANCE

If you use temporary tables, there are several steps that you can take to improve their performance, including:

- **Index appropriate columns.** Just because a table is temporary doesn't mean that it shouldn't be indexed. If you create an explicit temporary table, and then plan to access its information, try creating indexes on your search columns. You can use the same indexing guidelines for temporary tables as you use for permanent tables.
- **Turning off logging.** If you have transaction logging enabled on your database, and you create an explicit temporary table, you can improve performance by specifying WITH NO LOG in the CREATE TEMP TABLE or SELECT INTO TEMP statements. This stops the database engine from unnecessarily logging modifications to the temporary table. You benefit by reducing overhead, as well as by not using excess log space.

- **Temporary table placement** Another way to speed up explicit temporary tables is to put them on your system's fastest devices.
  For SE, your CREATE TEMP TABLE syntax would look like this:

  ```
  CREATE TEMP TABLE TEMP_ADDRESSES
  (
     COL1 CHAR(10),
     .     .
     .     .
  ) IN "/fast_drive/xxx";
  ```

  where "/fast_drive/xxx" is the actual path and filename that you want to use.

  For OnLine version 6.0 and newer, you can set the DBSPACETEMP environment variable to tell the engine which dbspace to use when creating temporary tables. You can specify a series of dbspaces as follows:

  ```
  setenv DBSPACETEMP dbspacetmp1: dbspacetmp2: ...
  ```

  You can also set the DBSPACETEMP configuration parameter in your ONCONFIG file.

- **UPDATE STATISTICS** If you explicitly create a temporary table, and plan to repeatedly use it over a period of time, consider running UPDATE STATISTICS on the temporary table to give the optimizer more information about the new temporary table:

  ```
  CREATE TEMP TABLE XXX (COL1 CHAR(10)...);

  INSERT INTO XXX SELECT * FROM YYY;

  UPDATE STATISTICS FOR TABLE XXX;
  ```

  If you're using 6.00 engines, you may even want to consider creating distributions for the columns within your temporary table. For more information about UPDATE STATISTICS and data distributions, see the "Understanding the Informix optimizer" section.

In summary, temporary tables by themselves are not necessarily a bad thing. They only become a problem when the database engine is repeatedly forced to create dozens of them because there is no other way to process the data. If you have an existing application, try to find all places where the server creates temporary tables. Turn on SET

EXPLAIN for a day and monitor the "sqexplain.out" file. You may be surprised with what you learn.

Subqueries

Subqueries let you pass search criteria into a filter condition. This greatly increases the power and flexibility of your queries. For example, the following query lets us retrieve all column names for a table, even though we only know the table name:

```
SELECT COLNAME FROM SYSCOLUMNS
WHERE  TABID =
 (SELECT TABID
  FROM SYSTABLES
  WHERE TABNAME = "inventory_detail");
```

The output from this query is:

```
colname

location
part_number
part_count
```

The subquery is processed first. In this case, it returns the "tabid" for the "inventory_detail" table. The outer query then uses this information to locate the column names from the "syscolumns" table.

This type of subquery is known as an "uncorrelated" subquery, because the inner SELECT doesn't rely on the outer SELECT for information.

Correlated subqueries, on the other hand, need information from the outer SELECT to locate rows. This means that the engine runs the inner query after every row that the outer query returns. This can greatly degrade performance, especially on a large table, with a non-indexed selection criteria. Therefore, try to avoid correlated subqueries whenever possible. If you must use them, make sure that the selection criteria columns are indexed.

Cost of views

Views provide DBAs and developers with a number of important benefits, including:

- **Enhanced security.** You can use views to restrict users from accessing certain rows or columns.

- **Simpler picture of the database.** You can use a view to join a number of related tables, and thereby present a less-complex picture of the database to programmers or end-users.

Sometimes, however, views have the potential to hurt performance. This is especially true when a programmer or user uses a view when they should work on the underlying tables instead. Let's look at an example to illustrate this potential problem:

Suppose that you have an application that tracks service calls. The database is made up of four tables and one view:

Table 3.5 Employees

employee_num	first_name	last_name ....
104	Carl	Lafong
1265	Ed	DeBevic
1926	Lee	Kwan

Table 3.6 Service_calls

service_num	customer_num	employee_num	service_date ....
73	496	1265	01/30/1995
74	92	104	01/31/1995

Table 3.7 Customers

customer_num	company_name	address1 ....
92	ABC Inc.	77 Sunset Strip
93	Bob's Flowers	155 E. 79th St.

Table 3.8 Responses

response_num	service_num	comments ....
11	73	Technician was great!
12	194	We're calling our lawyers

```
CREATE VIEW SERVICE_STATUS AS
   SELECT S.SERVICE_NUM,
          S.SERVICE_DATE,
          R.COMMENTS,
```

```
        C.CUSTOMER_NUM,
        C.COMPANY_NAME,
        E.FIRST_NAME,
        E.LAST_NAME
FROM    SERVICE_CALLS S,
        RESPONSES R,
        CUSTOMERS C,
        EMPLOYEES E
WHERE   S.EMPLOYEE_NUM = E.EMPLOYEE_NUM
AND     S.SERVICE_NUM  = R.SERVICE_NUM
AND     S.CUSTOMER_NUM = C.CUSTOMER_NUM;
```

The view was created by the DBA for programmers. It masks the relationships among the tables. Generally, this is not a problem. However, if a programmer only wants one or two columns from the view, it would be better to simply retrieve those columns from the base tables, instead of using the view and forcing the engine to join all the tables.

For example, assume that a user requests a simple report, showing the service number, date, and any comments. If the programmer retrieves this information from the view, the query plan looks like this:

```
    QUERY:
    ------
    SELECT SERVICE_NUM, SERVICE_DATE, COMMENTS FROM
     SERVICE_STATUS

Estimated Cost: 18
Estimated # of Rows Returned: 51

(1) db_user.service_calls: INDEX PATH

    (1) Index Keys: service_num

(2) db_user.customers: INDEX PATH

    (1) Index Keys: customer_num
      Lower Index Filter:
         db_user.customers.customer_num =
         db_user.service_calls.customer_num

(3) db_user.employees: INDEX PATH

    (1) Index Keys: employee_num
```

```
        Lower Index Filter:
         db_user.employees.employee_num =
         db_user.service_calls.employee_num

(4) db_user.responses: SEQUENTIAL SCAN

SORT SCAN: db_user.responses.service_num

MERGE JOIN
   Merge Filters:
   db_user.responses.service_num =
   db_user.service_calls.service_num
```

If, on the other hand, you run the query against the two base tables, your query plan looks like this:

```
QUERY:
------
SELECT S.SERVICE_NUM, S.SERVICE_DATE, R.COMMENTS
FROM   SERVICE_CALLS S, RESPONSES R
WHERE  S.SERVICE_NUM = R.SERVICE_NUM

Estimated Cost: 6
Estimated # of Rows Returned: 17

1) db_user.r: SEQUENTIAL SCAN

2) db_user.s: INDEX PATH

    (1) Index Keys: service_num
        Lower Index Filter: db_user.s.service_num =
                                db_user.r.service_num
```

The savings in processing time that the latter query provides could be substantial on a large system. If you make extensive use of views, consider documenting their underlying structure. Place this documentation in a location where programmers have easy access to it.

Using math inside SQL

There are times where you want to perform mathematical operations on a column(s) stored in a table. For example, assume that you have the following table that tracks labor costs:

Table 3.9 Resources

resource_id	resource_desc	resource_cost ....
CL1	Clerk level I	12.55
CL2	Clerk level II	14.03
AA1	Admin level I	13.39
AA2	Admin level II	16.39

During the design of a labor scheduling system, you learn that one report allows management to specify an across-the-board raise on an input screen. Your program then uses this value to produce a "what-if" report, showing what the "resource_cost" column would contain if the raise was applied. You could write your query this way (assuming that the raise is 20 percent):

```
SELECT RESOURCE_DESC,
       RESOURCE_COST OLD,
       RESOURCE_COST + (RESOURCE_COST * .2) NEW
FROM   RESOURCES;
```

If you are operating against a small to midsize table (less than 10,000 rows; for example), this type of query is fine. On larger tables, however, you can get better performance by moving the math outside of the SQL and into your application code. Using INFORMIX-4GL, for example, you could structure your code as follows:

```
    .           .            .
    .           .            .
DEFINE G_RESOURCE RECORD
   RESOURCE_DESC LIKE RESOURCES.RESOURCE_DESC,
   RESOURCE_COST LIKE RESOURCES.RESOURCE_COST
END RECORD
    .           .            .
    .           .            .

DECLARE CURSOR1 CURSOR FOR
SELECT RESOURCE_DESC, RESOURCE_COST
FROM   RESOURCES

FOREACH CURSOR1 INTO G_RESOURCE.*
   LET G_RESOURCE.RESOURCE_COST =
       G_RESOURCE.RESOURCE_COST +
        (G_RESOURCE.RESOURCE_COST * .2)
```

```
END FOREACH
        .           .            .
        .           .            .
```

In a client/server processing environment, the above change might not be optimal, however. This is because moving the math processing from server to client can add extra cost, namely:

- Extra network traffic. If there are a large number of rows being sent between client and server, application performance might suffer.
- Extra client load. If your client machines are not powerful, this type of change could subject them to unnecessary added processing load.

With this in mind, conduct some analysis before you move math calculations out of SQL, especially if you're using client/server processing.

NEW MATH FUNCTIONS

Version 6.0 of the Informix servers provides numerous additional SQL mathematical functions, including:

- ABS (absolute value)
- MOD (modulus)
- POW (raise to a power)
- SQRT (square root)
- SIN (sine)
- COS (cosine)
- TAN (tangent)

Unions

There are times when you can use unions to speed query retrieval speed. One instance is when you are retrieving two distinct sets of data (separated by an OR). Consider dividing the query into two different queries, and use a UNION to merge the results.

In this case, you have a table containing parts for outboard motors. There are indexes on the "part_num" and "part_cost" columns. You want to retrieve two sets of rows in one query:

- All rows that have a part number between 1 and 50 and cost more than $100.00

  - or -

- All rows where the cost is greater than $55.00

Table 3.10 Parts

part_num	part_description	part_cost ....
22905	4-blade propeller	165.03
3467	engine cowling	205.44
910	interior gasket	.58
1093	drive shaft	443.00
.	.	.
.	.	.
.	.	.
.	.	.
22906	3-blade propeller	145.99
911	lower unit gasket	3.00
.	.	.
.	.	.

Writing the query using an OR produces the following query plan:

```
QUERY:
------
SELECT * FROM PARTS
WHERE (PART_NUM BETWEEN 1 AND 50 AND
    PART_ COST > 100.00)
OR    PART_COST > 55.00


Estimated Cost: 2
Estimated # of Rows Returned: 2

   1) db_user.parts: SEQUENTIAL SCAN

    Filters: (((db_user.parts.part_num >= 1 AND
            db_user.parts.part_num <= 50 ) AND
            db_user.parts.part_cost > 100 ) OR
            db_user.parts.part_cost > 55 )
```

You can force the optimizer to use the indexes by simply rewriting the query as follows:

```
QUERY:
```

```
------
SELECT * FROM PARTS
WHERE PART_NUM BETWEEN 1 AND 50 AND
    PART_ COST > 100.00

UNION

SELECT * FROM PARTS
WHERE PART_COST > 55.00


Estimated Cost: 5
Estimated # of Rows Returned: 2

1) db_user.parts: INDEX PATH

    Filters: db_user.parts.part_cost > 100

    (1) Index Keys: part_num
        Lower Index Filter: db_user.parts.part_num >= 1
        Upper Index Filter:
           db_user.parts.part_ num <= 50


Union Query:
------------

1) db_user.parts: INDEX PATH

    (1) Index Keys: part_cost
        Lower Index Filter:
           db_user.parts.part_ cost > 55
```

Review your slow-running queries to see if they are candidates for this type of enhancement.

Sorting

No matter how much research and analysis you put into your database design, someone is going to want data sorted in an order you never imagined. This is not necessarily a bad thing; perhaps your existing indexes will be sufficient. More likely, however, a new sorting request means more work for you.

One of the most dangerous types of sorts occurs when a user or application requests an enormous set of data, sorted by a non-indexed column(s). For example, assume that you have a million-row transaction history table, defined as follows:

Table 3.11 pos_detail

sku_no	store_no	sale_date	amount ....
5409	636	11/01/94	1.55
112	636	11/01/94	32.00
.	.	.	
.	.	.	
1154	709	11/02/94	93.99
5903	709	11/03/94	5.87
.	.	.	
.	.	.	

This table has a composite index on sku_no, store_no, and sale_date. After the system has been in use for several weeks, management requests a report showing all rows in the table, sorted by the "amount" and "sale_date" fields:

```
QUERY:
------
SELECT *
FROM   POS_DETAIL
ORDER BY AMOUNT, SALE_DATE

Estimated Cost: 5
Estimated # of Rows Returned: 10
Temporary Files Required For: Order By

1) db_user.pos_detail: SEQUENTIAL SCAN
```

This is an especially dangerous situation. The query returns all rows in the table. What is worse is that the optimizer constructs a temporary table that is as big as the original table itself. It is entirely possible that you will run out of space to store the temporary table, and the query will "crash."

Fortunately, there are ways to prevent this situation:

1. For large table sorts, always try to have an index in place on the sort columns. Run SET EXPLAIN to make sure that the index is being used for the sort. Keep in mind that this change won't always help. For example, if the index is

already being used to resolve a filter or join condition, the optimizer may still need to create a temporary table. Let's look at an example to see what we mean.

Suppose that you have a generic header and detail table. These tables are created with the following SQL:

```
CREATE TABLE HEADER
(
   HEADER_ID   SERIAL PRIMARY KEY,
   HEADER_DATE DATE,
      .   .   .
);

CREATE TABLE DETAIL
(
   DETAIL_ID   SERIAL PRIMARY KEY,
   HEADER_ID   INTEGER,
   DETAIL_AMT  DECIMAL(8,2),
      .   .   .
   FOREIGN KEY (HEADER_ID) REFERENCES HEADER
);
```

The “header_id” column is indexed in both tables. Even though “header_id” is indexed in both places, there still are certain cases where the optimizer creates a temporary table. Look at the following query plan:

```
QUERY:
------

SELECT H.HEADER_ID,
       H.HEADER_DATE,
       D.DETAIL_AMT
FROM   HEADER H,
       DETAIL D
WHERE  H.HEADER_ID = D.HEADER_ID

Estimated Cost: 6
Estimate # of Rows Returned: 17

1) db_user.h : SEQUENTIAL SCAN

2) db_user.d : INDEX PATH
```

```
    (1) Index Keys : header_id
    Lower Index Filter: db_user.d.header_id =
      db_user.h.header_id
```

The index on header_id is used to join the two tables. Once we add an ORDER BY H.HEADER_ID to the query, the query plan changes:

```
QUERY:
------

SELECT H.HEADER_ID,
       H.HEADER_DATE,
       D.DETAIL_AMT
FROM   HEADER H,
       DETAIL D
WHERE  H.HEADER_ID = D.HEADER_ID
ORDER BY H.HEADER_ID

Estimated Cost: 11
Estimate # of Rows Returned: 17
Temporary Files Required For: Order By

1) db_user.h : SEQUENTIAL SCAN

2) db_user.d : INDEX PATH

    (1) Index Keys : header_id
    Lower Index Filter: db_user.d.header_id =
  db_user.h.header_id
```

Keep this in mind if you can't figure out why you still sometimes see temporary tables.

2. If you cannot afford a full-time index on the sort columns, consider creating a temporary index, running your report, and then dropping the index.
3. Try to limit the use of SELECT * on large tables. Determine if you really need all those columns.
4. Try to limit wildcard searches of tables without any filter conditions. Consider prompting users to be more selective, or at least warn them that their query may run slowly. For more information on this topic, see the "General tips" section.

COMPOSITE INDEXES AND SORTING

Composite indexes have a big impact on sorting. To learn more about this topic, see the "Indexing strategies" section.

ASCENDING VERSUS DESCENDING INDEXES

If your application makes use of descending sorts, be aware that the Informix optimizer only uses descending indexes for descending sorts; having an ascending (default) index will not help you in this situation. Instead, if you run the same sort over and over, consider placing a descending index on the column(s) in question.

For example, let's look at actual SET EXPLAIN results for some sample queries. Assume that you have an employee table, as follows:

Table 3.12 Employees

employee_last	employee_first	employee_num...
Gibbs	Ellen	1160
.	.	.
Katt	Isidore	1788
.	.	.
Zlotnick	Sidney	43

When you created this table, you placed a ascending index on "employee_last". A query that sorts on this column would have the following query plan:

```
QUERY:
------
   SELECT * FROM EMPLOYEES ORDER BY EMPLOYEE_LAST

   Estimated Cost: 12
   Estimated # of Rows Returned: 10

   1) db_user.employees: INDEX PATH

       (1) Index Keys: employee_last
```

The query plan shows you that the optimizer uses your index on "employee_last".

As time proceeds, you receive a request from a user who wants a report from the "employees" table to be sorted by last name descending. If you run the report, you'll see a query plan similar to this:

```
QUERY:
------
SELECT * FROM EMPLOYEES ORDER BY EMPLOYEE_LAST DESC

Estimated Cost: 5
Estimated # of Rows Returned: 10
Temporary Files Required For: Order By

1) db_user.employees: SEQUENTIAL SCAN
```

The optimizer creates a temporary table to hold the sorted contents. This is not necessarily a problem if the "employees" table contains less than a few thousand rows. However, on bigger tables, you might end up with an enormous, resource-consuming implicit temporary table. If you create a descending on the "employee_last" column, and rerun the query, the optimizer produces this output:

```
QUERY:
------
SELECT * FROM EMPLOYEES ORDER BY EMPLOYEE_LAST DESC

Estimated Cost: 12
Estimated # of Rows Returned: 10

1) db_user.employees: INDEX PATH

    (1) Index Keys: employee_last (desc)
```

The optimizer no longer creates a temporary table to hold the results of your query.

In summary, make sure that you examine the query plans for all of your SELECT statements. You may be surprised with what you learn.

CONTROLLING SORT MEMORY USAGE

When you request a sort on a column or group of columns that isn't indexed, the database server uses the sort package to return the information in the order you requested. This procedure can consume a great deal of system memory, and possibly slow down other processes.

Fortunately, beginning with version 5.01, the database engines let you control how much system memory the sorting package uses. You do this by setting the PSORT_MAXALLOC environment variable to the maximum number of kilobytes that you want the sort package to use. Since PSORT_MAXALLOC is an environment variable, you can grant certain users more memory for their queries, while limiting the amount of memory for other users.

General Tips

In this section, we continue our discussion about general application coding techniques that can help improve the performance of your programs. These suggestions can help improve your application's performance regardless of the database engine or front-end tool that you use.

We first cover the important topic of transactions, which are crucial for any application that depends on database integrity. We discuss how to make the best use of transactions, the value of adding transactions to existing applications, along with some traps that you should avoid in the process. Since error checking is such an important part of transactions, we also use this section to explore how to place comprehensive error checking inside your programs.

Since cursors are such an important tool in developing robust database applications, we describe ways to improve cursor performance. These include the PREPARE statement and scroll cursors.

In a multi-user environment, it's important that your application maximize concurrency. In the next section, we discuss several methods you can use to increase the level of concurrency in your applications. We explain what concurrency is, how locking effects concurrency, and the importance of isolation levels in programs that use the OnLine database server.

Next, we study ways to reduce the amount of pipe traffic between your application and the database server. These methods include lowering the amount of data that your program sends to the server, along with decreasing the amount of data that the server sends to your program. This includes a discussion on the benefits of joining between tables, instead of using single table SELECTs.

Finally, in the "Miscellaneous tips" section of this chapter, we suggest ways to minimize the amount of memory that your programs use in areas such as arrays, cursors, and executable sizes. We also discuss the high cost of screen I/O.

Transactions

If your goal is to develop robust applications that guarantee the integrity of your data as well as provide predictably good service to your user community, you should use transactions in your programs.

Regardless of the role you play in your organization's data-processing environment, transactions are a key aid in performing your job. As an administrator, you should insist that any application that modifies data in the database use transactions. As a programmer, you should insist that your underlying database support transactions.

No discussion on transactions would be complete without exploring error-checking issues. For more information about error checking, see the "Error checking" section of this chapter.

Let's look at a situation where an application program that doesn't use transactions damages the referential integrity of a database. In this example, you're maintaining a truck rental system. Customers call in to reserve a certain type of vehicle for a certain day. Two of the key tables in the system are the "reservations" table, which contains entries for all reservations, and the "vehicle_status" table, which stores the status for each vehicle for each day:

Table 3.13 reservations

res_num	vehicle_id	res_date
11095	15	11/12/1994 ......
11096	16	11/12/1994 ......
11097	17	11/13/1994 ......
.	.	.
.	.	.

Table 3.14 vehicle_status

vehicle_id	vehicle_type	vehicle_date	vehicle_status
15	Pickup truck	11/11/1994	Available
15	Pickup truck	11/12/1994	Booked
16	Pickup truck	11/12/1994	Booked
17	12000 pound truck	11/12/1994	Available
17	12000 pound truck	11/13/1994	Booked
.	.	.	.
.	.	.	.

When a customer calls in to request a truck for a certain date, your program first checks the "vehicle_status" table to see if there are any available trucks of the desired type for that date. If it finds any, you make an entry into the "reservations" table, and also update the status for the selected vehicle in the "vehicle_status" table.

Suppose that one day, during the middle of a reservation, you lose power, and your system goes down. What happens if the power loss happens after the entry into the "reservations" table, but before the update of the "vehicle_status" table? Since you're not using transactions, you've damaged the referential integrity of your database. In real-world terms, your customer is going to arrive on the designated day and expect the designated type of vehicle. Since you didn't get the chance to update the "vehicle_status" table for this customer's reservations, chances are there won't be a truck there for her when she arrives.

It's very easy to prevent these types of problems from occurring: use transaction logging for multi-table operations. For the case described above, your pseudocode would look like this:

```
check for vehicle availability
begin work
insert into reservations table
check error status
if no error
   update vehicle_status table
   check error status
   if no error
      commit work
   else
      rollback work
else
   rollback work
end if
```

Next, we'll look at some important issues to consider when you use transactions in your applications.

PREVENTING LONG TRANSACTIONS

One particularly crucial transaction issue is the length of time that your transactions take. It is extremely important to keep your transactions as brief as possible. This is even more important if you are using the OnLine engine, because of the way OnLine handles transactions and logical logs.

Let's look at an example of the dangers of long, open transactions. Suppose you develop a client support application for a large insurance company. Customers call in, requesting information about their policies. This information includes benefits, payments, and refunds. One day, an operator is working with a customer, using your payment record screen to modify the customer's record. The customer states that she paid her bill two days earlier than your company said that they received her check. After researching the case, the operator agrees, and offers to correct the record. The customer thanks your operator, and hangs up. Since it is so close to the end of the day, your operator decides to leave the customer's record on the screen, and make the change the next morning. If your 4GL code looks like the following example, can you spot the potential problem?

```
DEFINE QUERY_STMT CHAR(200)
```

```
{ Operator gets the customers name and account number }
CONSTRUCT CUST_QUERY
ON   CUSTOMER_NO, ACCOUNT_NO
FROM CUSTOMER_NO, ACCOUNT_NO

{ Start the transaction                                }
BEGIN WORK

{ Prepare the statement and declare a cursor           }
LET QUERY_STMT = "SELECT * FROM PAYMENT_INFO WHERE
    ",CUST_QUERY
PREPARE CUST_PREP FROM QUERY_STMT
DECLARE CUST_CUR CURSOR FOR CUST_PREP

{ Program retrieves payment record into 'pmt_info'     }
{ record, and then displays the information to the     }
{ sr_pmt_info' screen record                           }
    .           .           .           .
    .           .           .           .

{ Prompt the user to make any changes to the record    }
INPUT BY NAME PMT_INFO.* WITHOUT DEFAULTS FROM
    SR_PMT_INFO.*

{ Update the record                                    }
UPDATE PAYMENT_INFO
SET * = PMT_INFO.*
WHERE PAYMENT_INFO.CUSTOMER_NO = PMT_INFO.CUSTOMER_NO

{ Check for errors, and finish the transaction         }
IF SQLCA.SQLERRCODE = 0 THEN
   COMMIT WORK
   MESSAGE "RECORD UPDATED"
ELSE
   ROLLBACK WORK
   MESSAGE "RECORD UPDATE FAILED ",SQLCA.SQLCODE
END IF
```

If the operator goes home (or to lunch, or on break) after pulling up the record but before changing it, you have a long transaction. If you are using the OnLine engine, the current logical log cannot be freed until this transaction completes.

Modifying the above example to avoid the long transaction problem produces the following code:

```
DEFINE QUERY_STMT CHAR(200)

{ Operator gets the customers name and account number }
CONSTRUCT CUST_QUERY
ON   CUSTOMER_NO, ACCOUNT_NO
FROM CUSTOMER_NO, ACCOUNT_NO

{ Prepare the statement and declare a cursor          }
LET QUERY_STMT = "SELECT * FROM PAYMENT_INFO WHERE
    ",CUST_QUERY
PREPARE CUST_PREP FROM QUERY_STMT
DECLARE CUST_CUR CURSOR FOR CUST_PREP

{ Program retrieves payment record into 'pmt_info'    }
{ record and then displays the information to the     }
{  'sr_pmt_info' screen record                        }
.           .           .           .
   .           .           .           .

{ Prompt the user to make any changes to the record   }
INPUT BY NAME PMT_INFO.* WITHOUT DEFAULTS FROM
    SR_PMT_INFO.*

{ Start the transaction                               }
BEGIN WORK

{ Update the record                                   }
UPDATE PAYMENT_INFO
SET * = PMT_INFO.*
WHERE PAYMENT_INFO.CUSTOMER_NO = PMT_INFO.CUSTOMER_NO

{ Check for errors, and finish the transaction        }
IF SQLCA.SQLERRCODE = 0 THEN
   COMMIT WORK
   MESSAGE "RECORD UPDATED"
ELSE
   ROLLBACK WORK
   MESSAGE "RECORD UPDATE FAILED ",SQLCA.SQLCODE
END IF
```

By making this simple change, you eliminate the potential for a long transaction. You might want to add some logic to this code to make sure that the contents of the "payment_info" record haven't been changed by someone else between the time you select it and the time you update it.

WHEN NOT TO USE TRANSACTIONS

There are some situations where you should not use transactions. In fact, using transactions may actually hurt your performance in these instances:

- **Queries.** Remember that you only need to use transactions if your program modifies the database. If you're running a query, and it doesn't have any INSERT/UPDATE/DELETE statements, you can omit transactions.
- **Reports.** Many programmers make the mistake of issuing BEGIN WORK statements at the start of reports. Running a report inside a transaction does nothing to help the report (unless you are also updating the table(s) as you proceed through the report). In fact, an open transaction during a report may even hurt your system's performance. See the "Long transactions" section of this chapter for more information.

TRANSACTIONS AND TEMPORARY TABLES

If you explicitly create temporary tables as part of your application, remember to use the WITH NO LOG option in the CREATE TEMP TABLE/SELECT INTO TEMP statements. This prevents the database engine from logging any changes made to the temporary table, thereby conserving both CPU time and log space. For more information on this topic, see the "Temporary tables" section of the "Optimizing Application Code" chapter.

LOCATION OF BEGIN WORK & COMMIT WORK STATEMENTS

You can greatly improve the clarity and maintainability of your programs by making it easy to locate the beginning and end of any transactions that you use. It's hard enough to debug programs; having to search for the start and end of a transaction adds unnecessary difficulty to the process. Consequently, always try to have your BEGIN and COMMIT/ROLLBACK WORK commands in the same block. For example, see how hard it would be to debug the following section of 4GL code:

```
INPUT BY NAME G_CONTACT.* FROM SR_CONTACT.*

BEGIN WORK

CALL INSERT_CONTACT(G_CONTACT.*)

.          .          .

FUNCTION INSERT_CONTACT(P_CONTACT.*)
```

```
   DEFINE P_CONTACT RECORD LIKE CONTACT.*

   INSERT INTO CONTACT VALUES (P_CONTACT.*)

   IF SQLCA.SQLCODE = 0 THEN
      COMMIT WORK
   ELSE
      ROLLBACK WORK
   END IF

END FUNCTION
```

The difficulty would be compounded for each nested function that you call. Imagine what it would look like if the function calls went four or five levels down.

A much cleaner way of achieving the same goal would look like this:

```
BEGIN WORK

CALL INSERT_CONTACT (G_CONTACT.*) RETURNING
    ERROR_STATUS

IF ERROR_STATUS = 0 THEN
   COMMIT WORK
ELSE
   ROLLBACK WORK
END IF

FUNCTION INSERT_CONTACT(P_CONTACT.*)

   DEFINE P_CONTACT RECORD LIKE CONTACT.*

   INSERT INTO CONTACT VALUES (P_CONTACT.*)

   IF SQLCA.SQLCODE = 0 THEN
      RETURN 0
   ELSE
      RETURN 1
   END IF

END FUNCTION
```

By providing a single point of control for your transactions, you make the job of maintaining your code much easier.

ADDING TRANSACTIONS TO EXISTING APPLICATIONS

If you're maintaining an existing application that doesn't use transactions, you should consider adding this powerful feature to your programs. While retrofitting existing code is usually an unenviable chore, adding transactions is one enhancement that aids you in the long run. Transactions (and error checking) benefit you and your users by increasing the reliability, data integrity, and ease of maintenance of your applications.

Error checking

While it is a known fact that programmers never make mistakes, it is still a good idea to humor the users by checking for errors at critical points in your programs. If you aren't checking for errors, your programs may still fail, and you then have the added burden of trying to figure out what went wrong without the benefit of the information that error checking provides you.

Let's demonstrate what we mean with a simple example. Suppose you are maintaining an ESQL/C program that listens to a communication line, collects data, and then inserts rows into a table. The segment of code of interest looks like this:

```
EXEC SQL BEGIN DECLARE SECTION;
   struct input_record {
      int  comm_line;
      char data[30];
   } current_record;
EXEC SQL END DECLARE SECTION;

EXEC SQL database xxx;

/* open communication line */
while (1)
{
   /* pick up a record off of the communication line */
        .        .        .        .
     .        .        .        .
   EXEC SQL insert into received_data values
    (:current_record.*);
        .        .        .        .
        .        .        .        .
}
```

This program is fine if you never encounter an error, but realistically, you can expect that your code will run into problems from time to time. What happens in the above example if, while attempting to insert a new row into the table, the database returns an error indicating a duplicate value in a unique index? Since the program has no error checking, the data contained in the buffer is lost, potentially forever. It's especially dangerous not to check for errors when the data that you are working with is transitory in nature, since if you lose it you may not be able to replicate it. Adding error checking to the above sample is a simple task, but it greatly improves your program's ability to recover from a communication or database error:

```
EXEC SQL BEGIN DECLARE SECTION;
   struct input_record {
   int  comm_line;
   char data[35];
   } current_record;

   struct input_record error_record;
EXEC SQL END DECLARE SECTION;

EXEC SQL database xxx;

/* open communication line */
while (1)
{
   /* pick up a record off of the communication line */

   EXEC SQL insert into received_data values
    (:current_record.*);

   if (sqlca.sqlcode)
   {
      memcpy(error_record,&current_record,sizeof
        (struct input_record);
      fputs(error_log, "Database error occured
        at%s\n",error_record);
      /* Show date and timestamp as well */
   }
}
```

INCOMPLETE ERROR CHECKING

Just adding error checking to your programs is not enough. You also must make sure that you're checking for errors in all places where they might occur. It's all too common to take over the maintenance of an existing application, notice that the application has error checking in place, and then, later, realize that the error checking logic is incomplete.

Let's look at an example of this. In this example, your program inserts records into a shipment request table, and then logs this information into a table that tracks user access to the data. You use transaction logging, and also check for errors.

```
.              .              .
.              .              .

BEGIN WORK

INSERT INTO SHIPMENT_REQUESTS VALUES (....)

.              .              .
.              .              .

INSERT INTO TRANSACTION_AUDITS VALUES (....)

IF SQLCA.SQLCODE = 0 THEN
   COMMIT WORK
   MESSAGE "RECORDS UPDATED"
ELSE
   ROLLBACK WORK
   MESSAGE "RECORD UPDATE FAILED", SQLCA.SQLCODE
END IF

.              .              .
.              .              .
```

While this example does check for errors, it only checks for errors just prior to issuing a COMMIT WORK or ROLLBACK WORK command. If any errors occur earlier on in the program, they might pass unnoticed if the last SQL statement executes correctly. When using transactions, always make sure to check for errors along the way, as well as immediately before finishing the transaction:

```
.              .              .
.              .              .

BEGIN WORK

INSERT INTO SHIPMENT_REQUESTS VALUES (....)

IF SQLCA.SQLCODE <> 0 THEN
   ROLLBACK WORK
   MESSAGE "RECORD UPDATE FAILED ",SQLCA.SQLCODE
```

```
ELSE
   INSERT INTO TRANSACTION_AUDITS VALUES (....)
   IF SQLCA.SQLCODE <> 0 THEN
      ROLLBACK WORK
      MESSAGE "RECORD UPDATE FAILED", SQLCA.SQLCODE
   ELSE
      COMMIT WORK
      MESSAGE "RECORDS UPDATED"
   END IF
END IF

.               .               .
.               .               .
```

Remember to check for errors after any of the following statements:

- INSERT
- UPDATE
- DELETE
- SELECT
- PREPARE
- DECLARE
- OPEN CURSOR
- CLOSE CURSOR
- BEGIN WORK
- COMMIT WORK
- ROLLBACK WORK

TIMING OF ERROR CHECKING

So far, we've learned that your programs should check for errors, and that you should check for errors after all appropriate statements. There's one more thing to consider: the timing of your error checking.

Generally, to determine if your program has encountered a database-related error, you check the value of the SQLCA.SQLCODE variable. This variable is maintained for you by Informix; you only need to examine its contents. Be aware, however, that you may run into problems if you delay checking SQLCA.SQLCODE. This is because many operations reset SQLCA.SQLCODE, and by the time you check it, it may have been changed. SQLCA.SQLCODE gets reset by more operations than you may realize.

For example, let's look at a section of 4GL code to see how you might run into this type of problem. In this example, you are deleting a row from a table based on the value contained in a variable:

```
DEFINE ID_TO_DELETE LIKE INFO_REQUESTS.INFO_REQ_ID
.             .             .
.             .             .

DELETE FROM INFO_REQUESTS
WHERE INFO_REQ_ID = ID_TO_DELETE

MESSAGE "DELETING RECORD"

IF SQLCA.SQLCODE <> 0 THEN
   ERROR "ERROR DURING DELETE OPERATION ",
    SQLCA.SQLCODE
END IF
```

Can you see what is wrong with this example? The problem is that you check the SQLCA.SQLCODE value too late. You execute the SQL DELETE statement, then place a message on the screen, and only then check the SQLCA.SQLCODE value. Many operations reset the SQLCA.SQLCODE value, and the MESSAGE statement is one of them. This means that even if there is a problem with the DELETE statement, and the SQLCA.SQLCODE is set to an error status, you lose the error status by executing the MESSAGE statement, because that statement also resets the value.

Therefore, it's crucial that you don't wait too long to check the value of SQLCA.SQLCODE. You can do this by checking it after each operation, or you can save it off into your own variable:

```
DEFINE ID_TO_DELETE LIKE INFO_REQUESTS.INFO_REQ_ID
DEFINE SAVED_SQL_CODE INTEGER
.             .             .
.             .             .

DELETE FROM INFO_REQUESTS
   WHERE INFO_REQ_ID = ID_TO_DELETE

LET SAVED_SQL_CODE = SQLCA.SQLCODE

MESSAGE "DELETING RECORD"

IF SAVED_SQL_CODE <> 0 THEN
```

```
    ERROR "ERROR DURING DELETE OPERATION ",
     SAVED_SQL_CODE
END IF
```

By saving the value of SQLCA.SQLCODE into a variable that you maintain, you preserve the state of your program during the operation in question. You can then check the contents of your variable when appropriate.

USING THE WHENEVER STATEMENT TO HANDLE ERRORS

As an alternative to checking for errors after all appropriate statements, you can use the WHENEVER command to trap any errors that you might encounter. This command instructs your program to take a certain action after finding one of the following conditions:

- **SQLERROR.** This condition occurs when the server returns an SQL error. This covers just about any potential problem you can have accessing data.
- **NOT FOUND.** When you attempt to retrieve information that isn't in the database, the server returns this status (SQLCODE = 100).
- **SQLWARNING.** This is an Informix extension to the ANSI-89 SQL standard, and covers conditions when your statement completes successfully, but with an attached warning. This includes situations such as string truncation, disconnect errors, and null data removed from a set operation, such as SUM(), COUNT(), or MAX().

You can instruct your program, upon encountering one of the above conditions, to perform any one of the following actions:

- Stop
- Go to (an error-handling routine)
- Call (an error-handling routine)
- Continue

You can combine the WHENEVER statement to handle all of the above conditions in the same program. This helps you to develop a powerful error-handling strategy. In the following example, you've placed the following set of WHENEVER statements at the start of an ESQL/C program:

```
main()
{

   EXEC SQL WHENEVER SQLERROR call ErrorHandler();
   EXEC SQL WHENEVER NOTFOUND continue;
   EXEC SQL WHENEVER SQLWARNING call WarnProgrammer();
```

```
        .          .          .          .
        .          .          .          .
    }
```

Once your program begins, any SQL error (with the exception of a NOTFOUND condition) results in a call to the "ErrorHandler()" function. If the NOTFOUND condition occurs, your program simply continues, and if any SQLWARNINGs happen, you call the "WarnProgrammer()" routine. The benefit of this approach is that you need only develop the "ErrorHandler" and "WarnProgrammer" routines once.

Be careful with the WHENEVER ERROR CONTINUE statement, especially when developing 4GL applications. When you are developing and testing systems, knowing when errors happen enable you to (hopefully) eliminate them. By using WHENEVER ERROR CONTINUE during the development phase, you run the risk of ignoring potentially serious problems with your applications. It's better for programs to fail (perhaps even spectacularly) during the development and testing phase than for them to be released to your users with undiscovered bugs. Keep in mind that WHENEVER ERROR CONTINUE also suppresses automatic error logging by STARTLOG(). You can instruct your program to halt when it encounters an error by using the WHENEVER ERROR STOP command.

Cursors

THE PREPARE STATEMENT

With the exception of index enhancements, adding statement preparation to your applications yields the easiest, fastest performance improvements. The reason this relatively simple change has so much of an impact lies in the way that the engine processes SQL statements. When you submit SQL statements to the engine, several operations happen:

- The engine parses the statement, checking for invalid syntax.
- The engine optimizes the statement, to handle your request as efficiently as possible.
- The engine checks to make sure that the user running the SQL statement has all appropriate permissions.

All of these operations take precious time. When you repeatedly run an SQL statement, even if it doesn't change between each run, the engine still performs all of the above tasks. How can you prevent this expensive, unnecessary work? By using the PREPARE statement.

When you PREPARE an SQL statement, the engine still does all of the above tasks, but it only needs to do them once.

Let's look at some examples where using PREPARE helps improve your application's performance.

In this example, you are writing a 4GL report that prints a sales report. Your program contains two cursors: one outer cursor that retrieves stock keeping unit (SKU) information from a sales header table. After retrieving this data, you then call the report, where you DECLARE an inner cursor to locate all records in a detail table that match the SKU of the outer cursor.

```
MAIN

     DEFINE G_SALES_HEADER RECORD LIKE SALES_HEADER.*
       .              .                  .
       .              .                  .


   DECLARE HEADER_CUR CURSOR FOR
      SELECT * FROM SALES_HEADER

   START REPORT SALES_DETAIL_REP
   FOREACH HEADER_CUR INTO G_SALES_HEADER.*
      OUTPUT TO REPORT SALES_DETAIL_REP
        (G_SALES_HEADER.*)
   END FOREACH
   FINISH REPORT SALES_DETAIL_REP

       .              .                  .
       .              .                  .

END MAIN


REPORT SALES_DETAIL_REP(HEADER_REC)

   DEFINE HEADER_REC RECORD LIKE SALES_HEADER.*
   DEFINE DETAIL_REC RECORD LIKE SALES_DETAIL.*

   DECLARE DETAIL_CUR CURSOR FOR
       "SELECT TRANS_DATE, TRANS_AMOUNT
        FROM   SALES_DETAIL
        WHERE  SALES_DETAIL.SKU = HEADER_REC.SKU"

   FOREACH DETAIL_CUR INTO DETAIL_REC.*
      PRINT HEADER_REC.SKU, HEADER_REC.SKU_DESC,
```

```
                    DETAIL_REC.TRANS_DATE,
                      DETAIL_ REC.TRANS_AMOUNT
      END FOREACH

   END REPORT
```

If there are 5,000 individual SKUs in your inventory, your program declares the SALES_CURSOR 4,999 times more than necessary. Nothing about the SQL statement changes between iterations, except the value contained in G_SALES_HEADER.SKU. It's much simpler and faster to PREPARE and DECLARE the SALES_CURSOR once, and then open it with new values for each SKU:

```
   MAIN

       DEFINE G_SALES_HEADER RECORD LIKE SALES_HEADER.*
        .              .                  .
        .              .                  .


      DECLARE HEADER_CUR CURSOR FOR
         SELECT * FROM SALES_HEADER

      PREPARE DETAIL_CUR_PREP FROM
          "SELECT TRANS_DATE, TRANS_AMOUNT
           FROM   SALES_DETAIL
           WHERE  SALES_DETAIL.SKU = ?"
      DECLARE DETAIL_CUR CURSOR FOR DETAIL_CUR_PREP

      START REPORT SALES_DETAIL_REP
      FOREACH HEADER_CUR INTO G_SALES_HEADER.*
         OUTPUT TO REPORT
           SALES_DETAIL_ REP(G_SALES_HEADER.*)
      END FOREACH
      FINISH REPORT SALES_DETAIL_REP

        .              .                  .
        .              .                  .

   END MAIN


   REPORT SALES_DETAIL_REP(HEADER_REC)
```

```
    DEFINE HEADER_REC RECORD LIKE SALES_HEADER.*
    DEFINE DETAIL_REC RECORD LIKE SALES_DETAIL.*

    OPEN DETAIL_CUR USING HEADER_REC.SKU

    FOREACH DETAIL_CUR INTO DETAIL_REC.*
       PRINT HEADER_REC.SKU, HEADER_REC.SKU_DESC,
               DETAIL_REC.TRANS_DATE,
                 DETAIL_ REC.TRANS_AMOUNT
    END FOREACH

    CLOSE DETAIL_CUR

END REPORT
```

SELECT statements aren't the only areas where PREPARE can help you. You can also improve the response of INSERT, UPDATE, and DELETE statements. Let's look at a segment of code that updates a payroll status table:

```
.     .     .     .
.     .     .     .
/* You only need to prepare this statement once      */
/* The engine only needs to parse and optimize the ..*/
statement one time.                                  */
EXEC SQL prepare upd_prep from
"update pay_status set ytd_pay = ? where emp_id = ?";

.     .     .     .
.     .     .     .
/* You can execute it as many times as you need, and */
/* you won't incur any additional optimization costs */
EXEC SQL execute upd_prep using :calculated_pay,
    :employee_id;
.     .     .     .
.     .     .     .
```

For an example of how to use an INSERT cursor, see the "Bulk data loading" portion of this chapter.

IMPLEMENTING PREPARE

One way to implement PREPARE in your programs is to set up a function that issues all these commands at once. Typically, this takes place in an initial setup function that you call when your program starts. Once the program has implemented PREPARE in these statements, they are available for use.

SCROLL CURSORS

Scroll cursors allow you to move forward and backward through a set of data. This flexibility comes at a price, however: scroll cursors consume more resources and create temporary tables. With that in mind, let's examine a few types of situations to see where scroll cursors fit in.

In the first situation, you are developing a loan management application that tracks customer payments. One of the most commonly used screens is the account lookup screen. Customers call in, and give their last names to your operators. The operators then enter the last names onto the lookup screen, and your program returns the customers' records. This approach is fine if you have no customers with the same last name, but what happens if there are multiple customers with the same name? When you raise this possibility with your users, they tell you that if there are duplicate last names, they want to be presented with a list of all possible customers. They also want to be able to move backwards and forwards through the list. Finally, they inform you that the most common last name in the database has no more than 10 separate records. Based on this information, you determine that this case warrants using scroll cursors, for the following reasons:

- **Data set size.** The most common name in the database has no more than 10 distinct records. This means that the temporary table created by the scroll cursor will be small and manageable.
- **User requirements.** The users want to be able to move around in the list of possible customer records. You could store the information in an array, and navigate within the array instead of using a scroll cursor. While this may be faster than a scroll cursor, it also complicates your program, and introduces a new potential failure point.

In another situation, suppose that you are developing an application that tracks cellular phone calls. One important report in your application lists all phone calls that your customers make by time. The output of the report is huge; it fills up hundreds of pages. Your report's logic is simple: it moves through the data once, and uses an existing index on the phone call table to sort it. Should you use a scroll cursor in this case? Definitely not, for the following reasons:

- **Size of data set.** The amount of data that you process in this report is enormous; the size of the temporary table that a scroll cursor would create could be a problem.
- **Program flow.** You already know that you pass through the data once. With that in mind, there's no reason to incur the overhead of a scroll cursor, since you only move forward through the data.

For more information about the costs and benefits of temporary tables, see the "Temporary tables" section of the "Optimizing Application Code" chapter.

One final word of caution regarding scroll cursors. If you use scroll cursors to navigate through data, and decide to update a particular record by using its primary key, make sure that the underlying record in the database hasn't changed since you created your scroll cursor. The only exceptions to this rule occur when you use an isolation level of repeatable read, or cursor stability if you're updating the current row. Repeatable read holds locks on all rows of your scroll cursor until you release them, while cursor stability locks the current row. For more information about this topic, see the isolation levels section of this chapter.

Reducing traffic between client process and server process

Informix uses a variety of methods to communicate between the front-end process (the client) and the back-end process (the server). One way to improve your application's performance is to minimize the amount of data flowing between these processes. In this section, we explore several ways to achieve this result. We first look at server to client traffic, and then examine client to server communication.

SERVER TO CLIENT

Selecting only needed rows

Even if your database and program designs are optimal, your system can still get bogged down if your users always ask to look at all rows from all tables. Requesting such enormous data sets results in tremendous traffic, as the server dutifully sends huge amounts of data to the client. From your users" perspective, the system's response is horrible, since it may take several minutes to get the information they requested. How can you, as an administrator or programmer, prevent this problem? There are several ways:

- **Monitor user-entered selection criteria.**
  When you develop applications that allow users to enter free-form queries, let the users know (either through a message at runtime or in the documentation) that they should always specify a search criteria, rather than asking for all rows. If you're developing a 4GL application, see the "Optimizing Application Code" chapter for an example of how to do this.
- **Let the engine do the filtering, rather than your program.**
  Some programmers request all rows from a table, and then filter these rows through their conditional clauses inside their programs, instead of using the WHERE clause to reduce the number of rows that the engine returns. This definitely impairs system performance, as the server sends large volumes of data to the client, which then performs the CPU-intensive task of filtering out unneeded data. In a distributed processing environment, this may cause a drastic degradation of response time. It's much better to build up a WHERE clause in your program, and let the engine do the

filtering for you. Let's look at an example that demonstrates what we mean:

In this case, you're developing a sales tracking system for a clothing manufacturer. One report tracks outerwear sales. Your program reads through the very large "sales_history" table, and only prints outerwear records:

```
MAIN

   DEFINE SALES_RECORD RECORD LIKE SALES_HISTORY.*

   DECLARE SUMMARY_CURS CURSOR FOR
   SELECT * FROM SALES_HISTORY

   START REPORT OUTERWEAR_SUMMARY
   FOREACH SUMMARY_CURS INTO SALES_RECORD
       OUTPUT TO REPORT OUTERWEAR SUMMARY(SALES_RECORD.*)
   END FOREACH
   FINISH REPORT OUTERWEAR_SUMMARY

END MAIN

REPORT OUTERWEAR_SUMMARY(SALES_RECORD.*)

   DEFINE SALES_RECORD RECORD LIKE SALES_HISTORY.*

   IF SALES_RECORD.GARMENT_TYPE = "O" THEN
       PRINT...
   END IF

END REPORT
```

This design is inherently inefficient, because the engine returns all rows from the "sales_history" table, and then your report has to apply the filter on the "sales_record.garment_type" element. It's better to let the server do the work of data filtering:

```
MAIN

   DEFINE SALES_RECORD RECORD LIKE SALES_HISTORY.*

   DECLARE SUMMARY_CURS CURSOR FOR
   SELECT * FROM SALES_HISTORY
   WHERE  SALES_HISTORY.GARMENT_TYPE = "O"
```

```
START REPORT OUTERWEAR_SUMMARY
   FOREACH SUMMARY_CURS INTO SALES_RECORD
       OUTPUT TO REPORT OUTERWEAR_SUMMARY(SALES_RECORD.*)
   END FOREACH
   FINISH REPORT OUTERWEAR_SUMMARY

END MAIN

REPORT OUTERWEAR_SUMMARY(SALES_RECORD.*)

   DEFINE SALES_RECORD RECORD LIKE SALES_HISTORY.*

      PRINT...

END REPORT
```

Selecting only needed columns

Just as you should strive to reduce the number of rows that your users request, you should also attempt to minimize the number of columns that are transported between the server and client. This isn't always that easy, because when you develop applications that use SQL to retrieve information, it's tempting to request all columns from a table, whether or not you need them in your program. After all, SELECT * requires far less typing than specifying each column that you need. With 4GL, it's also very easy to DEFINE records to exactly match table layouts.

Unfortunately, SELECT * "costs" more than requesting individual columns, since returning all columns in a table results in higher traffic between the front-end and engine processes.

You can still SELECT only those columns that you need and DEFINE your records to look like a table, as follows:

```
DEFINE G_CLIENTS RECORD LIKE CLIENTS.*

SELECT CLIENTS.CLIENT_NUM,
       CLIENTS.CLIENT_FIRST,
       CLIENTS.CLIENT_LAST
INTO   G_CLIENTS.CLIENT_NUM,
       G_CLIENTS.CLIENT_FIRST,
       G_CLIENTS.CLIENT_LAST
```

While SELECTing only those columns that you need does add some extra typing to your development effort, it also pays off in reduced traffic between the front end and back end processes. This is especially true in a networked environment, where hundreds of miles may separate the client from the server.

Joining versus sequential SELECTs

Many programmers, especially those with a mainframe COBOL background, avoid joining between tables and instead process database records sequentially. While this approach may be comfortable, and easier to visualize, you're not using the full power of the database and the SQL programming language. We can illustrate this with an example.

For the purposes of this example, assume that you are developing a system to track sales calls by your company's representatives. To write the report, you work with two tables, "personnel" and "sales_calls". The "personnel" table contains information about each representative, and the "sales_calls" table tracks individual sales call statistics:

Table 3.15 personnel

personnel_id	**first_name**	**last_name**	**date_of_hire.....**
805	Sylvia	Migdal	08/02/1984
.	.	.	.
.	.	.	.
1109	Robert	Gordon	11/08/1992

Table 3.16 sales_calls

call_id	**personnel_id**	**date_of_call**	**company_name....**
1309	805	01/30/1994	Hasenffefer Corp.
.	.	.	.
.	.	.	.
2709	1509	08/15/1994	Freedom Rider, Inc.

Your task as the programmer is to produce a report that shows all sales calls that an employee has made, between January 1 and December 31 1994. Your output from the report must look like this:

```
    .                 .                    .
    .                 .                    .

Employee number:   nnnnn
Employee name  :   last, first

Sales call date         Company name......
------------------------------------------
mm/dd/yyyy              xxxxxxxxxxxxxxxxxxx
mm/dd/yyyy              xxxxxxxxxxxxxxxxxxx
```

If you processed the report without joins, your pseudocode looks something like this:

```
declare cursor to get records from 'personnel' table
open cursor
foreach cursor into host variable structure (personnel)
    print employee name and number and header info
    declare cursor to get records from 'sales_ calls'
       table
    open cursor using the contents of personnel
       host variable as key into sales_calls table
    foreach cursor into host variable structure
       (sales_calls)
       print sales call information
    end foreach
    close cursor
end foreach
close cursor
```

Can you see all the extra engine work that this process contains? For every employee found in the "personnel" table, you declare, open, and close a cursor to get data from the "sales_call" table. If you only have a few employees, this extra engine work may not be much of a problem. On the other hand, what happens if you have many thousands of employees that you need to report on?

In this case, you could use the PREPARE statement to reduce the number of times that the engine must parse and optimize the inner cursor (get records from "sales_calls" table). However, a better approach would be to let the database engine handle the joining of records between the "personnel" and "sales_calls" tables. You can do this by using the "personnel_id" column as a foreign key. Your new pseudocode now looks like this:

```
declare a cursor to get records from 'personnel' and
'sales_calls' tables
open cursor
foreach cursor into host variable structure
    (personnel + sales_calls)
    print employee name, number and header info
    (only once)
    print sales call information
end foreach
close cursor
```

What happens if a particular employee made no sales calls during this period, but you still want him to appear on the report? It's true that the sequential processing approach makes handling this situation easy, but it's also fairly simple to process it using an SQL, join-based method. Instead of performing a normal join between the tables, use an OUTER join, with the "personnel" table as primary, and the "sales_calls" table as outer:

```
SELECT *
FROM   PERSONNEL, OUTER SALES_CALLS
WHERE  PERSONNEL.PERSONNEL_ID =
    SALES_ CALLS.PERSONNEL_ID
```

By joining between tables, you take better advantage of database engine performance features. This is especially true if you're using the OnLine engine, which has sophisticated shared memory buffering.

Take advantage of stored procedures

One way to reduce overall traffic between the client and server process is to use stored procedures. You can write stored procedures to perform a number of important tasks, including:

- Summarization
- Aggregation
- Data collection
- Auditing
- Remote operations

For more information about these powerful tools, see the "Stored Procedures and Triggers" section.

CLIENT TO SERVER

Update only columns that have changed

Just as it's "easier" to SELECT * from a table rather than itemize the columns that you need, it's also "easier" to UPDATE all columns in a table, whether or not more than one of them has changed. Just as using a wildcard in your SELECT statement increases traffic between the front-end and engine processes, so does a wildcard UPDATE statement.

For example, suppose that you are writing an ESQL/C program to track the status of shipments. You maintain a table that stores the current location of each package. As the package moves between different sites, you update this table with the package's current location, along with the date and time the package arrived. The table that tracks these packages is large, having both many rows and many columns. It's your task as the programmer to make the update process as rapid as possible.

One of the easiest ways to do this is to UPDATE only those columns that need to be changed. In this example, since the only modified data is the package's current location and timestamp, you should only change those columns. This means that instead of issuing a wildcard UPDATE statement:

```
EXEC SQL UPDATE PACKAGE_STATUS
SET * = :g_package.*
WHERE PACKAGE_STATUS.PACKAGE_ID = :g_package.package_id
```

You only update those columns that you need to:

```
EXEC SQL UPDATE PACKAGE_STATUS
SET PACKAGE_STATUS.LOCATION_CODE =
    :g_package.location_code,
  PACKAGE_STATUS.TIMESTAMP        = CURRENT
```

While this approach results in somewhat longer SQL statements, it's still worth the effort.

Another reason to avoid wildcard UPDATE statements is that they may fail if you've set up referential integrity relationships for the table. For example, suppose that you have another table that has a referential integrity relationship with the "package_status" table, and you attempt to run the above wildcard UPDATE statement. The database server detects that the relationship is about to be violated, and returns the following error:

```
692: Key value for constraint (db_user.u110_8) is still being
referenced.
111: ISAM error:  no record found.
```

Concurrency

Concurrency can be thought of as the ability of your programs to peacefully co-exist with other programs running at the same time. In this section, we discuss how to maximize concurrency in your application environment.

When you design a single user application, you generally don't give concurrency much thought. This is only natural: the one user is king, and has exclusive control over all system resources. Problems can arise, however, when you port this application to, or develop a new application for, a multi-user environment. Before we discuss how to improve concurrency, however, let's look at a typical problem situation that illustrates how concurrency can become an issue:

Suppose that you have a ticket reservation application. Customers call in, and request seats for a particular event. Two of the more heavily accessed tables in the application are:

Table 3.17 events

event_id	event_title	event_date	seats_left
1105	A Night with Sammy Spear	12/07/1994	405
1106	Air Supply: The Reunion	12/19/1994	25034
1107	Featuring Nikki Sierra	12/30/1994	18
.	.	.	.
.	.	.	.

Table 3.18 purchases

purchase_id	event_id	amount_paid	payment_type.....
23098	1107	25.99	V
23099	1144	203.99	C
23100	1104	63.99	A

Your application processes ticket requests as follows:

- You determine what event the customer would like to see. This entails locating the correct row in the "events" table.
- If "seats_left" is greater than zero, you add a row into the "purchases" table.
- You update the "events" table to lower the number of "seats_left". Your UPDATE statement uses the "event_id" to find the correct row to change.

During development, everything seemed fine with this approach. Once the system rolls out, however, you begin hearing complaints from your users. Periodically, they receive "record locked" error messages from the applications. When this happens, they must re-enter the data into the system. Some customers have even lost out on fast-selling events. What is happening, and how can you correct it?

When you update the "events" table, you briefly hold a lock on the updated row. With the OnLine engine, you may even hold a lock on that row's data page. If other users are trying to update the same row, or, in the case of OnLine, other rows on the same page, their application will receive an error message from the engine. This error message tells the front-end process that the engine is unable to make the modification because the row is locked.

If your programs aren't specifically coded to gracefully handle locked records, they may fail at this point. Let's move on and learn more about locks, and how to code your programs to work with them.

LOCKING ISSUES

Locks are a powerful mechanism that allow the database engine to guarantee the integrity of changes to data. With this power comes responsibility, however, because you must design your programs to gracefully cope with locking. If you fail to do this, you can expect your applications to either abort or finish incorrectly when they encounter a lock.

In this section, we discuss how to implement graceful lock handling in your programs, as well as how to avoid running out of locks.

The most powerful tool that you can use in developing programs to gracefully handle locked rows is the SET LOCK MODE TO WAIT statement. Placing this statement inside your code tells the front-end process to wait upon encountering a lock, rather than abort or proceed without the lock.

Let's review an example of a program that doesn't use this statement. In this case, you have an ESQL/C program that deletes a parent record, and then goes on to delete all child records of the newly-deleted parent. The section of code that performs this task looks like:

```
DeleteServiceRecs()
{
.       .       .       .
.       .       .       .
   EXEC SQL delete from service_header
    where service_header.service_call_id = :id_to_delete;

   EXEC SQL delete from service_detail
    where service_detail.service_call_id = :id_to_delete;
.       .       .       .
.       .       .       .
}
```

This program runs smoothly, as long as there are no problems during execution. However, what happens if someone else holds a lock on the parent row while your program attempts to delete it? Since you have no error checking in place, your program fails to delete the parent row, but still moves on to delete any child rows. The worst part of this situation is that no one knows that the problem even exists while it is occurring. It's likely that this referential integrity violation won't be discovered until much later, when your users complain that there are "missing" child records. As a developer, you then have the unenviable task of digging through your application to learn what went wrong.

There are several ways to prevent this kind of problem from happening:

- Set up referential constraints between the parent and child tables. For more information about this topic, see the "Relational Database Design" section of the book.
- Enable error checking in the program. We discussed the benefits of error checking earlier in this chapter.
- Implement transactions for this program. We learned about using transactions earlier in this chapter as well.
- SET LOCK MODE TO WAIT. If you add this statement to the example above, the new code looks like this:

```
DeleteServiceRecs()
{
.        .        .        .
.        .        .        .
   EXEC SQL set lock mode to wait;

   EXEC SQL delete from service_header
    where service_header.service_call_id =
     :id_to_delete;

   EXEC SQL delete from service_detail
    where service_detail.service_call_id =
     :id_to_delete;
.        .        .        .
.        .        .        .
}
```

The OnLine database server handles SET LOCK MODE TO WAIT differently than the SE server. If you're developing for the OnLine database environment, you have the added benefit of being able to specify a maximum number of seconds to wait. If your program encounters a lock, it waits up to the number of seconds that you specify. If the data becomes available before the specified number of seconds elapse, your program proceeds. For example, if you code your program to wait for 60 seconds when it hits a lock, and the lock actually frees up in five seconds, your program continues as soon as the resource is available. If, on the other hand, the locked resource is still not available after the specified number of seconds has passed, your program receives an error back from the database. On the SE server, SET LOCK MODE TO WAIT waits indefinitely.

Given that SET LOCK MODE TO WAIT may potentially expire with the OnLine engine, you should provide lock handling logic. A good way to do this is to retry the operation a few times in conjunction with SET LOCK MODE TO WAIT n SECONDS. If, after a few tries, the resource is still not available, chances are that it won't be available anytime soon. As an administrator, it's in your best interest to know about these types of situations while they're happening. You can design your programs so that they send you electronic mail when they run into this type of problem. The pseudocode for this type of operation looks like:

```
for i = 1 to the maximum number of retries
   put the table name into a host variable
   update the record(s)
   if no errors
      set the status flag to success
      exit the for loop
   else
      if i is the maximum number of retries
         build up a mail message, showing date,
           time, table name, error number, etc.
         if your server is the OnLine engine
            run 'tbstat -u' and add the output
            to the mail message
         end if
         mail this message to the administrator
          display an error message on the screen for
            the user
            set the status flag to failure
         else
            continue the for loop
         end if
      end if
  end for
```

In summary, you can minimize failures due to locked records in several ways:

- Always code your programs to gracefully handle locks.
- Try to minimize the length of time that you hold locks. See the "Long transactions" section of this chapter for more detail.
- If you are using the OnLine engine, consider using row level locks instead of page level locks. This increases concurrency, but uses up more locks in the process.

Unfortunately, even if your programs are extremely efficient users of locks, they can still fail if they exceed the maximum number of available locks on the system. We now turn our attention to minimizing these types of problems.

Avoiding running out of locks

For a database administrator, no application failure is particularly pleasant. But when a large, multi-hour batch job fails due to a lack of locks, the administrator's job is especially difficult. These batch jobs are often crucial operations, in applications such as payroll, billing, end-of-month posting, etc. If they fail, you are often under a great deal of pressure to make them succeed. Often, one major problem in fixing these types of problems is the amount of time the application must run before encountering the error. For example, if you're running an end-of-month payroll, processing 12,000 employees, you may not run out of locks until the job has been running for several hours. If you "fix" the problem, you must re-run the job, and wait another few hours to see if the error was indeed corrected. What happens if it wasn't? The process continues, often seemingly endlessly. This highlights the importance of proactively designing your programs to avoid running out of locks.

There are three main ways to prevent this problem from occurring:

- **Lock the table.** If you are running a large batch job and running out of locks, consider locking the table. Other users can still see the table (assuming that you lock it in SHARE mode), but they can't make any changes. In this case, you might need to lock the table in EXCLUSIVE mode, since your batch job is modifying data. The engine places an exclusive row level lock on every updated or deleted row, even if the table is locked in SHARE mode. This means that the only way to guarantee one lock is to lock the table in EXCLUSIVE mode. Unfortunately, locking the table (in either SHARE or EXCLUSIVE mode) may not be acceptable, because your users may need to update the table while your batch job is running.
- **Change the table's lock mode.** The OnLine engine supports the concepts of lock modes. When you create a table, OnLine uses page level locking as a default. This means that when user A wants to update a single row on a page, she locks the entire page. If she updates several rows on that page, she still only needs to hold one lock. If user B wants to update another row on the same

page, however, he must wait until user A releases the lock. This has the effect of reducing the system's concurrency, since users end up waiting for each other to release locks on pages.

In an effort to improve concurrency, which in turn improves performance, database administrators can change the lock mode of heavily updated tables to row level. This means that user B can update his row on a page at the same time user A is updating hers. The net effect of row level locking is an increased lock requirement.

If you start running out of locks while running a batch program that updates a table that has a lock mode of row, consider changing the lock mode of the table to page. You could make this change before running your batch program, and change the table back after you finish.

- **Increase locks.** On certain UNIX platforms, Informix-SE uses kernel locking. If your system is one of these platforms, you can increase the number of locks by raising the maximum number of locks that are specified in your kernel configuration file and then rebuilding the kernel. Keep in mind that there are a limited number of locks available, so it's fairly likely that this type of change won't help on a relatively large job.

  With OnLine, however, you may be able to raise the number of locks high enough to support very large batch jobs. Keep in mind that with OnLine versions 5.01 and older, to increase the number of locks, your administrator needs to bring down the engine. This may be unacceptable in your production environment. With OnLine version 6.0 and newer, the administrator can change the number of locks without shutting the engine down.

ISOLATION LEVELS

A common area for concern when developing multi-user applications is "trusting" the data that your program sees. For example, what if two users, user A and user B, are working on the same record? How can you ensure that each user is seeing "real" data? Furthermore, what happens if user A changes a row while user B is searching for it? The number of potential data access and reliability problems is virtually unlimited. Fortunately, if you develop applications that run using the OnLine database engine, you can use isolation levels to help mitigate these types of situations.

Determining current isolation levels

You can easily determine your users" isolation levels. If you're using OnLine version 5.0x and earlier, use the **tbstat -u** command:

```
RSAM Version 5.01.UD1   -- On-Line -- Up 00:06:26 -- 2736 Kbytes

Users
address  flags   pid     user     tty       wait      tout locks nreads
nwrites
c0bf6120 ------D 13076   b        pty/ttyv 0         0    0     36        3
c0bf6194 ------D 0       b        pty/ttyv 0         0    0     0         0
c0bf6208 ------- 13157   informix pty/ttyv 0         0    1     88      104
c0bf627c ------- 13199   informix pty/ttyv 0         0    1     0         0
c0bf62f0 ------- 13211   informix pty/ttyv 0         0    1     0         0
c0bf6364 ------- 13224   informix pty/ttyv 0         0    1     0         0
 6 active, 20 total

Transactions
address  flags user     locks log begin isolation retrys coordinator
c0bf6a30 A---- c0bf6120 0     0         NOTRANS   0
c0bf6df0 A---- c0bf6194 0     0         NOTRANS   0
c0bf71b0 A---- c0bf6208 1     0         REPEAT    0
c0bf7570 A---- c0bf627c 1     0         DIRTY     0
c0bf7930 A---- c0bf62f0 1     0         CURSOR    0
c0bf7cf0 A---- c0bf6364 1     0         COMMIT    0
 6 active, 20 total
```

If you're using OnLine version 6.0 and newer, use the **onstat -ux** command:

```
RSAM Version 6.00.UD1 -- On-Line -- Up 20 days 21:57:22 -- 10032
     Kbytes

Userthreads
address  flags   sessid  user     tty      wait     tout locks
     nreads   nwrites
c01ee854 ---P--D 0       informix -        0        0    0  21  8
c01eebb8 ---P--F 0       informix -        0        0    0  0   0
c01eef1c Y--P--- 15      informix ttyvb    c0437250 0    1  0   0
c01ef280 ---P--B 0       informix -        0        0    0  0   1
c01f1e94 Y--P--- 17      informix ttyvb    c049d110 0    1  0   0
c01f21f8 Y--P--- 13      informix ttyvb    c02e5850 0    1  0   0
c01f255c ---P--D 0       informix -        0        0    0  0   0
 7 active, 20 total

Transactions
address  flags userthread locks log begin isolation retrys coordinator
c01f2c24 A---- c01ee854   0     0         COMMIT    0
c01f2d88 A---- c01eebb8   0     0         COMMIT    0
c01f2eec A---- c01eef1c   1     0         DIRTY     0
c01f3050 A---- c01ef280   0     0         COMMIT    0
c01f31b4 A---- c01f255c   0     0         COMMIT    0
c01f347c A---- c01f21f8   1     0         CURSOR    0
c01f35e0 A---- c01f1e94   1     0         REPEAT    0
 7 active, 20 total
```

At this point, let's go over each of the four isolation levels, and identify scenarios where each would be appropriate:

1. **DIRTY READ** This is the lowest level of isolation. Your program holds no locks on data rows. If it encounters a lock being held by another process, it disregards that lock and retrieves the row anyway. While this is the fastest and most efficient way to retrieve data, it also means that you may occasionally see a row that was never truly in the database. For example, assume that there are two users on your system, A and B. B is inserting rows into a table via a transaction. A has an isolation level of dirty read, and is looking at some of the same rows that B is inserting. If B later rolls back his transaction, A saw rows that were never really there. These types of data are known as "phantom rows", and can confuse your users and complicate your job responsibilities. Even with this in mind, there are still certain circumstances where an isolation level of dirty read is appropriate:
   - **Single user batch jobs.** If you're running a job that you know will be the only process working with a table(s), you can safely set isolation mode to dirty read.
   - **Non-changing tables.** If you're running a process that reads static, non-changing tables, there's no need to use any higher isolation level than dirty read.
   - **Summary reports.** If you're running a report that can tolerate the slim possibilities of finding a phantom row, such as a large scale summary report, you can improve performance by setting your isolation level to dirty read for the duration of the report.
2. **COMMITTED READ** This is the next higher level of isolation. In this case, before returning a row, the engine tests it to see if there are any update locks on it. If there aren't, the engine returns the row. This level of isolation is almost as efficient as dirty read; it is also the default isolation level for a database that is not ANSI-compliant. If your application must never receive a phantom row, use this isolation level.
3. **CURSOR STABILITY** What if you're running a program that must ensure that the current row doesn't change while you're looking at it? This situation calls for an isolation level of cursor stability. When a cursor fetches a row, the server places a lock on that row. If your cursor is an update cursor, the server places a promotable lock on the row. This means that the server reserves the right to update the row. If the cursor is a standard read-only cursor, the server places a shared lock on the row. In either case, no other process can change the row while you hold a lock on it. As soon as you fetch the next row, the server releases the lock on the row you were working with.

   Because cursor stability places (and then releases) locks on each row you work with, it consumes more resources and time. Consequently, use this isolation level only if you're running a multi-user system where it's possible that two or more users might try to update the same value. For example, when user A is viewing a row, the cursor stability isolation level places a lock on the row. If user B attempts to update the same row while user A still holds the lock, user B's process receives a locked row error message from the server. User B can then look at the changes made by user A, and decide how to proceed.

4. **REPEATABLE READ** This is the highest level of isolation. The only difference between repeatable read and cursor stability is the length of time that the lock is held. With cursor stability, the lock is only help while you look at the row. With repeatable read, the lock is held until you release it, either with COMMIT WORK or ROLLBACK WORK. If your program examines a large number of rows, you could easily run out of locks with this level of isolation. Therefore, you should reserve repeatable read isolation for only those circumstances that warrant it. Generally, these types of situations involve distinct groupings of records that must all be updated together, such as a header/detail relationship. You should not use this isolation level for any of the following types of processing:

   - **Reports.** There is no need to lock each row (and hold the lock until completed) in a report. In addition, if you're running a large report, you'll probably run out of locks long before your program can complete.
   - **Lookup screens.** If you're reading data from static tables, repeatable read isolation makes no sense. In fact, you'll probably cause other programs that read the same table to fail, as they wait for your session to free up the locks.
   - **Query by example.** It's very dangerous to allow users to enter in free-form query criteria, and then hold locks on the rows that the query returns. What if the user requests all rows in the database? Do you really want to lock these rows for the duration of the users query?

   Note that if you're using an ANSI-compliant database, repeatable read is the default isolation level.

Remember that you can change the isolation level within the same program. For example, this means that you could set your isolation to dirty read for a lookup, and then change it to repeatable read when you actually modify heavily accessed data.

Miscellaneous tips

BULK DATA LOADING

Regardless of the type of application that you're developing or maintaining, there's a good chance that you periodically need to load large amounts of data into your database. There are a number of ways to perform this task. In this section, we discuss the benefits and drawbacks of each method.

First, no matter what method you choose to load your data, you can improve throughput by performing the following steps:

1. Try to schedule the bulk data loading during off hours. Dropping indexes or changing OnLine shared memory parameters during peak hours will not make you very popular with your user community.
2. If the table size after the INSERT operation will be at least 10 percent larger than before the operation, drop any indexes on the table. This is because if there are indexes in place, the engine must update these indexes after each new row is added. This is highly inefficient; it is much better to simply re-create the indexes after you finish loading the data.
3. If you are running OnLine, consider allocating more shared memory buffers. This can help speed up the operation by reducing disk I/O. OnLine versions 6.0 and newer let you do this without restarting the engine; older versions require a shutdown and restart.
4. Using whichever method you choose, load the data.
5. Re-create the indexes (if you first dropped them).
6. Run UPDATE STATISTICS for the table. Many administrators forget this important step after loading data. Unfortunately, this can lead to drastically degraded performance. See the "Understanding the Informix optimizer" section for more detail about UPDATE STATISTICS.

Note that the dropping and recreating indexes suggestion applies to sites running Informix servers versions 5.0 and newer; these versions have much faster index creation speeds than earlier versions of OnLine.

SQL LOAD

The easiest and fastest way to load data into your database is the SQL LOAD statement. The syntax for this statement is:

```
LOAD FROM <filename> INSERT INTO <tablename>
```

This statement reads in data from the filename that you provide. Normally, these are flat, ASCII files that use the pipe character (|) to delimit each field. If you want to use another character as a delimiter instead of the pipe, just change your DBDELIMIT environment variable to match the new character.

While this is the simplest and fastest way to load data, it does have several drawbacks:

- **Failure detection.** If there is an error in your load file, the LOAD statement will abort. This can be complicated to handle whether or not you're using transaction logging.

  If you're using transaction logging, the entire loading process is rolled back. If the error occurs 95% of the way through a large file, you've wasted a substantial amount of time.

  If you're not using transaction logging, all the rows up to the failure point are loaded, while all rows from the failure point forward are not. It might be very difficult for you to determine exactly where the problem occurred. This means that after you fix the problem and re-run the LOAD, you might either duplicate some already-loaded rows, or you might omit some rows that never made it into the database. In either case, you can damage the integrity of your database.
- **Long transactions.** If you're using transaction logging, the LOAD statement can cause a long transaction to occur. This is because LOAD, in a database that uses transaction logging, implicitly begins a transaction when it starts loading data. If your load file is too large, or if your available logical log space is too small, there's a good chance that your load process will fail. You can get around this by turning off transaction logging for the database before you run the load. After it completes, you can turn logging back on. Remember that this technique won't work if your database is ANSI-compliant.
- **Delimiters.** Not all data files are delimited; there are many cases where you may receive a file containing fixed-length records with no delimiters. The LOAD statement can't easily handle this type of file.
- **Multiple table inserts.** If each line in your data file needs to be broken up and inserted into two or more tables, the LOAD statement won't be able to meet your needs.

If any of the above issues apply to your situation, consider using DBLOAD instead.

DBLOAD

DBLOAD is especially useful when you have files that are not delimited by any special characters. In these cases, DBLOAD lets you avoid writing any special programs to parse the files. Instead, you set up a command file that defines the layout of your input file. DBLOAD is more flexible than the LOAD statement in the following ways:

- **Error handling.** You can specify the number of errors that DBLOAD can receive during the loading process. If the number of errors exceeds your stated limit, DBLOAD stops processing the input file.
- **Status logging.** You can instruct DBLOAD to write erroneous rows and other diagnostic information to a log file. You can then inspect this log file at a later point in time.
- **Transaction length.** You can tell DBLOAD to commit the transaction (if you're using transaction logging) after a certain number of rows. This minimizes the possibility of a long transaction.
- **File offset.** If you don't want to process a number of rows at the start of your input file, you can request that DBLOAD skip those rows. It then inserts data after bypassing the number of rows that you specify. This is useful when you are inserting the contents of a report into your database, and you want to skip the page header and only process the actual report data.

In spite of the LOAD statement and DBLOAD utility, many programmers choose to write their own load programs. In the next section, we discuss how to optimize these types of applications.

Procedural languages

The most commonly used procedural language for bulk data loading is ESQL/C, so our example program in this chapter is written in this language. Assume that you have a transaction table that has 10 million rows. Each night, you expect to receive enough rows to grow the table by 15 percent:

Table 3.19 transactions

trans_id	trans_type	cust_id	trans_amount
106534	D	109964	407.33
106535	C	9011	87.08
106536	B	78665	1229.86
.	.	.	.
.	.	.	.
.	.	.	.

You could write an ESQL/C program to INSERT these rows, one at a time. However, you can use an INSERT cursor to greatly speed up the process. This is one way you could write the program:

```
/*****************************************************/

#include <stdio.h>

$include sqlca;

/* This is the number of records to                              */
/* process before COMMITting                                     */
#define MAX_TRANS 100

main()
{

   /* Host variables                                              */
   $int  trans_id;
   $char trans_type[2];
   $int  cust_id;
   $float trans_amount;

   /* Program variables                                           */
   int i;
   int counter = 0;
   int last_good_record = 0;

   $database sample;

   $prepare b from "insert into transactions values
        (?,?,?,?)";
   $declare insert_cur cursor with hold for b;

   $begin work;

   $open insert_cur;

   while (1)
   {

        .    .    .    .    .    .
        .    .    .    .    .    .
```

```
   /*
   ** You would read in each line of the input file,
   ** and populate any necessary host variables
   ** At the end of file marker, you would break out
   ** of the while loop
   */
    .   .   .   .   .   .
    .   .   .   .   .   .

   $put insert_cur from
      $trans_id, $trans_type, $cust_id,
         $trans_amount;

   if (counter <= MAX_TRANS)
   {
      counter++;
   }
   else
   {
      $flush insert_cur;
      if (sqlca.sqlcode == 0)
/* If everything is ok, we commit work and start  */
/*another.transaction.... .......................*/
      {
         last_good_record += counter;
         counter = 0;
         $commit work;
         $begin work;
      }
      else
      {             /* Otherwise, we rollback     */
         $rollback work;
         fprintf (stderr, "Error during insert
            operation\n");
         fprintf (stderr, "Last good record:
            %d\n", last_good_record);
         exit(-1);
      }
   }

}

/* Final flush to clear the buffer                */
```

```
    $flush insert_cur;
    /* Final commit                                         */
    $commit work;
}

/****************************************************************/
```

It's important to keep track of what the last successful inserted record was. If the program fails in the middle, you need to determine the correct restart point.

MEMORY MANAGEMENT

We can subdivide the topic of memory management into the following areas of interest:

- Arrays
- The FREE statement
- Reducing executable sizes

Arrays

Arrays are useful when you need to store more than one data record in memory. In an effort to allocate enough potential storage, however, many programmers define arrays that are much larger than necessary, and end up wasting valuable memory in the process.

ESQL/C programmers are aided by the numerous dynamic memory allocation functions (such as malloc()) that the C function library provides. Many experienced C programmers use these functions at runtime when their programs need more memory, instead of hard-coding fixed length arrays during development. If you're developing ESQL/C code, and you expect to define arrays to hold data, instead consider using one of the memory management functions to control your storage areas. You may find that your programs require far less memory when you dynamically allocate memory rather than define large arrays. See the "ESQL/C Tips" section for more detail about memory management and ESQL/C.

The topic of memory management becomes a little more complicated when we turn to INFORMIX-4GL, because 4GL doesn't provide for runtime memory allocation. Despite this, however, there are still some ways that you can conserve memory while developing 4GL applications:

- Limit array length. Try to keep your arrays as small as possible. Don't define an array consisting of 500 entries if you're not sure that you'll ever need space for that many records. Instead, consider using a counter to track how many records you actually end up using in production, and then modify your program accordingly.

- Limit array width. Remember that in addition to conserving the number of entries in your program arrays, you should minimize the number of columns or elements defined in each array member. For example, if you only need two columns from a 20-column table, don't define your array records to hold all 20 columns from the table. For more information on the benefits of only selecting those columns that you truly need, see the "Reducing pipe traffic" section of this chapter.

FREE

The FREE statement lets you free up the resources used by prepared statements and cursors. Note that while PREPARE allocates resources immediately, declaring a cursor doesn't allocate any resources until you open it. This means that if you declare (and then open) a cursor for a prepared statement, you can only free all the memory if you perform the following steps:

1. Free the prepared statement id.
2. Close the cursor.
3. Free the cursor's id.

If you prepared a statement but never declared a cursor for it (e.g., for an UPDATE or DELETE statement), you only need to free the statement id.

Reducing executable sizes

One way to conserve system memory is to keep the sizes of your executables as small as possible. You can do this in several ways:

- Avoid all-in-one executables for multi-faceted systems. For example, assume that you're developing a system that contains a number of completely separate functional modules that are tied together by a main menu. Instead of linking all these separate modules into one giant executable, consider grouping them into their own executables. Your main menu program could then start the appropriate, smaller executable when it is needed.
- Use shared libraries whenever possible. This allows you to develop a rich suite of functions and store them in a library. Your executable size is smaller because the functions in the library are not linked into your executable when you build your application. Instead, the functions are only retrieved from the library at runtime.

AVOIDING EXCESS SCREEN I/O

Screen I/O is very expensive. This is especially true if you are running in a client/server environment, where you may need to send the data over the network. Therefore, try to limit the number of times your application performs screen I/O. While this may not be possible in many cases, there are certain times where you can significantly reduce this operation.

One case involves programs that load data in bulk into the database. Many programmers provide status messages to the user, letting them know how many rows have been loaded. This is fine in moderation, but if you repaint the message after every processed row, you can drastically affect performance. Instead of displaying the message after every row, consider keeping a counter and only displaying the message after every 100, 1,000, or 10,0000 rows.

4GL SPECIFIC TIPS

Many organizations use INFORMIX-4GL to develop quality production applications quickly. Even though you can rapidly develop systems using 4GL, you still need to consider performance when you build or maintain your programs. In the "General Tips" section, we addressed a number of performance-enhancing techniques that you can incorporate into your applications, regardless of the programming language that you use. In this section, we turn our attention to tips that apply only to INFORMIX-4GL.

We begin our discussion with an analysis of several general 4GL topics. These include the benefits of rapid development system 4GL versus compiled 4GL, along with how you can best compile your 4GL programs. Next, we explore when to use the LET statement and when to use the INITIALIZE statement to reduce a program's running time. Many programmers don't realize that 4GL lets you take advantage of UNIX's multiprocessing capabilities. We examine how you can use RUN WITHOUT WAITING to fully utilize multiprocessing. Finally, even though 4GL is a powerful and flexible programming language, there are certain cases where you should think about using a lower-level language, such as ESQL/C. We close out this section by illustrating some of these situations.

In the next section, we highlight several easy steps you can take to speed up your 4GL forms. Users really like using query by example to locate information. As a programmer, there are certain controls that you should put in place to prevent users from entering "dangerous queries". We discuss two techniques that you can employ to intervene in this type of situation. Next, we point out why you should consider redefining the ACCEPT key to something other than <escape>.

Later in this chapter, we note that, unfortunately, programmers sometimes validate data too frequently. This can lead to substantially degraded performance. We reveal how you can reduce your overall calls to the database while still maintaining data integrity. Finally, we discuss how you can use variables to hold form names and titles, letting you create generic form-handling routines.

We close out this chapter by reviewing how you can write more efficient 4GL reports. We reiterate the importance of the PREPARE statement, especially as it relates to reports, then focus on how you can use ORDER EXTERNAL BY to eliminate unnecessary temporary tables from your reports. Our last report recommendation deals with using format strings to increase report maintainability and readability while reducing memory requirements.

General language tips

INTERPRETED VERSUS COMPILED 4GL

Many developers use the Informix Rapid Development System (RDS) when building and testing applications. It shortens the development cycle by letting you quickly compile and debug your programs. The compile cycle is the main reason for RDS's speed benefits. Standard 4GL follows these steps when generating an executable:

1. The 4GL source code is converted into ESQL/C statements, producing a corresponding embedded SQL (.ec) file.
2. The ESQL/C code is converted into C language, producing a standard C (.c) file.
3. The C compiler processes the C code, yielding an object (.o) file.
4. The linker links the object files together with all appropriate libraries (.a files), and creates the actual executable program, which usually has a ".4ge" suffix.

In contrast, RDS skips steps 2 through 4. It processes your 4GL code, and produces a "p-code" file (.4go or .4gi, depending on how you compiled your program). You can then run and debug this program. This takes much less time than the more traditional full compile process. In addition, you can step through your code one line at a time using the debugger, which helps you produce higher quality code.

Once you've finished the compiling and debugging cycle, however, it's a good idea to go back and follow the standard 4GL compiling procedure to produce an executable. Compiled C code generally executes faster than interpreted p-code. In addition, C compilers introduce more rigid type checking, which can help point out instances where you might have been careless when initializing variables. Specifically, p-code initializes all locally-defined variables to 0, while compiled C code doesn't automatically initialize any variables. This explains why many applications mysteriously "fail" when converted to compiled C code. The reason behind these failures is usually uninitialized variables.

While we're on the subject of compiled 4GL, remember that 4GL programs actually create ESQL/C and then C code before becoming executables. This means that you can decrease 4GL executable size by utilizing the same compiler flags that you can use when compiling ESQL/C programs. For more information about ESQL/C compiler flags, see the "ESQL/C tips" section.

INITIALIZE VERSUS LET

If you need to initialize a large number of variables or records, or if you need to repeatedly initialize the same variable or record, consider using the LET statement instead of the INITIALIZE statement. INITIALIZE uses several C-level function calls, while LET has much less overhead.

For example, look at the following portion of 4GL code:

```
# Initial setup, called only once
.          .          .
.          .          .
DEFINE I                                                    SMALLINT
DEFINE MACHINE_STAT_ARR ARRAY[300] OF RECORD LIKE MACHINE_STATUS.*
DEFINE MACHINE_LOOKUP                            LIKE MACHINE.MACHINE_ID
.          .          .
.          .          .

DECLARE MACHINE_STAT_CUR CURSOR FOR
   SELECT *
   FROM   MACHINE_STATUS
   WHERE  MACHINE_ID = MACHINE_LOOKUP
.          .          .
.          .          .

# The rest of this code is executed thousands of times a day
FOR I = 1 TO 300
   INITIALIZE MACHINE_STAT_ARR[I].* TO NULL
END FOR

LET MACHINE_LOOKUP = <user supplied>

OPEN MACHINE_STAT_CUR
LET I = 1

WHILE (SQLCA.SQLCODE = 0)
   FETCH MACHINE_STAT_CUR INTO MACHINE_STAT_ARR[I].*
   LET I = I + 1
   IF I = 300 THEN
      ERROR "ARRAY BOUNDS EXCEEDED: CONTACT IS DEPT."
      EXIT WHILE
   END IF
END WHILE
```

If your program activates this section of code 4000 times a day, and you use the INITIALIZE command to clear out each of the 300 array members, you can prevent over one million unnecessary function calls by simply using the LET statement instead:

```
# Initial setup, only called once
.          .          .
.          .          .
DEFINE I                                                 SMALLINT
DEFINE MACHINE_LOOKUP                               LIKE
MACHINE.MACHINE_ID
DEFINE MACHINE_STAT_ARR ARRAY[300] OF RECORD LIKE MACHINE_STATUS.*
DEFINE MACHINE_STAT_NULL              RECORD LIKE MACHINE_STATUS.*
.          .          .
.          .          .
INITIALIZE MACHINE_STAT_NULL.* TO NULL
.          .          .
.          .          .
DECLARE MACHINE_STAT_CUR CURSOR FOR
   SELECT *
   FROM   MACHINE_STATUS
   WHERE  MACHINE_ID = MACHINE_LOOKUP
.          .          .
.          .          .

# The rest of this code is executed thousands of times a day
FOR I = 1 TO 300
   LET MACHINE_STAT_ARR[I].* = MACHINE_STAT_NULL.*
END FOR

LET MACHINE_LOOKUP = <user supplied>

OPEN MACHINE_STAT_CUR
LET I = 1

WHILE (SQLCA.SQLCODE = 0)
   FETCH MACHINE_STAT_CUR INTO MACHINE_STAT_ARR[I].*
   LET I = I + 1
   IF I = 300 THEN
      ERROR "ARRAY BOUNDS EXCEEDED: CONTACT IS DEPT."
      EXIT WHILE
   END IF
END WHILE
```

If you follow this strategy, the only extra code you need to add is the one-time definition and initialization of any necessary null records.

RUN WITHOUT WAITING

One way to squeeze extra performance out of your UNIX platforms is to take full advantage of the operating system's multi-tasking features. If you have a 4GL program that issues operating system level calls, consider using the RUN WITHOUT WAITING command instead of the RUN command.

For example, suppose you're maintaining a point-of-sale system. When users run the daily transaction report, you want to send a copy of the report to your London site, using the UNIX "rcp" command:

```
.    .    .    .    .
.    .    .    .    .

LET SITE_ID = "07904"

DECLARE TRANSACTION_CUR CURSOR FOR
SELECT *
FROM   POS_TRANSACTIONS
WHERE  TRANSACTION_DATE = TODAY

START REPORT TRANSACTION_SUMMARY

FOREACH TRANSACTION_CUR INTO TRANSACTION_REC.*
   OUTPUT TO REPORT TRANSACTION_SUMMARY (TRANSACTION_REC.*)
END FOREACH

FINISH REPORT TRANSACTION_SUMMARY

LET OS_STRING = "rcp /tmp/report
    london:/usr/site_reports/report.",SITE_ID

RUN OS_STRING

RETURN
.    .    .    .    .
.    .    .    .    .
```

The above code forces the user to wait until the remote copy has finished. If the report is large, or the network is slow, the user may wait several minutes for the command to finish. In many cases, however, there's no reason that the user can't move on to other work. Unless your users absolutely must wait for operating system commands to end, use RUN WITHOUT WAITING instead:

```
   .    .    .    .    .
   .    .    .    .    .

LET SITE_ID = "07904"

DECLARE TRANSACTION_CUR CURSOR FOR
SELECT *
FROM   POS_TRANSACTIONS
WHERE  TRANSACTION_DATE = TODAY

START REPORT TRANSACTION_SUMMARY

FOREACH TRANSACTION_CUR INTO TRANSACTION_REC.*
   OUTPUT TO REPORT TRANSACTION_SUMMARY (TRANSACTION_REC.*)
END FOREACH

FINISH REPORT TRANSACTION_SUMMARY

LET OS_STRING = "rcp /tmp/report
 london:/usr/site_reports/report.",SITE_ID

RUN OS_STRING WITHOUT WAITING

RETURN
   .    .    .    .    .
   .    .    .    .    .
```

RUN WITHOUT WAITING still issues a system call, but it requests that UNIX run the request in the background. If you need to know the results of your operating system call, you can always redirect the command's output to a file. You can review the file later if you wish.

WHEN TO "JUMP OUT" TO C

You can write efficient 4GL code for most tasks. There are, however, certain cases where you should consider using a third generation language, typically ESQL/C. These situations include:

- **Extensive looping.** When you write a loop statement in 4GL (e.g., FOR, WHILE), the generated ESQL/C code is more cumbersome than if you write the looping logic in ESQL/C itself. For most applications, this extra cost isn't that significant. However, if you're trying to squeeze every last bit of speed out of your application, consider using ESQL/C if you make heavy use of looping.

- **Direct filesystem access.** If you need to read or write directly from or to operating system files, you'll generally get better response if you use ESQL/C. This is especially true if you're reading files, since 4GL doesn't contain any direct file operation statements.
- **Interprocess communication.** Certain types of applications, such as factory floor automation, telecommunications, etc. typically monitor an incoming data line and update a database with the received information. While you could conceivably write this kind of application using 4GL, you'll probably write faster and cleaner code if you use ESQL/C.

Forms tips

QUERY BY EXAMPLE

If you let your users search for information with query-by-example screens, you should first check to see if the user entered any selection criteria before you initiate the search. 4GL lets you do this at least two ways:

- **Check constructed clause**

If you use this method, you examine the constructed clause to see if the user has entered any information. If she hasn't, then the constructed clause contain " 1=1". This tells the database to return all rows, since 1 is always equal to 1:

```
.    .    .    .    .
.    .    .    .    .
define lookup_criteria char(300)
define sql_stmt        char(500)
.    .    .    .    .
.    .    .    .    .
.    .    .    .    .
   command "Search" "Search for transaction"
      while (1)
         construct by name lookup_criteria on transaction.*
            after field amount
               next field account_num
            after construct
               if lookup_criteria = " 1=1" then
                  error "No criteria entered.  Will search
                    entire database"
                  prompt "Continue? " for continue_flag
                  if continue_flag = "Y" or continue_flag =
```

```
                    "y" then
                       error "This may take some time"
                       exit while
                    else
                       error "Please try to be more selective"
                       sleep 1
                    end if
                 else
                    exit while
                 end if
           end construct
        end while

        let sql_stmt = "select * from transaction where ",
             lookup_criteria clipped
        prepare P1 from sql_stmt
        declare trans_cur cursor for P1
        open trans_cur
  .    .    .    .    .
  .    .    .    .    .
```

- **Use "field_touched()" operator**

You can use the built-in 4GL operator called "field_touched()" to see if the user entered any data:

```
  .    .    .    .    .
  .    .    .    .    .
  define lookup_criteria char(300)
  define sql_stmt        char(500)
  .    .    .    .    .
  .    .    .    .    .
  .    .    .    .    .
     command "Search" "Search for transaction"
        while (1)
           construct by name lookup_criteria on transaction.*
              after field amount
                 next field account_num
              after construct
                 if not field_touched(transaction.*) then
                    error "No criteria entered.  Will search
                      entire database"
                    prompt "Continue? " for continue_flag
                    if continue_flag = "Y" or continue_flag =
```

```
                    "y" then
                      error "This may take some time"
                      exit while
                    else
                      error "Please try to be more selective"
                      sleep 1
                    end if
                 else
                    exit while
                 end if
        end construct
     end while

     let sql_stmt = "select * from transaction where ",
          lookup_criteria clipped
     prepare P1 from sql_stmt
     declare trans_cur cursor for P1
     open trans_cur
.    .    .    .    .
.    .    .    .    .
```

You can use “field_touched()” for the entire table, or you can be more selective:

```
.    .    .    .    .
.    .    .    .    .
  after construct
       if not field_touched(trans_id, amount) then
         error "No criteria entered.  Please enter
           transaction id or amount"
         prompt "Continue? " for continue_flag
         if continue_flag = "Y" or continue_flag = "y" then
            error "This may take some time"
            exit while
         else
            error "Please try to be more selective"
            sleep 1
         end if
      else
         exit while
      end if
  end construct
.    .    .    .    .
.    .    .    .    .
```

ACCEPT KEY

In a 4GL program, the ACCEPT key signals that the user has finished working with a particular form. ACCEPT often signifies that the user is ready to insert/update the data, or begin the query. The default key for ACCEPT is <escape>.

Since the <escape> key is often used in conjunction with other keys to signal a special event, 4GL delays processing your form for one second after you press this key. This allows you enough time to press another key to complete the sequence. In most 4GL programs, however, you don't expect the user to enter another key in combination with <escape>. Despite this, 4GL still waits for one second, thereby introducing an automatic one-second delay into your form programs. To avoid this delay, map the ACCEPT key to either a function or control-sequence key. You can define this (and many other) keys when you open a form or window, in the "options" section.

VALIDATE ONLY WHEN NECESSARY

One common performance mistake that 4GL programmers make is to repeatedly validate forms fields, even if the user hasn't changed the fields" values. Let's look at an example.

In this example, you're maintaining a banking application. The tables that you use are:

```
create table accounts
(
   account_num integer primary key,
   last_name   char(30),
   first_name  char(15)
);


create table trans_codes
(
   trans_type char(1) primary key,
   trans_desc char(40)
);

create table transaction
(
   trans_id serial,
   account_num integer references accounts,
   trans_type char(1) references trans_codes,
   amount decimal(11,2)
);
```

In the following segment of code, you're validating a number of fields before allowing the user to commit the transaction:

```
.   .   .   .   .   .
.   .   .   .   .   .
define R_transaction record like transaction.*
define stop_processing smallint
.   .   .   .   .   .
.   .   .   .   .   .
.   .   .   .   .   .
   command "Add" "Add a new transaction"
      input by name R_transaction.* without defaults
         after field account_num
            call
              acct_validate(R_transaction.account_num)
              returning stop_processing
            if stop_processing then
               error "Invalid account number"
               next field account_num
            else
               next field trans_type
            end if
         after field trans_type
            call
              trans_validate(R_transaction.trans_type)
              returning stop_processing
            if stop_processing then
               error "Invalid transaction type"
               next field trans_type
            else
               next field amount
            end if
         after field amount
            next field account_num
      end input
      begin work
      insert into transaction values (R_transaction.*)
      if sqlca.sqlcode then
         error "Insert failed ", sqlca.sqlcode
         rollback work
      else
         let R_transaction.trans_id = sqlca.sqlerrd[2]
         display by name R_transaction.trans_id
```

```
         error "Insert succeeded"
         commit work
      end if
.   .   .   .   .   .
.   .   .   .   .   .
.   .   .   .   .   .
function acct_validate(key_value)

define key_value like accounts.account_num
define lookup_flag smallint
define record_count  smallint

let lookup_flag = 0
let record_count  = 0

select count(*)
into   record_count
from   accounts
where  accounts.account_num = key_value

case record_count
   when 0
      let lookup_flag = 1
      exit case
   when 1
      let lookup_flag = 0
      exit case
   otherwise
      let lookup_flag = 1
      exit case
end case

return lookup_flag

end function

function trans_validate(key_value)

define key_value like trans_codes.tran_type
define lookup_flag smallint
define record_count  smallint

let lookup_flag = 0
```

```
let record_count  = 0

select count(*)
into   record_count
from   trans_codes
where  trans_codes.tran_type = key_value

case record_count
   when 0
      let lookup_flag = 1
      exit case
   when 1
      let lookup_flag = 0
      exit case
   otherwise
      let lookup_flag = 1
      exit case
end case

return lookup_flag

end function
.    .    .    .    .    .
.    .    .    .    .    .
.    .    .    .    .    .
```

Can you see how this code can unnecessarily validate data? Suppose that the user enters data into a field, and then passes over that field several more times before deciding to commit the transaction. Even if he never changes the values in the <> , <>, or <> fields, you'll still validate those fields. This is bad enough if you're looking up information on the local system. It's even worse if you're running in a client/server or distributed environment, since you'll incur added network costs as well.

If your users complain of the cursor "sticking," or the screen "freezing" during data inserts or updates, check to see if you're repeatedly validating the same fields. If you are, you can avoid this type of extra processing with a few simple changes:

```
.    .    .    .    .    .
.    .    .    .    .    .
define R_transaction record like transaction.*
define S_transaction record like transaction.*
  # Shadow record for trans
define stop_processing smallint
```

```
let S_transaction.account_num = 0
let S_transaction.trans_type  = ""
.   .   .   .   .   .
.   .   .   .   .   .
.   .   .   .   .   .
   command "Add" "Add a new transaction"
      input by name R_transaction.* without defaults
         after field account_num
            if (R_transaction.account_num <>
               S_transaction.account_num) or
               (R_transaction.account_num = 0) then
               call acct_validate(R_transaction.account_num)
                  returning stop_processing
               if stop_processing then
                  error "Invalid account number"
                  next field account_num
               else
                  let S_transaction.account_num =
                     R_transaction.account_num
                  next field trans_type
               end if
            else
               next field trans_type
            end if
         after field trans_type
            if (R_transaction.trans_type <>
               S_transaction.trans_type) or
               (R_transaction.trans_type = "") then
            call trans_validate(R_transaction.trans_type)
              returning stop_processing
            if stop_processing then
               error "Invalid transaction type"
               next field trans_type
            else
               let S_transaction.trans_type =
                   R_transaction.trans_type
               next field amount
            end if
         after field amount
            next field account_num
      end input
      begin work
      insert into transaction values (R_transaction.*)
```

```
        if sqlca.sqlccde then
           error "Insert failed ", sqlca.sqlcode
           rollback work
        else
           let R_transaction.trans_id = sqlca.sqlerrd[2]
           display by name R_transaction.trans_id
           error "Insert succeeded"
           commit work
        end if
    .    .    .    .    .    .
    .    .    .    .    .    .
    .    .    .    .    .    .

function acct_validate(key_value)

   define key_value like accounts.account_num
   define lookup_flag smallint
   define record_count  smallint

   let lookup_flag = 0
   let record_count  = 0

   select count(*)
   into   record_count
   from   accounts
   where  accounts.account_num = key_value

   case record_count
      when 0
         let lookup_flag = 1
         exit case
      when 1
         let lookup_flag = 0
         exit case
      otherwise
         let lookup_flag = 1
         exit case
   end case

   return lookup_flag

end function
```

```
function trans_validate(key_value)

   define key_value like trans_codes.tran_type
   define lookup_flag smallint
   define record_count  smallint

   let lookup_flag = 0
   let record_count  = 0

   select count(*)
   into   record_count
   from   trans_codes
   where  trans_codes.tran_type = key_value

   case record_count
      when 0
         let lookup_flag = 1
         exit case
      when 1
         let lookup_flag = 0
         exit case
      otherwise
         let lookup_flag = 1
         exit case
   end case

   return lookup_flag

end function
   .   .   .   .   .   .
   .   .   .   .   .   .
   .   .   .   .   .   .
```

If you're querying for, and then updating a record, you can use the "field_touched()" operator to tell you if the user has changed the field's value:

```
   .   .   .   .   .   .
   .   .   .   .   .   .
   define R_transaction record like transaction.*
   define stop_processing smallint
   define record_on_screen smallint
   .   .   .   .   .   .
   .   .   .   .   .   .
   .   .   .   .   .   .
```

```
command "Update" "Update a transaction"
   if record_on_screen then
      input by name R_transaction.account_num,
                    R_transaction.trans_type,
                    R_transaction.amount without defaults
         after field account_num
            if field_touched(R_transaction.account_num) then
               call acct_validate(R_transaction.account_num)
                  returning stop_processing
               if stop_processing then
                  error "Invalid account number"
                  next field account_num
               else
                  next field trans_type
               end if
            else
               next field trans_type
            end if
      end input
      begin work
      update transaction set *     = R_transaction.*
      where  transaction.trans_id = R_transaction.trans_id
      if sqlca.sqlcode then
         error "Update failed ", sqlca.sqlcode
         rollback work
      else
         error "Update succeeded"
         commit work
      end if
   else
      error "You must first locate a record"
   end if
.  .  .  .  .  .
.  .  .  .  .  .
```

The drawback to "field_touched()" is that there's no way to "reset" its return code. This means that once the user modifies a field, this function will continually report that the field has changed, even after you've performed any necessary validation. Therefore, if you're updating data, consider using "field_touched()" in conjunction with other logic to prevent unnecessary field validation:

```
.  .  .  .  .  .
.  .  .  .  .  .
```

```
define R_transaction record like transaction.*
define S_transaction record like transaction.*
define stop_processing  smallint
define record_on_screen smallint
.   .   .   .   .   .
.   .   .   .   .   .
.   .   .   .   .   .
   command "Update" "Update a transaction"
      if record_on_screen then
         input by name R_transaction.account_num,
                       R_transaction.trans_type,
                       R_transaction.amount without defaults
            after field account_num
               if field_touched(R_transaction.account_num) then
                  call acct_validate(R_transaction.account_num)
                     returning stop_processing
                  if stop_processing then
                     error "Invalid account number"
                     next field account_num
                  else
                     next field trans_type
                  end if
               else
                  next field trans_type
               end if
         end input
         begin work
         update transaction set *     = R_transaction.*
         where  transaction.trans_id = R_transaction.trans_id
         if sqlca.sqlcode then
            error "Update failed ", sqlca.sqlcode
            rollback work
         else
            error "Update succeeded"
            commit work
         end if
      else
         error "You must first locate a record"
      end if
.   .   .   .   .   .
.   .   .   .   .   .
.   .   .   .   .   .
```

VARIABLES TO HOLD FORM NAMES

In earlier (pre-4.1) versions of 4GL, you had to hard-code form file names and handles (the name that you assign to the form). However, you can now assign these values to variables. This makes it easier to define generic form manipulation routines:

```
   .    .    .    .    .    .
   .    .    .    .    .    .
       command "Transaction" "Enter a transaction"
          call form_handler("transact", "transact", "O")
          call transaction_control()
       command "Account management" "Maintain an account"
          call form_handler("transact", "transact", "O")
          call account_control()
   .    .    .    .    .    .
   .    .    .    .    .    .

function form_handler(form_name, form_handle, action_code)

   define form_name   char(20)
   define form_handle char(20)
   define action_code char(2)

   case action_code
      when "O"
         open form form_handle from form_name options
           accept key "CONTROL-E"
         display form form_handle
         exit case
      when "C"
         close form form_handle
      otherwise
         error "Unknown action code"
         exit case
   end case

end function
```

While this type of enhancement won't necessarily improve performance, it does provide several benefits, such as reduced code complexity, increased maintainability, and fewer lines of code.

Report writer tips

PREPARED STATEMENTS

Remember that you can still use the PREPARE statement for statements that you run within your reports. For example, look at the following segment of code:

```
.    .    .    .    .    .
.    .    .    .    .    .
globals
   define g_accounts record like accounts.*
end globals


main
.    .    .    .    .    .
.    .    .    .    .    .
   declare c cursor for select * from accounts

   start report m1
   foreach c into g_accounts.*
      output to report m1(g_accounts.*)
   end foreach
   finish report m1
.    .    .    .    .    .
.    .    .    .    .    .

end main

report m1(x)

   define x record like accounts.*
   define y record like transaction.*

   format
   on every row
      declare g cursor for
      select * from transaction
      where transaction.account_num = x.account_num
      foreach g into y.*
         print y.trans_id, y.amount....
      end foreach

end report
```

This program unnecessarily re-declares the "g" cursor for each received row. A slight modification to the program can yield a big performance increase:

```
.   .   .   .   .   .
.   .   .   .   .   .
globals
   define g_accounts record like accounts.*
end globals


main
.   .   .   .   .   .
.   .   .   .   .   .
   declare c cursor for select * from accounts
   prepare P from
   "select * from transaction where transaction.account_num = ?"
   declare g cursor for P

   start report m1
   foreach c into g_accounts.*
      output to report m1(g_accounts.*)
   end foreach
   finish report m1
.   .   .   .   .   .
.   .   .   .   .   .

end main

report m1(x)

   define x record like accounts.*
   define y record like transaction.*

   format
   on every row
      open g using x.account_num
      foreach g into y.*
         print y.trans_id, y.amount....
      end foreach

end report
```

If you've got a report that seems to take a long time just to print out each row, see if your report code could benefit from the PREPARE statement.

EXTERNAL SORTING

If you've already sorted the data that you're sending to a report, remember to use the ORDER EXTERNAL BY clause in the body of the report. If you just use ORDER BY, the database engine first creates a temporary table to hold the report contents, and then sorts the temporary table to return the information in the correct order. This amounts to two passes through the data, which can be quite time-consuming for large reports.

For example, the following code segment produces a simple master-detail report:

```
DATABASE MANUF

MAIN

   DEFINE MACHINE_STAT_REC RECORD LIKE MACHINE_STATUS.*

   DECLARE MACHINE_STAT_CUR CURSOR FOR
   SELECT *
   FROM   MACHINE_STATUS
   ORDER BY MACHINE_ID

   START REPORT DETAIL_REPORT

   FOREACH MACHINE_STAT_CUR INTO MACHINE_STAT_REC.*
      OUTPUT TO REPORT DETAIL_REPORT(MACHINE_STAT_REC.*)
   END FOREACH

   FINISH REPORT DETAIL_REPORT

END MAIN

REPORT DETAIL_REPORT(DB_MACHINE_STATUS)

   DEFINE DB_MACHINE_STATUS RECORD LIKE MACHINE_STATUS.*

   ORDER BY DB_MACHINE_STATUS.MACHINE_ID

   FORMAT
      ON EVERY ROW
         PRINT COLUMN  5, DB_MACHINE_STATUS.MACHINE_ID,
               COLUMN 12, DB_MACHINE_STATUS.TOLERANCE,
               COLUMN 30, DB_MACHINE_STATUS.TIMESTAMP

END REPORT
```

Running SET EXPLAIN on this program yields the following output:

```
QUERY:
------
select * from machine_status order by machine_id

Estimated Cost: 12
Estimated # of Rows Returned: 10

1) db_user.machine_status: INDEX PATH

    (1) Index Keys: machine_id


QUERY:
------
select * from t_detail_report order by par1

Estimated Cost: 12
Estimated # of Rows Returned: 10

1) db_user.t_detail_report: INDEX PATH

    (1) Index Keys: par1
```

Notice that even though there's only one SQL statement in the program, there are two query plans. The report's ORDER BY clause causes the engine to create and index a temporary table "t_detail_report". Since the data is already sorted, there's no need for the report to sort it again.

```
DATABASE MANUF

MAIN

   DEFINE MACHINE_STAT_REC RECORD LIKE MACHINE_STATUS.*

   DECLARE MACHINE_STAT_CUR CURSOR FOR
   SELECT *
   FROM   MACHINE_STATUS
   ORDER BY MACHINE_ID

   START REPORT DETAIL_REPORT
```

```
    FOREACH MACHINE_STAT_CUR INTO MACHINE_STAT_REC.*
       OUTPUT TO REPORT DETAIL_REPORT(MACHINE_STAT_REC.*)
    END FOREACH

    FINISH REPORT DETAIL_REPORT

END MAIN


REPORT DETAIL_REPORT(DB_MACHINE_STATUS)

    DEFINE DB_MACHINE_STATUS RECORD LIKE MACHINE_STATUS.*

    ORDER EXTERNAL BY DB_MACHINE_STATUS.MACHINE_ID

    FORMAT
       ON EVERY ROW
          PRINT COLUMN  5, DB_MACHINE_STATUS.MACHINE_ID,
                COLUMN 12, DB_MACHINE_STATUS.TOLERANCE,
                COLUMN 30, DB_MACHINE_STATUS.TIMESTAMP

END REPORT
```

SET EXPLAIN for this version of the program yields this output:

```
QUERY:
------
select * from machine_status order by machine_id

Estimated Cost: 12
Estimated # of Rows Returned: 10

1) db_user.machine_status: INDEX PATH

    (1) Index Keys: machine_id
```

Since we alerted the report section of the program that the incoming data was already sorted, the optimizer didn't need to create a temporary table to process the report.

PREDEFINED FORMAT STRINGS

Format strings let you make your report's appearance more meaningful. You can specify a format string each time you print a variable:

```
REPORT MACHINE_TOLERANCE()
.    .    .    .    .
.    .    .    .    .
   FORMAT
      ON EVERY ROW
         PRINT COLUMN  5, DB_MACHINE_STATUS.MACHINE_ID
            USING "&&&&",
               COLUMN 12, DB_MACHINE_STATUS.ACT_TOLERANCE
                 USING "##.#####"
               COLUMN 30, DB_MACHINE_STATUS.TIMESTAMP
               COLUMN 42, DB_MACHINE_STATUS.OK_TOLERANCE
                 USING "##.#####"
.    .    .    .    .
.    .    .    .    .
END REPORT
```

This approach has some drawbacks, however. It can be somewhat tedious to keep typing in the full format string each time you want to use it. It's easy to make a typing mistake when entering the format string, but it's hard to track it down. Your program is harder to read and understand, as well. Finally, repeatedly entering the same format string can waste memory.

Fortunately, there's another way to specify format strings that provides better readability, reduces errors, and decreases memory requirements. You can set up variables to hold each format style, and then use the variables in the program instead of the actual format pictures:

```
DEFINE TOLERANCE_FMT CHAR(8)
DEFINE MACHINE_FMT   CHAR(4)

LET TOLERANCE_FMT = "##.####"
LET MACHINE_FMT   = "&&&&"

REPORT MACHINE_TOLERANCE()
.    .    .    .    .
.    .    .    .    .
   FORMAT
      ON EVERY ROW
         PRINT COLUMN  5, DB_MACHINE_STATUS.MACHINE_ID
            USING MACHINE_FMT,
               COLUMN 12, DB_MACHINE_STATUS.ACT_TOLERANCE
                 USING TOLERANCE_FMT
               COLUMN 30, DB_MACHINE_STATUS.TIMESTAMP
               COLUMN 42, DB_MACHINE_STATUS.OK_TOLERANCE
                 USING TOLERANCE_FMT
```

```
    .    .    .    .    .
    .    .    .    .    .
    END REPORT
```

If, at a later point, you need to change one or more variable's format, it's much easier and faster to make the change in one place rather than searching through the code for all occurrences. In addition, this approach reduces the overall amount of memory that your program requires, since you're re-using the same variable over and over, instead of continually defining "new" format strings.

ESQL/C SPECIFIC TIPS

ESQL/C combines the power of the C programming language with the superior data access capabilities of SQL. In this section, we examine a number of strategies that you can use to help improve your ESQL/C code's performance.

We begin by discussing ways that you can reduce your program's memory overhead. One way to reduce a program's memory requirements is to only prepare/declare those statements/cursors that you truly need. We examine how to use variables to store prepared statement ids and declared cursor names, instead of hard-coding them. We then look at the differences between linked lists and arrays, especially as they relate to memory usage. Next, we explore the different paths you can follow when defining variables to hold character information.

In the next section, we point out some of the many Informix written functions that you can easily integrate into your own applications. This not only helps you reduce development time, it can also improve performance. In addition to naming these functions, we discuss situations where you can best take advantage of them.

Next, we examine the system descriptor area versus sqlda approaches to dynamic SQL. We also point out dynamic SQL situations where you don't even need to use either of these solutions.

ESQL/C provides several process control functions that you can use to help realize performance gains as well enhanced program control. We learn more about how you can integrate these functions into your applications.

Finally, we investigate several compilation tactics that you can use to reduce program executable sizes. These include header files, libraries, and compile options.

Memory management

CURSOR DECLARATION

Prior to version 5.00 of ESQL/C, you couldn't use a variable to contain the name of a prepared or declared statement. This meant that programmers often declared many more cursors than necessary, since they couldn't dynamically name their prepared statement ids or declared cursors. Since the release of 5.00, however, you can now store statement ids and cursor names within ESQL/C host variables. This means that you no longer need PREPARE unnecessary statements, or DECLARE unnecessary cursors. Here's a segment of ESQL/C code that demonstrates how you can use variable names to hold statement and cursor ids, instead of having to hard-code them:

```
.    .    .    .    .
.    .    .    .    .

EXEC SQL BEGIN DECLARE SECTION;
   char sql_stmt[300];
   char PrepareName[20];
   char CursorName[20];
EXEC SQL END DECLARE SECTION;

strcpy(sql_stmt, "select * from machine_status");
strcpy(PrepareName, "Pmachine");
strcpy(CursorName, "Cmachine");

EXEC SQL prepare :PrepareName from :sql_stmt;

EXEC SQL declare :CursorName cursor for :PrepareName;

EXEC SQL open :CursorName;
.    .    .    .    .
.    .    .    .    .
```

Consider using a method similar to the above example if you're not sure which cursors you'll actually use during each invocation of your program.

You could easily expand the above approach to handle multiple cursors, by following these procedures:

1. Create an array or linked list to store all the statement ids and cursor names.
2. During program execution, whenever you need a cursor or prepared statement, check the array or list to see if you've already created the required cursor or statement.
3. If you haven't created the cursor or statement, create it, and then add it to the array or list.
4. If you have already created or prepared it, you can go ahead and use it.

HOST VARIABLES

Linked lists versus arrays

As a developer, one of your major goals should be to manage memory as wisely as possible. If you're building an application that retrieves large numbers of rows from a database, you've got to decide how to control process memory to handle these returned rows. Let's look at an example to learn more.

In this case, we're maintaining a factory floor automation system. Two dozen manufacturing robots continually insert information into the following table:

Table 3.20 machine_status

status_id	machine_id	tolerance	timestamp
1705	11	0.004303	1995-06-14 14:05:06.956501
1706	9	0.018955	1995-06-14 14:05:07.008751
1707	24	0.005622	1995-06-14 14:05:07.011911
.	.	.	.
.	.	.	.
.	.	.	.

This application is very time-sensitive, and collects a vast amount of data. In addition to the processes that insert data, you must develop a process that continually reads the table, retrieving all rows for a particular machine for a particular time period. One major difficulty you face is determining how to manage memory: you can't afford to waste any, yet you must be able to gracefully handle as many rows as your process finds. You could define an array to hold the rows that you fetch. However, what happens if your array is too small? What happens if you overestimate, and set up an overly large array?

Fortunately, the C programming language lets you allocate memory as you need it. When you're done with this memory, C also allows you to free it. Many experienced ESQL/C programmers use linked lists to efficiently store groups of records in memory. Let's look at some sample ESQL/C code to see how you can integrate linked lists with database communication to help design a solution for the above example:

```
#include <stdio.h>

EXEC SQL include sqlca;
EXEC SQL include sqlda;
EXEC SQL include datetime;
EXEC SQL include decimal;
```

```
/* Function declarations                                  */
void check_status();
void fetch_data();

struct linklist_mask
{
   int  status_id;
   short machine_id;
   float tolerance;
   dtime_t timestamp;
/* Pointer to next record in the list                     */
   struct linklist_mask *nextaddr;
};

EXEC SQL BEGIN DECLARE SECTION;
struct record_mask
{
   int  status_id;
   short machine_id;
   float tolerance;
   datetime timestamp;
} fetch_rec;
EXEC SQL END DECLARE SECTION;

main()
{
   /* Open the database                                   */
   EXEC SQL database manuf;

   /* Fetch data from the machine_status table            */
   fetch_data();

}

void fetch_data()
{
   struct linklist_mask *first_rec, *retrieve_rec;

   /* Grab storage for the first record that will        */
   /* be fetched                                          */
   first_rec = (struct linklist_mask *)
    malloc(sizeof(struct linklist_mask));
   /* Set the current record equal to the first           */
```

```
/* record                                                      */
retrieve_rec = first_rec;

/* Declare and then open a cursor                              */
EXEC SQL declare retrieve_curs cursor for
   select *
   from   machine_status;
check_status("declare cursor",sqlca.sqlcode);

EXEC SQL open retrieve_curs;
check_status("open cursor",sqlca.sqlcode);

/* Fetch the first record, and check status                    */
EXEC SQL fetch retrieve_curs
 into :fetch_rec.status_id,
      :fetch_rec.machine_id,
      :fetch_rec.tolerance,
      :fetch_rec.timestamp;

check_status("fetch first",sqlca.sqlcode);

while (sqlca.sqlcode == 0)
{
   /* Transfer the data from the fetched record   */
   /* into the linked list record (retrieve_rec)  */
   retrieve_rec->status_id  = fetch_rec.status_id;
   retrieve_rec->machine_id = fetch_rec.machine_id;
   retrieve_rec->tolerance  = fetch_rec.tolerance;
   retrieve_rec->timestamp  = fetch_rec.timestamp;

   /* Point the 'nextaddr' part of the memory     */
   /* record at the next linked list member       */
   retrieve_rec->nextaddr =
      (struct linklist_mask *) malloc(sizeof
         (struct linklist_mask));

   /* Set the current record to the next list     */
   /* member                                      */
   retrieve_rec = retrieve_rec->nextaddr;

   /* Fetch the next record from the database     */
   EXEC SQL fetch retrieve_curs
    into  :fetch_rec.status_id,
```

```
                :fetch_rec.machine_id,
                :fetch_rec.tolerance,
                :fetch_rec.timestamp;
    }

    /* Set the last 'nextaddr' to null - marks end     */
    /* of records                                      */
    retrieve_rec->nextaddr = NULL;

    EXEC SQL close retrieve_curs;
    check_status("close cursor",sqlca.sqlcode);


void check_status(action,stat_val)
char *action;
int stat_val;
{
    if (stat_val != 0)
    {
        printf ("Status error: %d on %s\n",stat val,
          action);
    }
}
```

For more information on memory management, see the "General Tips" section.

Character string storage

ESQL/C provides a choice of four different data types to handle character information. The following is a list of these data types, along with a brief description of how they handle retrieved character string data from the database engine:

- **CHAR.** This corresponds to the traditional null-terminated C language char data type. You should define char host variables to be the size of the column plus one byte for the terminating null. For example, if you have a 20-byte column in a table, define a char host variable to be 21 bytes wide. If you select a VARCHAR into this type of host variable, the database server doesn't strip out any trailing spaces.
- **VARCHAR.** This is a null-terminated string, similar to the CHAR data type. This means that you need to define this variable with an extra space to hold the trailing null. When you retrieve data from a varchar column into a VARCHAR host variable, OnLine strips out any trailing blanks, unless the user explicitly entered them.

- **STRING.** This data type is identical to the CHAR data type, except that the database engine removes any trailing blanks, whether they were intentionally entered or not. This is the most storage-efficient of the four character data types, since it never has any trailing blanks. If your application makes heavy use of character strings, consider using this data type.
- **FIXCHAR.** The only difference between this data type and the CHAR data type is that FIXCHAR doesn't need space for a trailing null value. This means that if you want to define a host variable for a column of char(20), you can define your host variable to be 20 bytes as well.

To illustrate the differences among the various character data types, we created a table called "char_test" in the "sample" database. This table contains only one column, which is defined as a CHAR(20). We inserted one row into the table with the following syntax:

```
INSERT INTO CHAR_TEST VALUES ("hello");
```

Next, we wrote a simple program to retrieve this row from the table into a variety of data types. Here is the program that we used, along with the output:

```
-------------------------------------------------------
#include <stdio.h>

main()
{
   EXEC SQL BEGIN DECLARE SECTION;
      string  string_var[20];
      varchar vc_var[20];
      char    char_var[20];
      fixchar fix_var[20];
   EXEC SQL END DECLARE SECTION;

   EXEC SQL database sample;

   EXEC SQL prepare p1 from "select * from char_test";

   EXEC SQL declare c1 cursor for p1;

   EXEC SQL open c1;
   EXEC SQL fetch c1 into :string_var;
   printf ("string :|%s| %d\n", string_var,
    strlen(string_var));
   EXEC SQL close c1;
```

```
    EXEC SQL open c1;
    EXEC SQL fetch c1 into :vc_var;
    printf ("varchar:|%s| %d\n", vc_var,
     strlen(vc_var));
    EXEC SQL close c1;

    EXEC SQL open c1;
    EXEC SQL fetch c1 into :char_var;
    printf ("char    :|%s| %d\n", char_var,
     strlen(char_var));
    EXEC SQL close c1;

    EXEC SQL open c1;
    EXEC SQL fetch c1 into :fix_var;
    printf ("fixchar:|%s| %d\n", fix_var,
     strlen(fix_var));
    EXEC SQL close c1;
}
-------------------------------------------------------

Output:

string :|hello| 5
varchar:|hello                | 19
char   :|hello                | 19
fixchar:|hello                | 20
```

Informix string-handling functions

Informix provides a number of string-handling functions that are generally faster than comparable C compiler library functions. This is because Informix specifically writes these functions in the assembly language of each supported platform.

These functions include:

Table 3.21

C	Informix	Purpose
strcpy	stcopy	Copy a string to another string.
strcat	stcat	Concatenate two strings together.
strlen	stleng	Determine the length of a string.
stcrmp	stcmpr	Compare two strings.

If your application repeatedly uses any of the above C library functions, consider switching to the Informix functions instead. While even a small number of calls to the Informix functions is faster than their C counterparts, you will really see the benefit of this type of change if you are calling the functions hundreds of thousands (or even millions) of times.

Informix provides other useful data comparison and manipulation functions that are also very fast; if you need to perform any of the following tasks, consider using the Informix function instead of writing your own:

Table 3.22 Data comparison

Function	Purpose
bycmpr	Compares two sets of contiguous bytes.
byleng	Counts the number of characters in a string. Omits trailing blanks.
risnull	Checks to see if a variable is null.

Table 3.23 Data manipulation

Function	**Purpose**
byfill	Fills a variable with a character.
bycopy	Copies bytes from one location to another.
ldchar	Copies a fixed-length string into a null-terminated string. Omits trailing blanks.
rdownshift	Changes all upper case in a string to lower case.
rupshift	Changes all lower case in a string to upper case.
rstod	Converts null-terminated string into a double.
rstoi	Converts null-terminated string into an integer.
rstol	Converts null-terminated string into a long.
rsetnull	Sets a variable to null.

While the above functions usually help speed up ESQL/C programs, it is somewhat time-consuming to alter an existing application to incorporate them. If you're maintaining an existing application, consider modifying a small segment of code, and then testing that code section for enhanced throughput. If you're pleased with the results, you can then proceed with confidence and propagate the changes to the rest of the application.

One final note regarding Informix-provided functions: Remember that these functions are specific to Informix. If your application only needs to work with Informix, this isn't a problem. On the other hand, if you plan to port your application to work with other databases, your code may need substantial rewriting to remove all calls to these functions.

Dynamic SQL

If you're developing an application that uses dynamic SQL, one important decision to make is whether to use the system descriptor area or the sqlda structure when you describe your SQL statements. In this section, we describe these two different approaches, especially as they relate to program design.

The system descriptor area stores the following information about each column:

- The actual data
- The type of data
- The length of the data
- Whether the data is null or not
- The column name
- The column's scale (if decimal or money)
- The column's precision (if decimal or money)

- Whether or not the column can contain null values
- The host variable's name
- The host variable's type
- The length of the host variable

The "sqlda" structure points to a linked list of "sqlvar_struct" structures. These structures store these attributes for each data column:

- The type of data
- The length of the data
- A pointer to the data
- A pointer to an indicator
- The column name
- The host variable's name
- The host variable's type
- The length of the host variable

Which of these two methods should you choose when implementing dynamic SQL? There are several strong arguments in favor of the system descriptor area approach:

- **Database portability.** If you're developing applications with database portability in mind, choose the system descriptor approach for dynamic SQL, because each database vendor's "sqlda" structure is slightly different.
- **Language portability.** The system descriptor method is language independent: What works for ESQL/C works for ESQL/COBOL and ESQL/Fortran. If you want to move all or part of your SQL between languages, and you've used the "sqlda" structure, you'll need to make substantial alterations, since the "sqlda" structure is a C language construct.
- **Standards.** The system descriptor area conforms to the X/Open standard.
- **Ease-of-use.** It's easier to develop and maintain ESQL/C programs that work with the system descriptor area instead of the "sqlda" structure. For example, compare the size and complexity of the next two programs, each of which displays information about the columns and data returned from a SELECT. The first example uses the X/Open system descriptor area. The second example uses the Informix sqlda structure.

First, the system descriptor example:

```
#include <stdio.h>

EXEC SQL include sqlca;
EXEC SQL include sqlda;
```

```
main()
{
   EXEC SQL BEGIN DECLARE SECTION;
   int j = 0;

/* String to hold the SQL statement                        */
   char SqlStatement[300];
/* Number of columns that the engine returns               */
   int  ColumnCount = 0;
/* The column's name   */
   char ColumnName[20];
/* The data that the engine returns                        */
   char ActualData[80];
/* The length of the returned data                         */
   int  DataLength = 0;
/* Is the data null?                                        */
   int  IsNowNull = 0;
   EXEC SQL END DECLARE SECTION;

   EXEC SQL database manuf;

   /* Build up an SQL statement.  This can either be */
   /* hard coded or it can be generated at runtime   */
   strcpy(SqlStatement, "select * from
    machine_status");

   /* Prepare a statement, and then declare a      */
   /* cursor */for it                             */
   EXEC SQL prepare P from :SqlStatement;
   EXEC SQL declare C cursor for P;

   /* Allocate a descriptor for the prepared       */
   /* statement.  To conserve memory, only allow for */
   /* 10 columns to be returned. You might want to   */
   /* use a larger number if you believe that the    */
   /* returned number of columns will be larger.     */
   EXEC SQL allocate descriptor 'machine_status'
    withmax 10;

   /* Open the cursor                                */
   EXEC SQL open C;

   /* Describe the prepared statement, and give it a */
```

```
    /* label of 'machine_status'                        */
    EXEC SQL describe P using sql descriptor
     'machine_status';

    /* Get the system descriptor for the                */
    /* 'machine_status' descriptor. Set the             */
    /* ColumnCount variable equal to the 'count'        */
    /* column at the head of the descriptor.            */
    EXEC SQL get descriptor 'machine_status'
     :ColumnCount = count;

    printf ("-------------------------------------\n");

    /* Loop through each returned row from the query   */
    while (1)
    {
       EXEC SQL fetch C using sql descriptor
     'machine_status';
       if (sqlca.sqlcode)
          break;

       /* Loop through each column in each row          */
       /* returned from the query. Copy some of the     */
       /* descriptor fields into host variables         */
       for (j = 1; j <= ColumnCount; j++)
       {
          EXEC SQL get descriptor 'machine_status'
             value :j
                :ColumnName  = name,
                :ActualData  = data,
                :DataLength  = length,
                :IsNowNull   = indicator;
          if (IsNowNull)
             strcpy(ActualData, "**NULL**");
          printf ("%s %s\n", ColumnName, ActualData);
       }
       printf ("\n\n");
    }
    printf ("-------------------------------------n");

 /* Show the contents of descriptor                     */
    DisplayDescriptor(ColumnCount);
```

```
/* Close the cursor                                    */
   EXEC SQL close C;
/* Free the prepared statement                         */
   EXEC SQL free P;
/* Deallocate the descriptor                           */
   EXEC SQL deallocate descriptor 'machine_status';

}

DisplayDescriptor(TotalColumns)
$int TotalColumns;
{
   EXEC SQL BEGIN DECLARE SECTION;
      int i;

      char name[20];
      int  type;
      int  length;
      int  indicator;
      int  scale;
      int  precision;
      int  nullable;
   EXEC SQL END DECLARE SECTION;

   /* Loop through all of the columns that the         */
   /* query returns, and print the value for each      */
   /* system descriptor field                          */
   for (i = 1; i <= TotalColumns; i++)
   {
      EXEC SQL get descriptor 'machine_status' value :i
         :name      = name,
         :type      = type,
         :length    = length,
         :indicator = indicator,
         :scale     = scale,
         :precision = precision,
         :nullable  = nullable;

      printf ("Column %d\n", i);
      printf ("name %s\n", name);
      printf ("type %d\n", type);
      printf ("length %d\n", length);
      printf ("indicator %d\n", indicator);
```

```
        printf ("scale %d\n", scale);
        printf ("precision %d\n", precision);
        printf ("nullable %d\n", nullable);
    }
}
```

Next, the "sqlda" program:

```
#include <stdio.h>
#include <decimal.h>

EXEC SQL include sqlca;
EXEC SQL include sqlda;
EXEC SQL include sqltypes;

#define DECIMALSIZE 30
char *calloc();
char *buffer;

struct sqlvar_struct *col;

int i;
int type;
char          string_var[256];
char          decstr[DECIMALSIZE];
long          loclong;
short         locshort;
double        locdouble;
float         locfloat;

main()
{
   int size;

   EXEC SQL BEGIN DECLARE SECTION;
/* String to hold the SQL statement                              */
      char SqlStatement[300];
   EXEC SQL END DECLARE SECTION;

/* Declare a pointer to the sqlda structure                      */
   struct sqlda *machine_status;

   EXEC SQL database manuf;
```

```
printf ("%d\n", sqlca.sqlcode);

/* Build up an SQL statement.  This can either be */
/* hard coded or it can be generated at runtime   */
strcpy(SqlStatement, "select * from
machine_status");

/* Prepare a statement, and then declare a cursor */
/* for it                                         */
EXEC SQL prepare P from :SqlStatement;
EXEC SQL declare C cursor for P;

/* Describe what the cursor will return           */
EXEC SQL describe C into machine_status;

/* Send the sqlda structure and an address in     */
/* which to place the size                        */
SizeStructure(machine_status, &size);

/* Allocate a buffer big enough to hold the       */
/* returned data                                  */
buffer = calloc((unsigned int) size,(unsigned int)
1);

/* If the 'calloc' fails, exit the program       */
if (!buffer)
{
   printf ("Out of memory\n");
   EXEC SQL close database
   exit(1);
}

/* Open the cursor                                */
EXEC SQL open C;

/* Bind memory for each column in the query       */
BindColumn(machine_status, buffer);

while (1)
{
   EXEC SQL fetch C using descriptor machine_status;
   if (sqlca.sqlcode)
      break;
```

```
printf ("-----------------------------------\n");
for (col = machine_status->sqlvar,i = 0;
     i < machine_status->sqld; col++, i++)
{
   /* Copy from the col->sqldata holding area  */
   /* into a variable that has been cast to    */
   /* character, for the appropriate length    */
   switch(col->sqltype)
   {
      case CLONGTYPE:
         bycopy(col->sqldata, (char *)&loclong,
         sizeof(long));
         printf ("%d", loclong);
         break;
      case CSHORTTYPE:
         bycopy(col->sqldata, (char *)&locshort,
         sizeof(short));
         printf ("%d", locshort);
         break;
      case CDOUBLETYPE:
         bycopy(col->sqldata, (char *)
         &locdouble, sizeof(double));
         printf ("%f", locdouble);
         break;
      case CFLOATTYPE:
         bycopy(col->sqldata, (char *)
         &locfloat, sizeof(float));
         printf ("%f", locfloat);
         break;
      case CDECIMALTYPE:
         dectoasc((dec_t *) col->sqldata,
          decstr, DECIMALSIZE, -1);
         ldchar(decstr, DECIMALSIZE, decstr);
         fputs(decstr, stdout);
         break;
      case CFIXCHARTYPE:
      case CSTRINGTYPE:
      case CDTIMETYPE:
         bycopy(col->sqldata, string_var,
         col->sqllen);
         string_var[col->sqllen] = 0;
         printf ("%s", string_var);
         break;
```

```
        }
        printf ("-----------------------------------\n");
        }

    }

    /*
    ** Print out the contents of the header, as well
    ** as column attributes for each column
    */
    DisplayDescriptor(machine_status);

/* Deallocate the descriptor                                */
    free (machine_status);
/* Close the cursor                                         */
    EXEC SQL close C;
/* Free the prepared statement                              */
    EXEC SQL free P;
}


/*
** This function accepts a pointer to an sqlda and a
** pointer to an integer variable.  It examines the
** described query, converts the specified rdsql type
** to the equivalent C type, calculates the amount of
** storage required for each including adjustments for
** necessary word boundaries, and stores the total
** length in the integer variable pointer at by psize
*/
SizeStructure(PtrSqlda, psize)
/* Pointer to sqlda structure                               */
struct sqlda *PtrSqlda;
/* Return address for size                                  */
int *psize;
{
/* Pointer to sqlvar_struct                                 */
    struct sqlvar_struct *col;
/* Byte counter                                             */
    register int pos;
/* C data type                                              */
    register int type;
    register int i;
```

```
   pos = 0;

   /*
   ** Run through each column structure - assign the
   ** correct data type to it
   */
   for (col = PtrSqlda->sqlvar, i = 0; i <
      PtrSqlda->sqld; col++, i++)
   {
/* What kind of SQL data type do we have?              */
      switch(col->sqltype)
      {
         case SQLINT:
         case SQLSERIAL:
            type = CLONGTYPE;
            break;
         case SQLSMINT:
            type = CSHORTTYPE;
            break;
         case SQLFLOAT:
            type = CDOUBLETYPE;
            break;
         case SQLSMFLOAT:
            type = CFLOATTYPE;
            break;
         case SQLMONEY:
         case SQLDECIMAL:
            type = CDECIMALTYPE;
            break;
         case SQLCHAR:
            type = CFIXCHARTYPE;
            break;
         case SQLVCHAR:
            type = CSTRINGTYPE;
            break;
/* Fixed type, but we also get the width               */
         case SQLDATE:
            type = CFIXCHARTYPE;
            col->sqllen = rtypwidth(col->sqltype,
            col->sqllen);
            break;
         case SQLDTIME:
            type = CSTRINGTYPE;
```

```
                col->sqllen = 40;
                break;
             default:
                printf ("Error, invalid data type found
                in sqlda\n");
                break;
          }
    /* Set the type in the record                              */
          col->sqltype = type;
    /* Align on proper data boundary                           */
          pos = rtypalign(pos, type);
    /* Cast to character                                       */
          col->sqldata = (char *) pos;
          if  ((type != CFIXCHARTYPE)
             ||(type != CSTRINGTYPE))
             col->sqllen = rtypmsize(type);
          else
             col->sqllen = 0;
    /* Increment the total byte count                         */
          pos += col->sqllen;
       }

    /* Set the return size value                               */
       *psize = pos;

    }

    /* Print the header and the detail for returned rows */
    DisplayDescriptor(p)
    struct sqlda *p;
    {
       printf ("\n%-20s\tsqltype\tsqllen\tsqldata\
         tsqlind\n", "sqlname");
       while (p->sqld--)
       {
          printf ("%-20s\t%d\t%d\t%x\t%x\n", p->sqlvar
          ->sqlname, p->sqlvar->sqltype, p->sqlvar->sqllen,
          p->sqlvar->sqldata, p->sqlvar->sqlind);
          p->sqlvar++;
       }

    }
```

```
/*
** This function allocates memory obtained from calloc
** and sets each sqlda pointer to the beginning of its
** buffer area
*/
BindColumn(PtrSqlda, buf)
/* The described sqlda structure                          */
struct sqlda *PtrSqlda;
/* The allocated buffer area                              */
char *buf;
{
/* sqlvar_struct column structures                        */
   struct sqlvar_struct *col;
/* Memory buffer                                          */
   register long longbuf;
   register int i;

   /*
   ** Run through each column structure - assign the
   ** correct memory address to it
   */
   for (col = PtrSqlda->sqlvar, i = 0; i < PtrSqlda
    ->sqld; col++, i++)
   {
      longbuf = (long) buf;
      col->sqldata += longbuf;
   }
}
```

One final note regarding the system descriptor area. The syntax for the ALLOCATE DESCRIPTOR statement is as follows:

```
ALLOCATE DESCRIPTOR <descriptor name> WITH MAX n
```

The letter "n" stands for the number of columns that you expect to handle. If you don't use the "WITH MAX" clause and specify a number, ESQL/C allocates memory for 100 columns. If you're only working with a few columns, this wastes memory. Try to specify as realistic a number as possible when allocating a descriptor.

Dynamic SQL without system descriptor area or sqlda

Remember that you can still use dynamic SQL without having to use the system descriptor area or the sqlda structure. If your SQL statement receives a fixed number of parameters at runtime, you can use the PREPARE statement to assign placeholders. For example, suppose that you want to write a general purpose DELETE statement to delete rows from a particular table. You know what the primary key of the table is when you develop the program, but you don't know the runtime value of the primary key. This is supplied by the user once the program is running. Once you receive the primary key, you delete any row that matches it.

In this case, you need only PREPARE a DELETE statement once. You can then execute the statement many times, and merely change the runtime value for each iteration:

```
EXEC SQL BEGIN DECLARE SECTION;
   sql_stmt char[300];
EXEC SQL END DECLARE SECTION;

.      .      .      .
.      .      .      .
strcpy(sql_stmt, "DELETE FROM TABLE_A WHERE
    RECORD_ID = ?";
EXEC SQL prepare D1 from :sql_stmt;
.      .      .      .
.      .      .      .
while (condition)
{
   /* Get the primary key */
   rec_id = nnn;
   delete_routine(rec_id);
}

.      .      .      .
.      .      .      .

delete_routine(rec_id)
EXEC SQL BEGIN DECLARE SECTION;
   int rec_id;
EXEC SQL END DECLARE SECTION;
{
   EXEC SQL execute D1 using :rec_id;
}
```

SETTING FETCH BUFFER SIZE

If you're using ESQL/C version 7.1 or newer, you can control the fetch buffer size. The database server uses the fetch buffer as a holding area when sending data to the application. If the server is returning only one row, the buffer size is equal to the size of the row. For more than one row, the buffer size is set as follows:

- If two of the rows are each larger than 2048 bytes, the buffer size is equal to the row size.
- If two of the rows taken together are larger than 1024 bytes, but less than 2048 bytes, the buffer size is 2048.
- If two of the rows can fit together in a 1024-byte buffer, the server uses 1024 as the buffer size.

You can override these settings in one of two ways:

- By setting the "FetBufSize" global variable. This variable is found in the "sqlhdr" include file.
- By setting the FET_BUF_SIZE environment variable.

In both cases, the unit of measurement is bytes. If you expect that your application will receive many rows from the database server, try tuning the fetch buffer size. Keep in mind that this is not ANSI-standard; other database products may implement fetch buffers in different ways. Finally, if your application only works with small amounts of data, tuning the fetch buffer won't have much of an effect on performance.

Process control

Informix provides a number of functions that give you greater control over your processes and their communication with the database. You can interrupt execution of an SQL statement, disconnect from the database server, and detach a child process from its parent process. Let's look at these operations in more detail.

INTERRUPTING A QUERY

Normally, when you issue a database request, you want the database server to complete its work before returning control to your program. However, there are cases where you may want to abort a database request while it's running. For example, suppose that you develop an application that lets users enter free-form queries. What happens if a user requests a very non-selective query on an enormous table, and then changes his mind while the query is running? The database server is busy servicing the request, and it's quite possible that other users are beginning to notice that the system is suddenly slowing down. How can you gracefully handle this problem? One of the best approaches you can take is to use the "sqlbreak()" function to interrupt the database server. When you call "sqlbreak()", your process sends an interrupt request to the database server. The server then aborts your current SQL statement and returns control to your program.

The best way to implement this function is to write a handler to trap the SIGINT signal. Once you receive a SIGINT (usually generated by a user pressing CTRL-C), you can call the sqlbreak() function and halt the current SQL statement.

TIMING OUT FROM A DATABASE OPERATION

If you're using ESQL/C version 7.1 or newer, you can instruct the database server to return control to your program after a certain interval, by using the "sqlbreakcallback()" function. You pass two parameters to this function:

1. A four-byte timeout interval, expressed in milliseconds.
2. A pointer to the timeout handler function that you want to call. This callback function then determines the next course of action to take:

- You can halt execution of the SQL statement by calling the "sqlbreak()" function.

-- or --

- You can let the database server continue working until your SQL is finished, or another timeout interval elapses. You can use the "sqldone()" function to learn whether the database server is still processing your request or not. See the next section of this chapter for more detail.

DETERMINING IF THE DATABASE SERVER IS STILL PROCESSING AN SQL REQUEST

Beginning with ESQL/C 7.1, Informix provided a function that you can call to see if the database server is still processing an SQLrequest. This function is called "sqldone()". Typically, you call "sqldone()" from within either:

- **A timeout callback handler function.** If your program times out (using the "sqlbreakcallback()" function), you can call "sqldone()" to see if the database server has finished its work.
- **A signal handler function.** If you've just called "sqlbreak()", for example, you can using "sqldone()" to see if the database server was still working on your request.

"sqldone()" returns one of two values:

1 : The database server is idle.

2 : The database server is currently working on an SQL statement.

DISCONNECTING FROM THE DATABASE SERVER

If you're developing an application that doesn't need a full-time connection to the database server, consider using the "sqlexit()" function. This function ends your database connection, which helps reduce resource requirements. Minimizing the number of database sessions can be quite important in a client/server environment, especially when the client and server are separated by a long distance. This strategy may even be able to reduce your network charges, since your clients will spend less time connected over the network to the server. How can you tell if your application is a candidate for "sqlexit()'? Use the following guidelines to help you decide:

- Do long intervals elapse between database calls? If your application only needs to access the database infrequently, or after relatively long intervals, try experimenting with "sqlexit()".
- Is your current environment overloaded? If you believe that your current system is spending too much time managing idle database sessions, you might benefit from "sqlexit()".
- Do you need to keep your place within a cursor over time? If you call "sqlexit()", and then reconnect to the database later, you'll have to reopen any cursors. This means that you'll have to start over at the beginning of the data set each time.
- Do you need the same transaction to remain open over time? Calling "sqlexit()" rolls back any open transactions. If your program does indeed require open transactions over long periods of time, you may experience long transactions. For more information about the dangers of long transactions, see the "General tips" section.
- Are your clients' processes separated from the server by a wide distance? If you answer "yes" to this question, you might be able to reduce overhead (and cost) with "sqlexit()".

DETACHING A CHILD PROCESS FROM A PARENT PROCESS

If you're developing an application that uses the UNIX "fork()" and "exec()" system calls to create and transfer control to child processes, consider using "sqldetach()" to end the database connection for all child processes that don't actually work with the database. Remember that if a parent program connects to a database and then spawns child processes, each child process has an open database connection. From the database server's perspective, however, there is only one client process. For clarity, use "sqldetach()" in all child processes except the one(s) that work(s) with the database server.

In the example illustrated in Figure 3.2 below, you've designed an application that first connects to the database server (parent process), and then spawns three children (children A, B, and C). Child processes A and C perform other tasks, while child B actually works with the database. In this case, use the "sqldetach()" function in child A and child C.

Figure 3.2

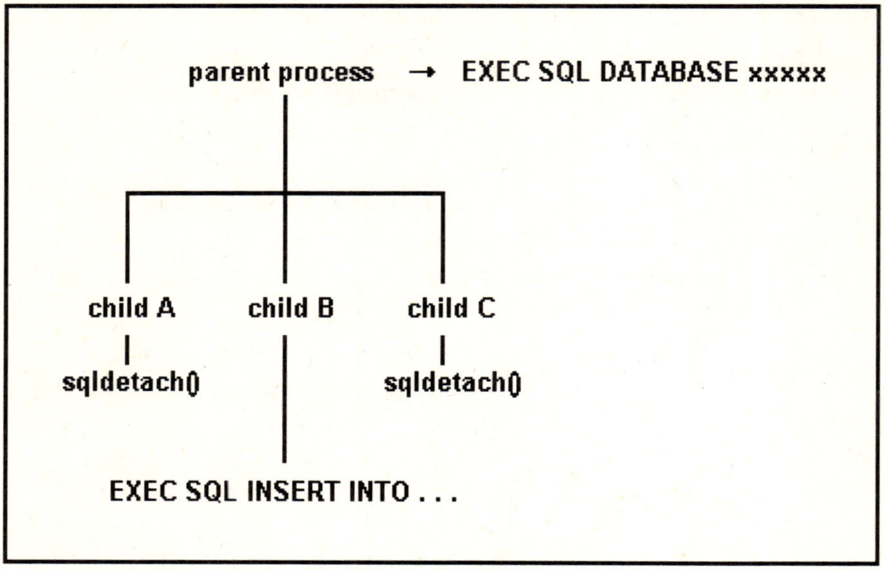

Compilation hints

Large program executables consume copious amounts of memory. One way to improve system response is to minimize the amount of memory that each user requires. Fortunately, if your application includes programs written in ESQL/C, you can "slim down" the executable size, by including only those header files that are necessary, as well as specifying certain compiler options.

INCLUDE FILES

When you compile an ESQL/ program, the Informix preprocessor automatically includes the "sqlca.h" header file. All other header files should only be included if you need them. Review the following list to see which header files you actually need:

Table 3.24

File name	Purpose
sqlca.h	Provides structures necessary to handle error codes; automatically included.
sqlda.h	Use for dynamically defined variables.
sqlstype.h	Provides integer constants for each type of SQL statement; used for DESCRIBE.
sqltypes.h	Has list of strings that correspond to C and SQL data types.
sqlxtype.h	Same as "sqltypes.h", except this file contains strings that conform to X/Open standards.
datetime.h	Supports DATETIME and INTERVAL data types.
decimal.h	Supports DECIMAL data type.
locator.h	Supports BLOBs.
varchar.h	Supports VARCHARs. Note: You only need to include this file if you are using its macros for VARCHAR length information.

LIBRARIES

Another way to minimize your program's executable size is to only link in those libraries that are absolutely necessary. Sometimes, you might be linking in more libraries than you realize, especially if you've used another project's makefile as a baseline for your project. If you're copying a makefile from another project, take the time to understand which libraries are actually being linked in.

For more information on controlling program executable size, see the "General tips" section.

COMPILER FLAGS

Normally, compiled ESQL/C programs include line numbers for each line of embedded SQL. The compiler provides these numbers for a debugger to use. If you use a debugger during development, and you need numbering for both SQL and C code statements, use the "-g" compiler option. Once you finish development and testing, consider recompiling your programs with the "-G" or "-nln" option. This removes all line numbers from the program executables, and can save substantial amounts of memory, especially for programs that make heavy use of SQL.

Stored Procedures, Triggers, and Cascading Deletes

Stored procedures and triggers are powerful tools that let you move program logic from your application code into your database. In this section, we discuss what stored procedures and triggers are, how they work, and situations where they can help you improve performance.

If you're using OnLine version 6.00 or newer, you have the additional power of cascading deletes to simplify and speed up your database applications. We review this topic at the end of the chapter.

Stored procedures

In a nutshell, stored procedures are functions composed of procedural language and SQL statements. The procedural language is known as Stored Procedure Language (SPL). You use SPL and SQL to create functions that are stored in the database engine, instead of in application code or libraries. This feature was first introduced in the OnLine and SE engines, version 5.0. You create stored procedures following these steps:

1. Connect to the database via "dbaccess". You need to have at least RESOURCE privilege to create stored procedures.
2. Using SPL, write a script that contains the stored procedure logic.
3. Run the script.

You can also create stored procedures using ESQL/C or any other Informix Embedded SQL tool. When you run the script to create your procedure(s), the database server performs these tasks:

1. Checks the syntax of the procedure.
2. Parses and optimizes the procedure.
3. Creates entries in the "sysprocedures" and "sysprocbody" tables. These tables act as header and detail tables, respectively, and have the following layouts:

Table 3.25 sysprocedures

column name	type	purpose
procname	char(18)	Name that you call the procedure.
owner	char(8)	The user id of the owner.
procid	serial	System-generated numeric identifier.
mode	char(1)	Type of procedure: D: DBA O: Owner P: Protected

continued next page

Table 3.25, continued

column name	type	purpose
retsize	integer	Compiled size of values.
symsize	integer	Compiled size of the symbol table.
datasize	integer	Compiled size of data segment (constants).
codesize	integer	Compiled size of stored procedure code (SPL).
numargs	integer	Number of arguments to the procedure.

Table 3.26 sysprocbody

column name	type	purpose
procid	integer	Numeric identifier, joins to sysprocedures.
datakey	char(1)	Type of data descriptor: D : User-entered document text. L : Literals, such as quoted strings. P : Interpreter instructions. R : List of return type values. S : Symbol table for procedure. T : Procedure source code.
seqno	integer	Line number in the procedure.
data	char(256)	Procedure's text.

Before you modify an existing procedure, you must remove it from the database server by dropping it. Then, you can modify the script and recreate the procedure.

Some of the major benefits of stored procedures are:

- Elimination of runtime parsing and optimizing. Since stored procedures are already parsed and optimized at creation time, the database engine can skip these time-consuming steps at runtime.
- DBA privileges for regular users. You can designate certain stored procedures to run with DBA privileges, even if the user running them does not have this level of security. This lets you combine a high level of data access with tight security.
- Centralization of commonly used operations. You can easily create libraries of functions, thereby reducing the amount of original code that your programmers must write.
- Reduction of traffic between server and client. In a distributed environment, stored procedures let you cut down the amount of information traveling

between the front end (client) and the back end (server). This can add up, especially if client and server are separated by a long distance.

Let's explore situations where you can use stored procedures specifically to improve system performance.

FREQUENTLY USED ROUTINES

In many applications, different programs often perform the same set of operations. Typically, these include several SQL statements, along with procedural language flow control. You can convert some of these heavily used operations into stored procedures, thereby simplifying and speeding up your application.

You can also use stored procedures to "customize" SQL, by adding new functions to your environment.

For example, suppose that you are developing a manufacturing application. One of your most important tables tracks the historical tolerances of various parts. Another table tracks the actual tolerances of these parts during particular manufacturing runs:

Table 3.27 parts

part_num	part_desc	part_tolerance
1	Drive shaft	0.01500
2	Manifold cover	0.12000
3	Main gasket	0.00200
.	.	.
.	.	.

Table 3.28 manuf_status

part_num	run_id	run_date	run_tolerance
2	17	1994-03-02 16:45	0.01600
3	18	1994-03-02 16:47	0.00700
1	19	1994-03-02 18:49	0.00100
1	20	1994-03-02 19:03	0.19000
.	.	.	.
.	.	.	.
.	.	.	.

You are asked to produce a report, displaying which manufacturing runs produced parts that met or failed to meet historical part tolerances. This entails joining the "parts" and "manuf_status" tables on the "part_num" key, and then comparing the "part_tolerance" (historical value) and the "run_tolerance" (actual batch value). Traditionally, you would tackle this problem by writing a program to do the joins and compare the values.

An alternate approach would be to let a stored procedure do the comparison for you:

```
CREATE PROCEDURE TOLERANCE(PART_NUM INTEGER,
                           RUN_TOLERANCE DECIMAL(6,5))
       RETURNING CHAR(10);

   DEFINE A DECIMAL(6,5);
   DEFINE RETURN_STATUS CHAR(10);

   SELECT PART_TOLERANCE
   INTO   A
   FROM   PARTS
   WHERE  PARTS.PART_NUM = PART_NUM;

   IF A >= RUN_TOLERANCE THEN
      LET RETURN_STATUS = "PASSED";
   ELSE
      LET RETURN_STATUS = "FAILED";
   END IF;

      RETURN RETURN_STATUS;

END PROCEDURE;
```

Your SQL statement would look like this:

```
SELECT PART_NUM, RUN_ID, RUN_DATE,
       RUN_TOLERANCE, TOLERANCE(PART_NUM,
        RUN_TOLERANCE)
FROM   MANUF_STATUS;
```

Using the data listed above, this query returns the following results:

Table 3.29

part_num	run_id run_date	run_tolerance	(expression)
2	17 1994-03-02 16:45	0.01600	PASSED
3	18 1994-03-02 16:47	0.00700	FAILED
1	19 1994-03-02 18:45	0.00100	PASSED
1	20 1994-03-02 19:03	0.19000	FAILED

You benefit from converting common functions into SPL in at least five ways:

- **Performance.** The stored procedure should yield better performance, especially in a distributed environment (see Client/Server section).
- **Development time.** Programmers no longer need to write their own versions of these routines, since they can now access the shared stored procedures.
- **Error reduction.** Since programmers no longer need to write, test, and support their own versions of the shared functions, you minimize the number of potential application errors.
- **Change control.** If you need to change the operation, you only change it in one place.
- **Simplicity.** New programmers do not need to learn the internal intricacies of these functions; they only need to know the name, parameters, return values, and purposes of your stored procedures.

How can you tell whether an operation is a good candidate for conversion to a stored procedure? Use these guidelines:

1. Does the operation contain several related SQL statements? It doesn't necessarily make sense to write a separate stored procedure for each SQL statement. Ideally, your stored procedures should contain several closely-tied database operations.

   For example, if you're writing a banking operation, you could write one stored procedure to handle the transfer of funds between accounts. The procedure would incorporate SQL statements to handle these operations:

   - Check existing balance in source account.
   - Update the target account by adding the transferred amount.
   - Update the source account by subtracting the transferred amount.

2. Is the operation used by more than one program? If only one program performs the task, it may not make sense to convert it into SPL.

3. Does SPL have the features that you need to replicate the logic of your existing routines? Only you can determine the answer to this question; try to learn as much as you can about the features of SPL before you start converting existing routines into stored procedures.
4. Will moving the operation into SPL simplify your application? In many cases, the answer to this question is a definite yes. If it is no, it may not pay to make the conversion.
5. Will moving the operation into SPL reduce network traffic? If excess network traffic is hurting performance, stored procedures may be the answer.
6. Does the operation require higher-level security? Stored procedures let you grant users temporary DBA authority.

Client/Server

One area that typically bogs down in a client/server configuration is data communication over the network. Clients often request enormous amounts of data from servers, only to process the data locally, and reduce it to a fraction of its original size. You can move much of this reduction process onto the server by using stored procedures.

For example, assume that you have an order-tracking application where PC-based Windows clients request line item detail information from a server. This information serves as raw data for a calculation routine that the client runs. After running the calculation, the client displays the results. The user on the client never needs to see the line item details.

By analyzing the situation, you realize that you are using up a tremendous amount of network bandwidth just in sending the data from the server to the client. You determine that by rewriting the calculation routine in SPL, you can move the entire processing operation onto the server. After the change, the client passes search criteria to the server's stored procedure, and waits for the server to return the calculated results. Once the client receives the results, it then displays the information. To the user, there is no change in functionality.

The benefit of this change is chiefly the elimination of the transfer of thousands of lines of detail data over the network. This conserves valuable network bandwidth. When you multiply this by all of the concurrent clients that perform this operation, you should see a noticeable network improvement.

The downside to this change is that the server now has more work to do. Therefore, you should only move logic from the client to the server if it is apparent that the savings from the network's speed improvement outweighs the cost of extra server processing.

Security

Stored procedures provide you with more options for data security. You can place very restrictive security on a table but still allow users to access its information via stored procedures.

For example, suppose that you are developing a sales prospecting system. One of the tables in the system contains very sensitive data, such as your prospect's contact names, telephone numbers, and expected revenue potential.

Table 3.30 prospects

contact_first	contact_last	company	phone	class....
Larry	Lashow	Valet 2U	415-555-3333	C
Nicole	Taylor	Baby Togs	510-966-0918	A
Sylvia	Midgal	Vision Intl	201-543-7765	A
.	.	.	.	.
.	.	.	.	.
.	.	.	.	.

Your user community has numerous tools available for reading information directly from tables. You are concerned that certain users may use SQL to bypass the security that you set up on your database, and provide your competitors with proprietary data.

To restrict access to this table, you could GRANT and REVOKE the SELECT, UPDATE, INSERT, or DELETE privileges for each user, or for PUBLIC. The problem is that sometimes, users really do have legitimate reasons for seeing this data. For example, you might allow junior employees to see only prospects with a class of C (not as much revenue potential as classes A or B). Another set of users may need to insert data into the table (via your application), but not actually see the other data in the table. You could, via a home-grown security application, dynamically GRANT and REVOKE privileges as needed. Instead, let's explore a stored, procedure-based alternative for the INSERT privilege:

- First, REVOKE all privileges on the table:

```
REVOKE ALL ON PROSPECTS FROM PUBLIC;
```

- Next, create a DBA-level procedure that allows the user to insert rows into the table:

```
CREATE PROCEDURE INSERT_P
(
    CONTACT_FIRST CHAR(10),
    CONTACT_LAST  CHAR(20),
```

```
        COMPANY         CHAR(20),
        PHONE           CHAR(10),
        CLASS           CHAR(1)
    )

       INSERT INTO PROSPECTS VALUES
       (
           CONTACT_FIRST,
           CONTACT_LAST,
           COMPANY,
           PHONE,
           CLASS
       );
    END PROCEDURE;
```

- Finally, allow only certain users to execute the procedure you just created:

```
GRANT EXECUTE ON INSERT_P TO (user, user,
  etc. (or public));
```

At this point, your programmers can replace the direct SQL entries in their programs with calls to this stored procedure. Other users, via their direct access tools, will not be able to directly retrieve information from this table.

Triggers

Triggers are statements that are invoked, or "triggered" when certain operations are performed on a table. Triggers can, in turn, invoke SQL or stored procedures. Triggers were first introduced in the OnLine and SE engines, version 5.01. You create triggers by following these steps:

1. Connect to the database via "dbaccess". You must have at least RESOURCE privilege.
2. Write a script that contains the trigger creation statements.
3. Run the script.

You can also create triggers using ESQL/C or any other Informix Embedded SQL tool. When you create a trigger, the database engine makes entries in the "systriggers" and "systrigbody" tables. These tables have the following layouts:

Table 3.31 systriggers

column name	type	purpose
trigid	serial	System-generated trigger identifier.
trigname	char(18)	User-supplied trigger name.
owner	char(8)	User id of trigger's owner.
tabid	integer	Table id of trigger's table.
event	char(1)	Type of trigger: I: INSERT D: DELETE U: UPDATE
old	char(18)	Value's name before update
new	char(18)	Value's name after update
mode	char	Reserved for future use.

Table 3.32 systrigbody

column name	type	purpose
trigid	integer	Trigger identifier, joins to systriggers.
datakey	char(1)	Type of data: A : Actual trigger body text B : ASCII text for trigger body. D : Actual text of trigger header. H : ASCII code for header. S : ASCII code for symbol table.
seqno	integer	Sequence number for this line.
data	char(256)	Actual or ASCII trigger code.

You can create triggers for INSERTs, UPDATEs, and DELETEs. Note that if you want your trigger to call a stored procedure(s), make sure that the stored procedure(s) exists before you create the trigger.

In this section, we discuss the benefits of triggers, especially as they relate to system performance. We focus on audit trails and data replication.

Note: Informix OnLine 6.0 now supports data replication at the server level, as well as detailed data auditing. In this chapter, however, we concentrate only on triggers as data replication and auditing features.

AUDIT TRAILS

There are many times when you want to track modifications to a table. You could code audit trail logging directly into your applications, but this approach has several drawbacks:

- Users could potentially modify the data by using an unsecured end-user tool. You would have no way of knowing what changes were made, and who made them.
- Programmers could omit audit trail logging from new applications, either accidentally or on purpose. Again, this allows unaudited access to your data.
- Even if programmers included audit trail logging in their programs, they could do so in a terribly inefficient way.

Instead of embedding audit trail logic into your applications, consider using a combination of triggers and SPL:

1. First, create a table to store audit trail records:

```
CREATE TABLE AUDIT_TRAIL
(
   SOURCE_TABLE      CHAR(18),
   USER_ID           CHAR(8),
   ACTION_CODE       CHAR(1),
   ACTION_TIMESTAMP  DATETIME YEAR TO SECOND,
   OLD_VALUE         CHAR(80),
   NEW_VALUE         CHAR(80)
);
```

The table above was designed to be a general purpose repository, instead of being specifically tailored to hold information about only one database table.

2. Next, write a stored procedure that receives audit information from triggers, and then inserts this data into the "audit_trail" table:

```
CREATE PROCEDURE AUDIT_LOGGER
(
   SOURCE_TABLE      CHAR(18),
   USER_ID           CHAR(8),
   ACTION_CODE       CHAR(1),
   ACTION_TIMESTAMP DATETIME YEAR TO SECOND,
   OLD_VALUE         CHAR(80),
   NEW_VALUE         CHAR(80)
)

   INSERT INTO AUDIT_TRAIL VALUES
   (
      SOURCE_TABLE,
      USER_ID,
      ACTION_CODE,
      ACTION_TIMESTAMP,
      OLD_VALUE,
      NEW_VALUE
   );
END PROCEDURE;
```

3. Finally, create triggers on any tables that you want to audit. The trigger listed below is for an INSERT on a table where we want to track one column's value:

```
CREATE TRIGGER EMPLOYEE_INS
INSERT ON EMPLOYEE
REFERENCING NEW AS NEW_VAL
FOR EACH ROW
(EXECUTE PROCEDURE AUDIT_LOGGER
   (
   "EMPLOYEE",        -- Table name
    USER,             -- Current user
    "I",              -- (I)nsert
    CURRENT,          -- Timestamp
    "",               -- Old value: null, since
                         we're inserting
    NEW_VAL.SALARY    -- Inserted salary value
   )
);
```

If you want to track more than one column's value, you can simply create a header/detail relationship in your audit tables. You would also modify your triggers and stored procedures accordingly.

By placing triggers on your sensitive tables, there is no possible way for users to modify data without generating an audit trail record.

DATA REPLICATION

In a multi-server environment, there may be certain critical tables that you want to copy among servers. If time is not an issue, you can always write batch programs to perform this task at off hours. For sites that are 24 x 7, this is not an option. Administrators at these sites often write "watchdog" programs or scripts to monitor key tables. When their programs detect changes, they update remote tables to reflect the new state of the database. This approach has several potential problems:

- **Overhead** Many of these approaches use daemon processes, which awaken every so often and determine whether any changes have happened. Usually, this involves running SELECT statements against the tables in question. This can be very resource intensive, and may bog down the system to a point where users complain.
- **Timeliness.** If your watchdog program does not awaken often enough, minutes or even hours could pass between the time of an update at the first location, and the copying of this data to the other locations.
- **Complexity.** Most watchdog programs are complex, and are written specifically for certain tables. Maintaining these programs can be an administrative nightmare.

Triggers can provide a simpler way of achieving data replication. You can create a series of replication triggers as follows:

1. Determine which tables you want to replicate.
2. Write stored procedures for each type of operation that you want to support. For example, you may decide that you only want to replicate INSERTs for a particular table. Therefore, you would only write a stored procedure to handle this particular database operation. Another approach would be to write a general purpose stored procedure that expects a flag to determine whether it will INSERT, UPDATE, or DELETE from the remote sites.
3. Create the necessary triggers on the tables that you want to replicate. Have these triggers call the appropriate stored procedures.

Cascading deletes

One goal of referential integrity is to eliminate the possibility of "orphaned" child records. This means that you generally need to delete the child records first, and then delete the appropriate parent record. Cascading deletes (available in OnLine 6.00 and newer) provide an easier and more flexible approach to deleting parent and child records.

If you've defined a cascading delete relationship between a parent and child table and then delete a record from the parent table, the database engine automatically deletes any corresponding child records. Let's look at some sample SQL that creates a parent and two child tables that have a cascading delete relationship:

```
CREATE TABLE PARENT
(
   PARENT_ID SERIAL PRIMARY KEY,
       .    .    .
);

CREATE TABLE CHILD1
(
   CHILD_ID INTEGER PRIMARY KEY,
   PARENT_ID INTEGER,
       .    .    .
   FOREIGN KEY (PARENT_ID) REFERENCES PARENT ON
    DELETE CASCADE
);

CREATE TABLE CHILD2
(
   CHILD_ID INTEGER PRIMARY KEY,
   PARENT_ID INTEGER,
       .    .    .
   FOREIGN KEY (PARENT_ID) REFERENCES PARENT ON
    DELETE CASCADE
);
```

OnLine still enforces referential integrity (for example, you can't add a child without first adding a parent), but you can now delete a parent record and have the engine remove all appropriate child records.

In addition to simplifying your applications, cascading deletes also help reduce traffic between the engine and application processes, since you only need one SQL statement to handle two delete operations. This can be especially important in a client/server system.

To use cascading deletes, you need:

- **Transaction logging.** If you don't have logging turned on for your database, OnLine won't perform cascading deletes.
- **Identical data types between parent and child.** If the data type of the parent and child don't match, OnLine won't perform cascading deletes. The only exception to this rule is if the parent's primary key is a serial. This same rule applies to references in general.

- **Cascading delete specified for all child tables.** You can't "mix-and-match" cascading deletes: either all child tables use cascading deletes, or none of them do.

DISTRIBUTED SYSTEM CONSIDERATIONS

Distributed systems are becoming more commonplace each day. Organizations are incorporating both client/server and peer-to-peer technology into their most vital processing operations. Along with this new power and technology, however, comes increased complexity. Unfortunately, many organizations have learned the hard way that developing distributed applications requires much more analysis than traditional single-computer systems. This is especially true with regard to performance.

In this section, we explore a number of strategies that you can apply to your distributed systems environments. We begin by discussing how you can assess your network's capabilities, because without a reliable and rapid network, you'll have a hard time creating a distributed application that performs well.

Regardless of what kind of network you have, it's always a good idea to reduce the amount of data you send between your machines. We conclude by citing several strategies that you can implement to diminish the possibility of delay.

Assessing your network's capabilities

A big factor in your distributed processing plan is your network's capabilities. You can think of capabilities as being composed of a number of features, including:

- **Network speed.** If you're connecting your systems at a relatively slow speed (9600 baud or lower), you may encounter built-in performance delays, especially if you move large quantities of data over the network. This can be very frustrating, since you might waste an enormous amount of time trying to optimize the application code, only to learn that the application was never part of the problem.
- **Network reliability.** If you're not confident about your network's data transmission reliability, you should seriously consider how much data you want to send between systems, as well as what kind of response you can expect. Most modern networks and communications devices have built-in error detection and correction. While this does reduce the chances of data corruption, it also delays the overall performance of the network.
- **Network complexity.** Networks that consist of leased lines are generally much easier to maintain than networks that rely on dialup connections. If you write programs that must repeatedly dial remote systems as part of normal operations, you can expect them to fail more frequently than if the remote systems were directly connected. This has the potential to introduce significant delays into your application, especially if your users are running transactions that rely on real-time response from these remote systems.

Even if you have a low speed, low quality network, you can still take advantage of distributed processing. You may, however, need to write your programs to perform their remote updates asynchronously, rather than synchronously.

For example, suppose that you're developing a car rental reservation system, using 4GL. You want your system to accept reservations from a central site, as well as walk-in reservations from any of your worldwide field offices. You want to develop this application using a decentralized client/server approach. Your network consists of some high speed, high quality data lines along with some 9600 baud lines of dubious integrity.

You could code your application to update the central database at the time of the field reservation:

```
.    .    .    .    .
.    .    .    .    .

BEGIN WORK

INSERT INTO RESERVATIONS@LOCAL_SITE:CUST_REV
VALUES (....)

LET STATUS_CODE = STATUS

IF STATUS_CODE = 0 THEN
   INSERT INTO RESERVATIONS@CENTRAL_SITE:CUST_REV
   VALUES (....)
   LET STATUS_CODE = STATUS
   IF STATUS_CODE = 0 THEN
      COMMIT WORK
      MESSAGE "RESERVATION ACCEPTED"
   ELSE
      ROLLBACK WORK
      MESSAGE "RESERVATION FAILED: COULD NOT CONNECT TO CENTRAL"
   END IF
ELSE
   ROLLBACK WORK
   MESSAGE "RESERVATION FAILED: COULD NOT INSERT LOCAL RECORD"
END IF

.    .    .    .    .
.    .    .    .    .
```

There are a number of drawbacks to this approach: the most glaring potential problem is how a network delay or failure would impact the customer waiting at the counter for her reservation to be accepted and confirmed.

Instead of linking your central and remote systems together within one transaction, you could easily modify your code to update the local database immediately, and then connect to and update the central database at a (slightly) later time:

```
.     .     .     .     .
.     .     .     .     .

BEGIN WORK

INSERT INTO RESERVATIONS@LOCAL_SITE:CUST_REV
VALUES (....)

LET STATUS_CODE = STATUS

IF STATUS_CODE = 0 THEN
   INSERT INTO RESERVATIONS@LOCAL_SITE:TRANSACTION_LOG
   VALUES (....)
   LET STATUS_CODE = STATUS
   IF STATUS_CODE = 0 THEN
      COMMIT WORK
      MESSAGE "RESERVATION ACCEPTED"
   ELSE
      ROLLBACK WORK
      MESSAGE "RESERVATION FAILED: COULD NOT INSERT INTO LOG"
   END IF
ELSE
   ROLLBACK WORK
   MESSAGE "RESERVATION FAILED: COULD NOT INSERT LOCAL RECORD"
END IF

.     .     .     .     .
.     .     .     .     .
```

The above segment of code writes a record into the "transaction_log" table at the time of the local reservation. To complete the transaction, a daemon process wakes up every few minutes, reads the "transaction_log" table, and executes a stored procedure to update the central database with the record of the reservation. If, for some reason, the procedure can't update the central system, it repeats the attempt several times. If it still can't get an acknowledgment, it reports an error. You could also implement this technique using triggers and stored procedures.

This approach lets you make local updates, but doesn't "hang up" the local process if the network or central system is down.

Minimizing network traffic

Even if you have a lightning-fast network, with unlimited bandwidth, you should still try to reduce the amount of traffic that you ask your network to handle. You can use any or all of these strategies to lower network traffic:

- Improve distributed SELECT statements. If you're running a high volume, transaction-intensive application, and you're experiencing slow queries, check to see if your queries are joining widely-separated tables. For example, suppose you have a query that joins between a few distributed tables that reside on different machines:

```
SELECT U.USER_COMPANY,
       L.LOCATION_NAME,
       A.TRANSACTION_DATE,
       A.TRANSACTION_AMOUNT
  FROM PROFILE@CORPORATE:USERS U,
       CUSTINFO@MARKETING:LOCATION L,
       ACCOUNTS@DATA_WAREHOUSE:ACCOUNT_HISTORY A
 WHERE U.LOCATION_ID = L.LOCATION_ID
  AND  U.ACCOUNT_NUM = A.ACCOUNT_NUM
  AND  A.TRANSACTION_DATE BETWEEN
       "01/01/1995" AND "12/31/1995"
```

  To assemble the information to service this query, the optimizer chooses the most efficient access method. The optimizer's goal is to reduce the overall amount of data sent among the various servers during query generation. For example, in the above case, assume that the "location" table on the "marketing" machine has the fewest rows, and that the "users" table on the "corporate" machine has many more. When joining between these two tables, the optimizer must choose between:

  - Sending the entire "users" table to the "marketing" machine, and then joining to the "location" table.
  - Sending the entire "location" table to the "corporate" machine, and then joining to the "users" table.

  If the optimizer has all the facts, it generally chooses the second option, since it results in the fewest rows passed among the machines. However, if the optimizer doesn't have all the facts, it might make an incorrect decision, and choose the first option. How might the optimizer miss certain important facts? If you haven't run UPDATE STATISTICS on **both** machines recently (or at all), the optimizer might not know that the "users" table is much larger than the "location" table. Without this important knowledge, the optimizer might decide to send all of the "users" table rows across the network, resulting in greatly degraded performance. For this reason alone, remember to run UPDATE STATISTICS on all database servers in your network. For more information about UPDATE STATISTICS, see the "Understanding the Informix optimizer" section.

Finally, don't join between distributed servers just for the sake of joining. There are times where it makes sense to distribute multiple copies of a table to all the database servers in your environment. This is especially true if the table(s) in question rarely change, and are used primarily for lookup. In the above example, the "location" table doesn't change very often. You could reduce the number of remote joins by copying this table to the "corporate" server. You would rewrite the query as follows:

```
SELECT U.USER_COMPANY,
       L.LOCATION_NAME,
       A.TRANSACTION_DATE,
       A.TRANSACTION_AMOUNT
  FROM PROFILE@CORPORATE:USERS U,
       CUSTINFO@CORPORATE:LOCATION L,
       ACCOUNTS@DATA_WAREHOUSE:ACCOUNT_HISTORY A
 WHERE U.LOCATION_ID = L.LOCATION_ID
  AND  U.ACCOUNT_NUM = A.ACCOUNT_NUM
  AND  A.TRANSACTION_DATE BETWEEN
       "01/01/1995" AND "12/31/1995"
```

- Don't use the network for local queries. If you're running a query directly on a database server, don't use the network when writing your SQL. If you use the network name, OnLine goes out through the network, and comes back in on the same machine to retrieve data! This adds a great deal of unnecessary overhead. For example, assume that a user on the "corporate" machine is running the previous query:

```
SELECT U.USER_COMPANY,
       L.LOCATION_NAME,
       A.TRANSACTION_DATE,
       A.TRANSACTION_AMOUNT
```

```
  FROM PROFILE@CORPORATE:USERS U,
       CUSTINFO@CORPORATE:LOCATION L,
       ACCOUNTS@DATA_WAREHOUSE:ACCOUNT_HISTORY A
 WHERE U.LOCATION_ID = L.LOCATION_ID
  AND  U.ACCOUNT_NUM = A.ACCOUNT_NUM
  AND  A.TRANSACTION_DATE BETWEEN
       "01/01/1995" AND "12/31/1995"
```

Since you specified "profile@corporate" for the "users" table and "custinfo@corporate" for the "location" table, OnLine uses TCP/IP to resolve the addresses of these databases, and then communicate with them. The only exception to this rule occurs if you're using OnLine 6.0 or newer, have a shared memory connection listed in your $INFORMIXDIR/etc/sqlhosts file, and have set your INFORMIXSERVER environment variable to point at that connection.

In this example, it's much faster to simply provide the database and table name:

```
SELECT U.USER_COMPANY,
       L.LOCATION_NAME,
       A.TRANSACTION_DATE,
       A.TRANSACTION_AMOUNT
  FROM PROFILE.USERS U,
       CUSTINFO.LOCATION L,
       ACCOUNTS@DATA_WAREHOUSE:ACCOUNT_HISTORY A
 WHERE U.LOCATION_ID = L.LOCATION_ID
  AND  U.ACCOUNT_NUM = A.ACCOUNT_NUM
  AND  A.TRANSACTION_DATE BETWEEN
       "01/01/1995" AND "12/31/1995"
```

Remember that you can build up SQL statements dynamically, which lets you maintain one code stream for programs that query both local and remote servers:

```
.   .   .   .   .
.   .   .   .   .
DEFINE MACHINE_NAME  CHAR(20)
DEFINE DATABASE_NAME CHAR(18)
DEFINE TABLE_NAME    CHAR(18)
DEFINE SQL_STMT      CHAR(300)

DEFINE RUNNING_ON_SERVER  SMALLINT
```

```
# Set RUNNING_ON_SERVER to 1 if the next database is
# found on the local server, otherwise set it to 0
LET RUNNING_ON_SERVER = ...

LET DATABASE_NAME = "PROFILE"
IF RUNNING_ON_SERVER THEN
   LET MACHINE_NAME = ""
   LET DATABASE_NAME = DATABASE_NAME,"."          # Add in any
ELSE
   LET MACHINE_NAME = "@",<variable or constant>  # special
   LET MACHINE_NAME = MACHINE_NAME CLIPPED, ":"   # characters
END IF

LET SQL_STMT = "SELECT U.USER_COMPANY,
                L.LOCATION_NAME,
                A.TRANSACTION_DATE,
                A.TRANSACTION_AMOUNT "

LET SQL_STMT = SQL_STMT, "FROM ", DATABASE_NAME CLIPPED
LET SQL_STMT = SQL_STMT, MACHINE_NAME, TABLE_NAME
.    .    .    .    .
.    .    .    .    .

PREPARE Q_PREP FROM SQL_STMT
DECLARE Q_CUR CURSOR FOR Q_PREP

OPEN Q_CUR USING....
.    .    .    .    .
.    .    .    .    .
```

One final note regarding not using the network for local queries: Before OnLine 6.00, you needed to install and configure Informix Star or Informix NET if you wanted to connect clients and servers. Beginning with the 6.0 servers, however, Informix bundled the networking software directly into the server products. You still need Informix NET/PC on PC-based clients, however.

If you have an Informix engine that's newer than version 6.00, you need to instruct remote clients to choose a network protocol from these options: TCP/IP, IPX, or sockets. For local clients (e.g., those users directly connected to the server), you have the added option of using shared memory to communicate with the server. In this case, you should always opt for a shared memory connection. Shared memory is the fastest protocol that you can use, since it doesn't have nearly as much of the overhead inherent with any of the other networking protocols. Therefore, make sure that all users running directly on the server use shared memory to access the database. Regardless of protocol, set all of the network parameters in the $INFORMIXDIR/etc/sqlhosts.

- Reduce the number of rows sent between client and server. We first reviewed this strategy in the "General tips" section, but it bears repeating here. If, as part of your application, you need to summarize a number of records before presenting information to the user, consider writing a stored procedure to run on the server. This procedure could handle most of the summarization work for the client, and then only return the actual summary information, rather than all of the detail data.

  For example, suppose that you're writing a PC client-based program that summarizes account activity for a particular client. You could follow this algorithm to collect and process the account detail:

client-based code

```
prepare a SELECT statement to retrieve information from
   the 'account_detail' table
declare a cursor for the prepared statement
while (1)
   get the account number from the user
   open the cursor using the account number
   while not end-of-cursor
      fetch detail record into host variable
      update summary information
   end while
   display summary information
   close the cursor
   if user is finished with program
      exit while
   end if
end while
```

server-based code

```
         *None*
```

This algorithm does provide us with the information that we need. However, it also has its drawbacks, primarily regarding network traffic.

Fortunately, it's not hard to rewrite this algorithm to consume minimal network resources:

client-based code

```
while (1)
   get the account number from the user
   execute the 'acct_summary' procedure, using the
      account number
   display summary information
   if user is finished with program
      exit while
   end if
end while
```

server-based code (stored procedure)

```
receive account number from calling process
declare a cursor to retrieve detail records
open the cursor using the received account number
while not end-of-cursor
  fetch detail record into host variable
  update summary information
end while
return summary information
```

Remember that if your clients are hard-wired to the server, reducing network traffic isn't quite as crucial as when a long distance or poor network separates them from the server.

- Reduce the number of times that the client and server must communicate. The approach is counter-intuitive: All the suggestions that we've made so far instruct you to reduce the number of rows sent between client and server, yet now we recommend that you send data, in bulk, between the server and client. Let's look at an example that explains the reasons for this strategy shift:

  Suppose you're developing an executive information system (EIS) for a department store chain. You have 125 stores in 11 countries. Figure 3.3 below provides a simplified network diagram:

Figure 3.3

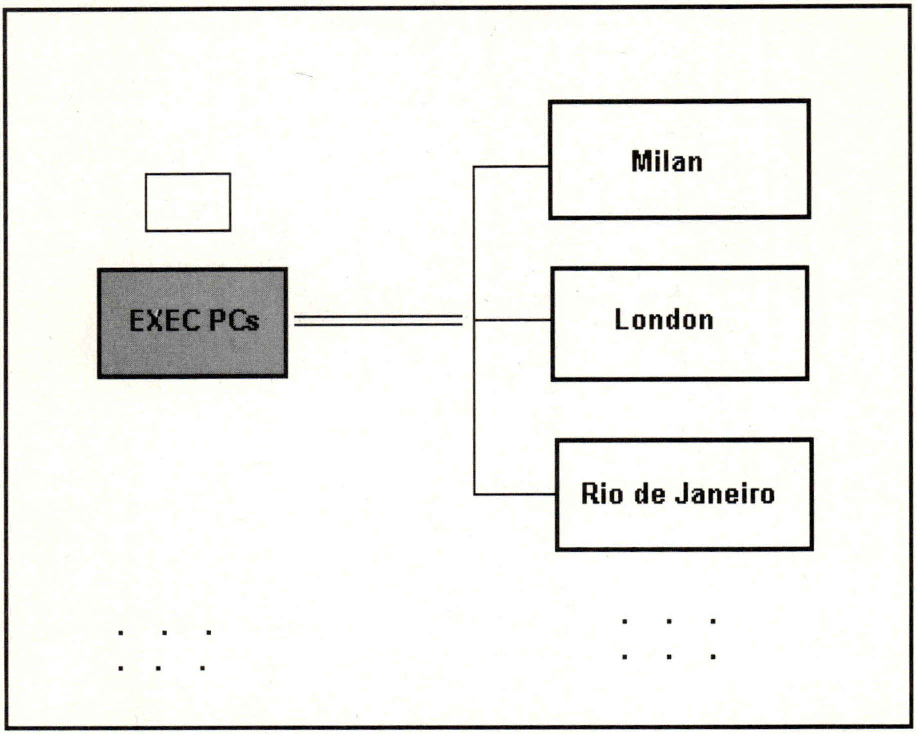

Executives are located around the world. They want to be able to run summary reports and queries for any or all stores in the chain. They expect very rapid response from this new system. The problem that you face is that your network is already overloaded. In addition, each store's processor is heavily taxed. What will happen when dozens of executives start running potentially enormous free-form queries that may contain dozens of joins between any number of systems?

One way that you can satisfy your user community while maintaining some semblance of acceptable system performance is to group all of the distributed data onto one machine, via a batch process. This one machine would be dedicated to the EIS project, which would lower the demand on the struggling in-store processors. Once a day, you'd run a process to retrieve, in bulk, all of the appropriate summary information from each site. As you pulled in this information, you would insert it into the summary database. Your EIS would only run against the summary database, rather than connecting to each separate store. This process is shown in Figure 3.4:

Figure 3.4

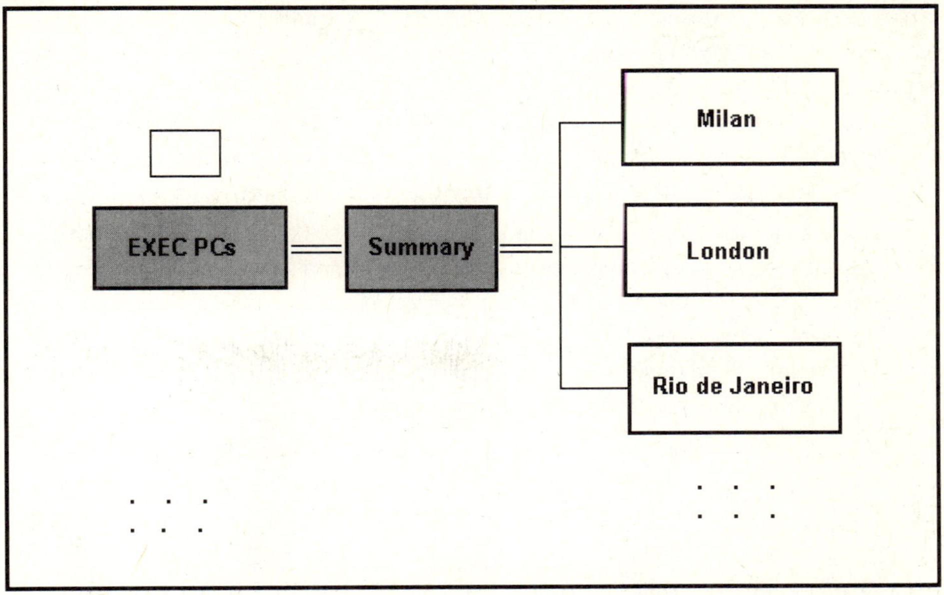

Taking this approach a step further, you could have a number of these "summary" machines. Each machine could service the PC users in a particular country or region. If the local summary machine failed, you could point the local PC users to the nearest summary machine.

By following this strategy, you can diminish your overall network load while increasing the amount and quality of data available for your users.

If you're using OnLine 6.0 or newer, you have the added power and flexibility of data replication. You can use this built-in feature to transparently distribute data among two or more systems.

Tuning your network

Today's networks are highly powerful and sophisticated. However, with this power and capability comes great complexity. As we've seen, your network can contain many potential bottlenecks that can act as unseen drags on performance. Consequently, as an administrator maintaining or programmer developing a distributed system, you may always wonder if program delays are the responsibility of the network or of the underlying code or database design. To remove this potential confusion, it's always a good idea to have a networking professional examine and tune your network. Unfortunately, many organizations ignore the network's impact on performance, and never analyze network throughput. This is a mistake, because sometimes a simple network tuning change leads to astounding performance improvements.

If you're running a distributed application, and you think that you have a performance problem, consider letting a network specialist analyze your environment. One easy way to tell if you have a network problem versus a program or database design problem is as follows:

1. Construct a test case that you can run on the client, as well as directly on the server. This may mean cutting the SQL components out from the programs, and running them alone, via a tool like “dbaccess” or “isql”.
2. Run the test case on the client, and then run it on the server. Make sure that you're looking at the same data on both the client and server. In addition, try to ensure that the number of users and processes on the server is approximately the same between test runs. See the “Setting up an optimization test environment” section for more details on good optimizing practices. When you've finished your tests, carefully record your results.
3. Compare the performance figures from the client test versus the performance figures from the server. If there's a substantial difference, you probably need to either rethink your application architecture or tune your network. Before you go to the trouble of redesigning your system, try tuning your network; you might be pleasantly surprised.

Chapter 4
The Informix Engines

INTRODUCTION

Optimal database systems and applications rely on well-tuned database engines. Your database design can be carefully planned, your SQL and procedural code can be perfect, yet your system can still be lethargic. This is very frustrating, especially in large organizations, where the application developers, database administrators, and system administrators may not communicate frequently (or may not be on speaking terms). In many cases, database administrators blame sluggish system performance on poor application code; system administrators ascribe the problem to inefficient database design or engine tuning, and the application developers decide that the performance issue is directly related to the operating system.

In this section, we devote our attention to ensuring that your database engine is as well-tuned as possible. We discuss both Informix database engines: Informix-SE, and Informix OnLine.

Informix-SE is a full-featured, yet easy to use and administer database engine. Most SE sites don't require a full-time DBA. In fact, SE is often bundled and resold inside other applications. Even though SE doesn't require much administration, there are still a number of steps you can take to improve its performance. In the first chapter, we discuss how you can implement these methods. Since SE uses the UNIX file system, we demonstrate why you should periodically de-fragment the file system, along with how you can use multiple disk drives to help balance your data. We also point out several of the UNIX kernel parameters that you can tune to improve SE's response. Finally, we describe some of the reasons commonly given by SE administrators who decide to upgrade to Informix OnLine.

Informix OnLine is a powerful database server that supports high-volume, high availability applications. You should consider many details when optimizing your OnLine configuration. For our discussion, we've divided these details into four major components: disk configuration, shared memory configuration, virtual processor administration, and miscellaneous topics.

In the disk configuration portion, we investigate some of the techniques that you can use to properly size your root dbspace, along with your physical and logical logs. We examine what happens if your root dbspace is too small, as well as what happens if it's too big. Since more environments now feature multiple disk drives, we illustrate how you can use multiple drives to help balance your data, as well as your temporary storage.

OnLine provides reports on table fragmentation, so our next topic relates to extent management, including several ways that you can de-fragment your tables.

In addition to the more traditional data types, OnLine lets you store binary large objects (BLOBs). We discuss some of the best approaches to take when you set up your disk environment to handle BLOBs.

When you define disk storage for OnLine, you can use the UNIX file system, or you can use a lower-level data access. The first method is known as "cooked files", and the second method is known as "raw devices". We point out the benefits and drawbacks of both approaches, as well as why you should use links instead of drive names when you name your storage areas.

Many administrators use mirroring as a powerful tool in constructing a reliable data environment. We address how mirroring impacts performance, as well as the differences in mirroring between OnLine 5.0x and older versus OnLine 6.00 and newer.

Turning our attention to shared memory, we first address what happens if you don't have enough shared memory versus what happens if there's too much shared memory. OnLine lets you tune the physical log and logical log buffer sizes, and we also examine how you can determine the optimal size for these buffers.

Since data buffers are the most important component of shared memory, we explore how you can choose the correct number of buffers for your environment. In addition, we explain the best way to set the LOCKS, USERS/USERTHREADS, and TBLSPACES parameters.

Page cleaners can greatly affect your system's performance, so we evaluate how to set the optimal number of page cleaners. Because LRU queues and page cleaners are closely related, we explain this relationship, along with how you can select the right page cleaner work parameters. It's important to set these parameters right, because if they're set incorrectly, your page cleaners might time out. We also discuss how to get the most performance out of your checkpoints. We conclude the shared memory section by examining the parallel sorting and spinning features that you can use on multi-processor machines.

Informix completely revamped OnLine's process architecture beginning with OnLine 6.00. We discuss new architecture, as well as how you can best tune the virtual processors that are at the heart of this new architecture.

Rounding out our chapter on the OnLine engine, we examine the tradeoffs between buffered and unbuffered logging, the concept of "key-only" reads, setting "sqlturbo" process priority, and parallel archive and recovery. We also devote some time to discussing some of the new statistics that you can use to monitor OnLine performance.

If you're using OnLine 7.00 or newer, you can take advantage of data fragmentation and parallel data query (PDQ) to streamline database performance. In the last section of this chapter, we review these new features. We begin by concentrating on fragmentation. This includes analysis of the two types of fragmentation that you can implement (round-robin and expression-based). Next, we evaluate PDQ. We discuss how the different types of applications have different needs for PDQ. We then examine how you can configure and monitor this feature.

STANDARD ENGINE SPECIFIC TIPS

The Informix-SE is an ideal database server for mid-sized and smaller databases and applications, as well as for remote sites that don't have system administrators.

Since SE is so easy to administer, there are only a few specific steps that you can take to improve performance. In this section, we discuss defragmenting your UNIX file system, controlling the size of the transaction log, moving heavily used tables and the transaction log to other devices, and kernel tuning. Finally, we explore how you can determine if you need to move to the OnLine engine.

Defragmenting database files

Since SE's files reside on the UNIX and DOS filesystems, the engine dynamically allocates disk space as needed. The only limits to the size of a table are the amount of space on the filesystem, or 2.1 billion rows.

If you are only working with one table, on a relatively empty filesystem, chances are that most of the table's allocated disk space will be nearly contiguous. However, it is rare to find a real-world application with only one table. It is more likely that your file systems contain many tables that are all growing at the same time, combined with hundreds of other UNIX files. In this case, it is easy for your file system to become fragmented, with tables scattered in numerous segments.

There are numerous utilities for defragmenting DOS disks. There are substantially fewer utilities under UNIX. If you don't have any available utilities on your system, you can still defragment your SE database by following these steps:

1. Determine which tables are most likely to be fragmented. These generally include tables that are frequently modified.
2. Back up your database.
3. Unload to ASCII files all tables that you want to defragment.
4. Use the "dbschema" utility to generate the SQL for each table that you are defragmenting.
5. Drop the tables.
6. Re-create, and then re-load each table. You must do this sequentially, not in parallel. If you do it in parallel, you will only interleave and fragment all your tables once again.

You'll want to periodically defragment your tables, especially if the net size of the database grows over time.

Transaction log

The transaction log file grows at a very rapid rate. In fact, depending on the transaction rate and filesystem free space, the log file can fill up your UNIX file system. If this happens, applications start failing, since they cannot begin transactions. Even if the filesystem doesn't reach 100 percent of capacity, UNIX still becomes progressively slower as the filesystem gets more full. In addition, the larger your log file, the longer it takes to recover from a disaster.

You can prevent these situations from happening by following these steps:

1. Back up the database periodically. Once you back up your database, you no longer need the log file.
2. After you have backed up your database, free up the log file's space with this command:

   ```
   cp /dev/null log_file_name
   ```

   This sets the log file's size to 0 bytes. Make sure that you run this command immediately after you back up the database and before users start new transactions. Otherwise, you might clear active transactions.

If you don't back up your database frequently, you can still clear transaction log space on a daily or even hourly basis with these steps:

1. Copy the log to a backup file:

   ```
   cp log_file_name log_file_name.datestamp
   ```

2. Free up the log file's space:

   ```
   cp /dev/null log_file_name
   ```

3. To free up even more disk space, compress the log file that you just moved:

   ```
   compress log_file_name.datestamp
   ```

Moving tables to other devices

On an active system, it is easy for processes to become I/O bound when they all compete for data on the same disk drive. If you have more than one disk and controller, you can improve I/O throughput by moving heavily used tables onto other disks.

For example, assume that you are administering a database on a system that has four disks and two controllers, as shown in Figure 4.1:

Figure 4.1

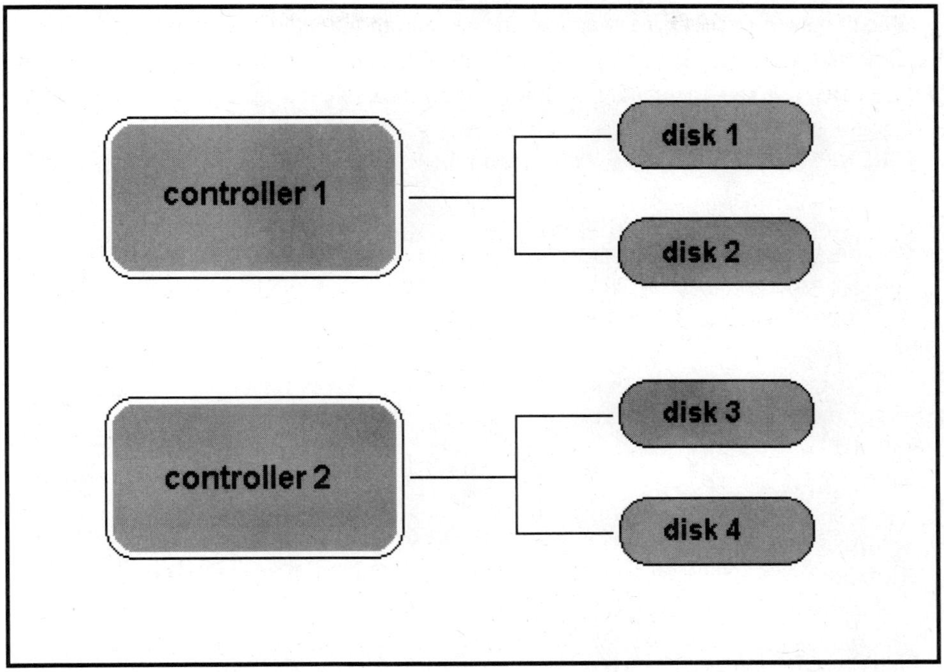

During the design of the system, you decided that disk 1 would hold most of your application code, disk 2 would hold your database, and disks 3 and 4 would hold your users' home directories.

Once you are in production, however, you monitor your system and learn that disks 1 and 2 are busy almost 100 percent of the time, while disks 3 and 4 are underutilized. You can use the "iostat", "sar", or other utilities to reach this conclusion. Fortunately, you can balance the disk load by moving some of your tables to either disk 3 or 4.

How would you decide which tables should stay, and which ones should move? The easiest way would be to identify the 10 most frequently accessed tables on your system. You could then move every other table in this list onto the other disks (e.g., tables 2, 4, 6, 8, and 10). You would then have a more balanced I/O profile. One benefit of this approach is that it is easy to experiment with table location: your applications will run normally regardless of the location of underlying tables.

If you are using transaction logging, you may find it beneficial to move the log file to another device as well.

The rest of this section describes the steps required to move new and existing tables to other devices.

NEW TABLES

For this example, assume that you are writing an application to process electronic mail. One of your tables stores message headers. If you create the table using standard SQL, the CREATE statement and "systables" entry look like this:

```
CREATE TABLE EMAIL_HEADERS
(
   MESSAGE_ID     INTEGER,
   MESSAGE_FROM   CHAR(8),
   MESSAGE_TO     CHAR(8),
   MESSAGE_DATE   DATETIME YEAR TO SECOND
);
```

```
tabname    email_headers
owner      db_user
dirpath    email_h137
tabid      137
rowsize    28
ncols      4
nindexes   0
nrows      0
created    03/08/1994
version    8978433
tabtype    T
audpath
```

If, in contrast, you specify another device to hold the table, your SQL would look like this:

```
CREATE TABLE EMAIL_HEADERS
(
   MESSAGE_ID     INTEGER,
   MESSAGE_FROM   CHAR(8),
   MESSAGE_TO     CHAR(8),
   MESSAGE_DATE   DATETIME YEAR TO SECOND
) IN "/db/email_h";
```

SE creates the table in the designated directory, using the filename that you specified. You may encounter problems with the length of your filename; if so, simply shorten the name until SE accepts it.

After creating the table, the "systables" entry looks like this:

```
tabname    email_headers
owner      db_user
dirpath    /db/email_h
tabid      146
rowsize    28
ncols      4
nindexes   0
nrows      0
created    03/08/1994
version    9568257
tabtype    T
audpath
```

This method works well for new tables; the next section discusses how to move existing tables.

EXISTING TABLES

Follow these steps to move existing tables to other devices:

1. Log in as the "informix" user. This user "owns" the "systables" table, no matter who created the database.
2. Determine what the original file names are. You can find this out by using the following SQL statement:

```
SELECT DIRPATH
FROM   SYSTABLES
WHERE  TABNAME = (table name)
```

3. Back up the original files. Copy the ".dat" and ".idx" files to another location, just for safekeeping. You may even want to back up the entire database.
4. Determine where you want to move the table(s) to. Make sure that there is enough space to hold the table, as well as allow for future growth.
5. Make sure that no database users are currently using the database. You can guarantee this by temporarily changing the directory's permissions to prevent modification by anyone other than root or informix.
6. Move the ".dat" and ".idx" files to the new directory.
7. UPDATE the "systables" entry by using one of the following two methods:

- **ISQL:**

  A. Create a form based on the "systables" table.

  B. Query for the entry based on the "tabname" column.

C. Change the “dirpath” column to reflect the new location of the table.

- **SQL:**

  Run this SQL statement:

```
UPDATE SYSTABLES
SET DIRPATH = (path and name of the file)
WHERE TABNAME = (table name)
```

Regardless of the method you choose, do not enter the “.dat” or “.idx” suffix into the “systables” table. Note that if you manually move the table to another place, both the index file (.idx) and the data file (.dat) must reside in the same location.

Be very careful when you move tables around. Pay special attention to the SQL statement you use to modify the “systables” entry. If you omit the WHERE clause, you change the expected location of all tables, not just the one you want to move. If this happens, you must reconstruct your “systables” entries by keying in the actual “.dat” filenames. Try getting some practice by creating and moving sample tables before actually moving live data.

KERNEL TUNING

One of the best things about SE is that you generally don't need to tune kernel parameters. However, if you experience performance problems, you should know what kernel parameters affect SE response. These include:

- **Open files.** If you receive error messages from SE that you exceeded the maximum number of open tables, try increasing this kernel parameter.
- **Inodes.** You should also raise this parameter if you experience open table problems.
- **Locks.** If you find that your programs are running out of locks, try raising this kernel parameter.

Be aware that modifying the above kernel parameters may have unanticipated side-effects on other areas of your system. Always save a copy of the previous kernel parameters before you make any changes.

When to move to OnLine

As we've seen, Informix SE is appropriate for many types of applications. However, there are also times when you need a more powerful database engine. How can you determine if you need to upgrade your database server? If you need one or more of the following features, consider moving to the OnLine engine:

- **Support for a large number of concurrent users**

  As the number of concurrent users increases, SE applications often run into operating system resource constraints. OnLine 6.0's multi-threaded process architecture lets you support hundreds of concurrent users. If you find that your system is collapsing under the load of all your users, investigate the OnLine engine. For more information about OnLine's multi-threaded architecture, see the "OnLine tips" section.

- **Fault-tolerance**
  Since the SE engine uses the UNIX file system, it relies on the kernel to write data. You can experience data corruption if any of the following problems occur:
  - Sudden power failure during data writing
  - System crash due to serious application failure
  - Hardware problems

  OnLine has a very sophisticated fault-tolerant architecture. This greatly reduces the chance of data or index corruption. If you believe that your power source is not stable, OnLine might be the better database server for your situation.

  Improved throughput
  OnLine uses shared memory, which greatly reduces the amount of I/O that the system performs. If user A retrieves information from a table, and user B then needs the same data, chances are that the data is already in shared memory. This has a large impact on performance, especially when multiplied by many users. If you suspect that your system is I/O bound, OnLine may help you squeeze more throughput from the same system.

- **Additional data types**
  OnLine provides several additional data types. These include:

Data type	Purpose
VARCHAR	Stores variable length character information.
BYTE	Stores non-text data, such as images, program executables, and sound.
TEXT	Stores text data, such as ASCII files and electronic mail.

  If you need to support any of the above data types in your application, use the OnLine engine.

- **Administrative and diagnostic tools**
  OnLine has numerous tools to provide DBAs with important administrative and diagnostic information. If your application or environment requires these types of tools, Online is the better choice.

ONLINE SPECIFIC TIPS

In this section, we focus on some of the methods you can use to improve your OnLine database engine's performance. For clarity, we've grouped our suggestions into these groups:

- Disk configuration
- Shared memory configuration
- Virtual processor configuration (OnLine 6.00 and newer)
- Miscellaneous suggestions

Your root dbspace configuration has a big impact on your OnLine system's productivity. We begin by delving into some techniques you can use to size your root dbspace. This section also includes suggestions on how to best size and arrange your physical and logical logs. If you have more than one disk drive, we propose some practices that you can use to upgrade your system's throughput. We also uncover the major costs and benefits of using the UNIX file system for data storage versus using raw devices, as well as some reasons why you should use links rather than direct device names.

OnLine offers many reports that you can use to monitor your data storage. One of the most important reports provides information about table fragmentation. We illustrate how you can use this data to determine which tables need defragmentation.

Blobs can negatively affect your system's response rate in a number of ways. In this section, we propose several methods that can help mitigate these potential problems. In addition, we discuss mirroring, which is becoming more common in today's computing environment. We spell out some of the performance advantages of mirroring, especially with OnLine version 6.00 and newer.

Disk configuration is only part of the OnLine administration picture. Administrators also need to configure and tune shared memory. We study shared memory's influence on your system's response, including what happens if you don't have enough shared memory versus what happens if there's too much shared memory. We cover the physical log buffer, the logical log buffer, and, most importantly, the data buffers. We explain how to set these consequential parameters, as well as how to best tune your page cleaners and LRU queues. We then discuss the PSORT_NPROCS and SPINCNT parameters. These are important if you're running OnLine on a multiprocessor machine.

There are substantial architectural changes in OnLine 6.00 and newer. We also examine virtual processors, and how you can best monitor and tune them.

Rounding out our section on the OnLine engine, we examine the tradeoffs between buffered and unbuffered logging, as well as the concept of "key-only" reads. If you're using OnLine 6.00 or newer, you can take advantage of parallel archiving and restoring, as well as enhanced user monitoring. We cover these two topics at the end of this chapter.

Conventions

5.0X AND OLDER VERSUS 6.00 AND NEWER

Beginning with version 6.00, Informix changed the names of all OnLine utilities, from "tb(utility)" to "on(utility)". In addition, the TBCONFIG environment variable was changed to ONCONFIG. For this chapter, we primarily use the original utility and environment names.

Note that if you're using 6.00, you can still use the old "tb" prefixes, since Informix provides links between the previous command names and the new names. In addition, you can query the "sysmaster" database in OnLine 6.00 and newer to obtain much of the same information that you get from the "onstat" utility. We'll demonstrate some of these queries in this chapter. Keep in mind that OnLine 6.00 introduces dozens of new statistics; for more information about these statistics, see the *OnLine DSA Administrators Guide*.

Disk configuration

Disk configuration is one of the most important facets of OnLine tuning. In this section, we explore this topic in detail, covering how to determine the best size for your root dbspace, as well as your physical log and logical logs. We examine what can happen if you incorrectly size these crucial areas, as well as how you can use multiple disk drives to improve your data distribution strategy. We also discuss how you can improve the performance of your temporary storage space, and how to handle fragmentation of your data.

Since many OnLine users now store more esoteric information in their database, we investigate how to store and process BLOBs as efficiently as possible. OnLine lets you use both raw devices and cooked files to store information, so we evaluate both types of storage, especially as they relate to performance. As part of this discussion, we also look at how you can use links to simplify your disk configuration.

Finally, disk mirroring is a valuable tool that you can use to ensure high availability of your systems. We address this important topic, with particular emphasis on mirroring's effect on system throughput.

OnLine 7.00 introduced data and index fragmentation, along with parallel data query (PDQ). We reference this topic several times in this chapter; for more detail, see the "Data fragmentation and PDQ" section.

SIZING THE ROOT DBSPACE

The size of your root dbspace is determined by a number of factors. These include:

- **Data distribution.** If you have more than one disk drive, it's a good idea to consider spreading your data across the drives. For further information about the benefits of data distribution, see the "Multiple drive considerations" section of this chapter.

Even if you don't have multiple disk drives, it's still a good idea to set up separate dbspaces for data. You can substantially reduce the size and complexity of your root dbspace if you decide to store your data elsewhere.

- **Log placement.** The physical and logical logs are among the most heavily accessed data structures in an OnLine system. There are a number of good reasons to move them out of the root dbspace. For more information on the benefits of this type of move, see the "Multiple drive considerations" of this chapter.

  Moving the physical and/or logical logs away from the root dbspace lets you minimize its size. Remember that even if you decide to move the logs, you'll still have to initialize your system for the first time with the physical log and at least three logical logs in the root dbspace. Once you've initialized the system, you can move the logs elsewhere.

- **Temporary tables.** One way to fill up the root dbspace, regardless of how large it is, is to create numerous, large, temporary tables. Fortunately, there are several steps you can take to reduce the impact of temporary tables on the root dbspace.

1. When you explicitly create temporary tables (with the CREATE TABLE statement), you can instruct OnLine to place the table in an alternate dbspace, instead of the root dbspace. However, implicit temporary tables still reside in the root dbspace.
2. If you're using OnLine version 6.00 or newer, you can set up special dbspaces for use only by temporary storage. You can then include this dbspace in the ONCONFIG file's DBSPACETEMP parameter. This parameter tells OnLine to store temporary tables in the listed dbspaces, which can be both regular and temporary dbspaces.
3. If you're using a parallel processor, consider setting the PSORT_DBTEMP parameter in the TBCONFIG file. This tells OnLine to use the UNIX filesystem to store temporary tables. For more information about this parameter, see the "Multiprocessor considerations" section.

Even if you're successful in avoiding the root dbspace for your temporary tables, remember that disk space is rarely unlimited; use temporary tables as judiciously as possible.

What if the root dbspace is too small?

If your root dbspace is too small, you'll find out in a number of ways:

- **Data storage shortfall.** If you store your data in the root dbspace (which is the default), and your root dbspace is too small, you'll experience problems as soon as OnLine attempts to add an extent for a table. Since there isn't enough space in the current dbspace (root), this operation will fail, and OnLine will return an error code to the process that was attempting to add data to the table.
- **Temporary table problems.** Unless you explicitly create temporary tables in alternate dbspaces, or use the DBSPACETEMP parameter in the 6.00 and newer ONCONFIG file, OnLine creates temporary tables in the root dbspace. If there isn't enough room in the root dbspace for OnLine to create the temporary table, it returns an error message to the process that requested the temporary table.
- **Log-sizing difficulties.** If you store your physical and/or logical logs in the root dbspace (which is their default location), and try to increase the size of the physical log or increase the number of logical logs, OnLine returns an error message if there isn't enough space to satisfy your request.

Don't worry too much about having a root dbspace that is too small. Remember that you can always enlarge the root dbspace; all you have to do is add a chunk.

What if the root dbspace is too big?

The only risk you face if you make your root dbspace bigger than necessary is wasted disk space. OnLine version 5.0x and older doesn't allow you to drop any chunks, even if they're empty. If you're using OnLine 6.0 or newer, you can drop a chunk (assuming that it's empty). Regardless of the engine that you're using, it's better to slowly increase the size of the root dbspace instead of allocating too much disk space to start.

PHYSICAL AND LOGICAL LOGS

Sizing the physical log

One of the most important factors to consider when you set up your physical log is the volatility of your data. Remember that OnLine writes copies of data pages to the physical log before changing them. These pages are known as "before-images". If your system primarily serves as an information repository, with relatively few real-time data modifications, you can make your physical log smaller than if you expect your data to be heavily modified as part of normal operations.

If you expect your data to be volatile, try dedicating 20 percent of your total disk space to your physical and logical logs. Within that space, allocate one quarter to the physical log, and three quarters to the pool of logical logs. For example, if your system has one gigabyte of storage space, and your data is volatile, use 200 megabytes for the logs. Use 50 megabytes for the physical log, and 150 megabytes for the pool of logical logs. If you use three logical logs, this works out to 50 megabytes per logical log.

If you expect your data to be relatively static, it's safe to use 10 percent instead of 20 percent of your total disk space for your physical and logical logs. In the above example, this works out to 100 megabytes for your logs, with 25 megabytes for the physical log, and 75 megabytes for the pool of logical logs.

On an existing system, the best way to tell if your physical log is sized correctly is to monitor your checkpoint frequency. As you may recall, OnLine is forced to begin a checkpoint when the physical log reaches 75 percent of capacity. If your physical log is too small, you'll observe checkpoints happening much sooner than the number of seconds you set in the CKPTINTVL parameter in the TBCONFIG file. If this happens, you probably need to enlarge your physical log file.

If, after analyzing the situation, you feel that you've incorrectly sized the physical log, remember that it's easy to increase or decrease its size. Just use the "tbmonitor" or "tbparams" utilities.

Sizing the logical log

There's no "hard and fast" rule about sizing your logical logs. Each environment is different; each application within each environment is different as well. You may have several databases on your OnLine system. Some of these databases might use buffered logging, some might use unbuffered logging, and some might not use any logging. All of these factor into your sizing decision.

With all of the above caveats in mind, how do you decide how large to make your logical logs? You can use the formulas listed in the "Sizing the physical log" section of this chapter as a start. Keep in mind that if you make your individual logical logs too small, you can always increase the total amount of available logical log space by adding more logical logs later.

If you're administering an existing system, there are a number of ways that you can tell that your logical logs are too small:

- **Long transactions.** If you are unable to complete certain transactions, even if you've made sure that they are as compact as possible, there's a chance that your logical logs are too small, or that you haven't defined enough logs.
- **All available logs fill up.** OnLine handles logical logs in a round-robin fashion: it loops back to the first logical log in the chain upon completing the last logical log. If, during normal processing, your logs are filling up so fast that you don't have time to free them (by backing them up to disk or tape), it's possible that you haven't defined enough logical log space.

Fortunately, if you determine that you don't have enough room in your logical logs, it's not difficult to add one or more additional logical logs, provided you have enough disk space.

Remember that no matter how large you make your logical logs, you can still encounter circumstances where the logs won't be big enough. You may still encounter long transactions and/or open transactions. For more information on avoiding these types of problems, see the "Transactions" sub-section of the "General tips"section. One of the most common causes of rapid logical log consumption is unbuffered logging; keep this in mind if you're experiencing "mysterious" full logs and long transactions.

Finally, until OnLine 6.00, you couldn't change the logical log size without re-initializing your system. Beginning with version 6.00, however, you can change the size of the logical log with minimal inconvenience. This reduces the importance of "getting it right the first time" when sizing your logical logs.

Number of logical logs

Generally, the actual number of logical logs is not as important as the total amount of space that these logs contain. For example, if you decide that you need 150 megabytes of logical log space, it doesn't matter if you have three 50-megabyte logical logs or ten 15-megabyte logical logs. This was not always the case, however. See the "Logical logs and long transactions" section of this chapter for more information about the problems this caused in earlier versions of OnLine, as well as how to set important TBCONFIG parameters to gracefully handle long transactions.

Even though it doesn't matter which approach you take, most OnLine administrators allocate three, relatively large logical logs rather than numerous, relatively small logical logs. This has the effect of reducing the number of logical logs that need to be backed up, since large logical logs fill more slowly than small logical logs. The drawback to this approach is you might lose more transactions if your disk fails before you get a chance to back up the large logical log file. This, by the way, is one of the stronger arguments in defense of mirroring your logical logs.

The LOGFILES parameter in the TBCONFIG file designates how many logical logs your system currently has, and the LOGSMAX entry determines the maximum number of logical logs that your system can have. Note that you can change the LOGSMAX entry as needed; you only need to restart the OnLine engine for your change to take effect.

Regardless of the approach you take, remember that you can always add more logical logs later, provided that you have enough disk space.

Logical logs and long transactions

In older versions of OnLine (pre-4.10), problems arose during long transaction rollbacks if OnLine didn't have enough logical log space to write all the rollback records. The workaround to this problem was to have many, relatively small logical logs, instead of only a few, large logical logs.

Beginning with version 4.10, Informix addressed this problem by adding two new TBCONFIG parameters: LTXHWM and LTXEHWM. LTXHWM stands for Long Transaction High Water Mark, and is expressed as a percentage of available logical log space. If a transaction causes the logical logs to reach this percentage of capacity, OnLine rolls back this long transaction without affecting any other active transactions. A long transaction rollback message in the OnLine system log looks like this:

```
16:09:53  Aborting Long Transaction: tx 0xc0433570 0
```

From the application's perspective, the engine tells it about the long transaction by returning an error code in the SQLERROR/sqlca.sqlcode system variable.

LTXEHWM stands for Long Transaction Exclusive High Water Mark, and is also expressed as a percentage of available logical log space. There is one difference between this parameter and LTXHWM: if the logical logs fill up to the higher LTXEHWM percentage, OnLine temporarily halts all other processing and grants exclusive logical log access to rollback process.

For example, suppose that you have three 20-megabyte logical logs, for a total of 60 megabytes of logical log space. Your LTXHWM and LTXEHWM parameters are set to the default: 80 and 90 percent, respectively. In this case, if OnLine detects that 48 megabytes (80 percent) of the available log space is being used, it searches for the transaction that is preventing the used logical logs from being freed. This transaction could be performing a great deal of work, or it could have simply issued a "begin work" statement without finishing the transaction. In either case, OnLine finds and rolls back the long transaction. If, during the rollback, the amount of used logical log space reaches 54 megabytes (90 percent), OnLine suspends all other applications to conserve log space for the rollback.

Clearly, you should strive to avoid long transactions wherever possible. If you're running a production system, make sure that you monitor your OnLine log to determine if the engine has rolled back any long transactions. Also, listen for any complaints from your users about "mysterious" program failures. If you're developing or testing a new system, one interesting approach that some OnLine administrators have taken is to set the values for LTXHWM and LTXEHWM to very low levels, 20 and 30, for example. This artificially low barrier helps "trap" any programs that might not have been coded to avoid long transactions. It's much better to discover and correct these programs during development than to suffer a failure during production. Once you have ensured that there are no programs that cause long transactions and are ready to put the system into production, you can then raise the values for these parameters to more realistic numbers, such as 70 and 80, for example.

For more information on how to prevent long transactions from occurring, see the "Preventing long transactions" sub-section of the "General tips" section.

MULTIPLE DRIVE CONSIDERATIONS

If you are fortunate enough to have more than one disk drive, there are several ways that you can use these drives to improve your system's performance. In this section, we discuss each of these methods.

Moving log files out of root dbspace

The physical and logical logs are the most heavily accessed portions of your OnLine database system, along with the other information normally found in the root dbspaces, such as system tables and OnLine reserved pages. Consequently, performance bottlenecks often arise when these three components (root dbspace, physical log, and logical logs) reside on the same device. As a database administrator, you can help minimize these bottlenecks by moving the log files out of the root dbspace device onto other devices. Let's look at a simple example to illustrate what we mean.

Assume that you've been the administrator for a system for the past few years. Up until now, you've only had one disk drive, but you've decided to purchase a second drive because your database has grown. This presents you with a golden opportunity to improve your system's performance. Let's call the two drives A and B. Drive A is the disk drive that you've had all along; drive B is the new one. Use the following procedures to move your log files:

1. Install disk drive B.
2. Set the owner and group for the drive to "informix".
3. Set the permissions for the device to 660by entering: chmod 660 <device name>
4. Consider using a link to reference the new device. See the "Using links instead of drive names" section of this chapter for more information on the value of links.
5. Using tbmonitor, create a new dbspace on drive B. Try to give this dbspace a meaningful name, such as "logdbs".
6. Using tbmonitor, move the physical log from the root dbspace to the newly-created dbspace.

Follow these procedures if you want to move your logical logs as well:

1. Using tbmonitor, create at least three additional logical logs in the newly-created dbspace.
2. Perform an archive to activate these new logs.
3. Delete the original logical logs from the root dbspace.

Dividing large tables among multiple disk drives

If your database contains more than one large, frequently used table, consider distributing these tables among your disk drives. This helps reduce the load on any one drive, often leading to improved performance. We can best illustrate this with an example.

Suppose you're developing a manufacturing application. Your database design contains dozens of tables, and you expect the size of the database to be around four gigabytes. However, only a few of these tables are large and heavily accessed:

Table 4.1

table name	size in megabytes
customer_requests	200
inventory	500
machinery_status	425
product_tracking	400
shipments	605
suppliers	335
Total	**2465**

Your disk configuration consists of three 2-gigabyte disk drives. For simplicity, let's call them drive_one, drive_two, and drive_three. You partition these drives as shown in Figure 4.2 below:

Figure 4.2

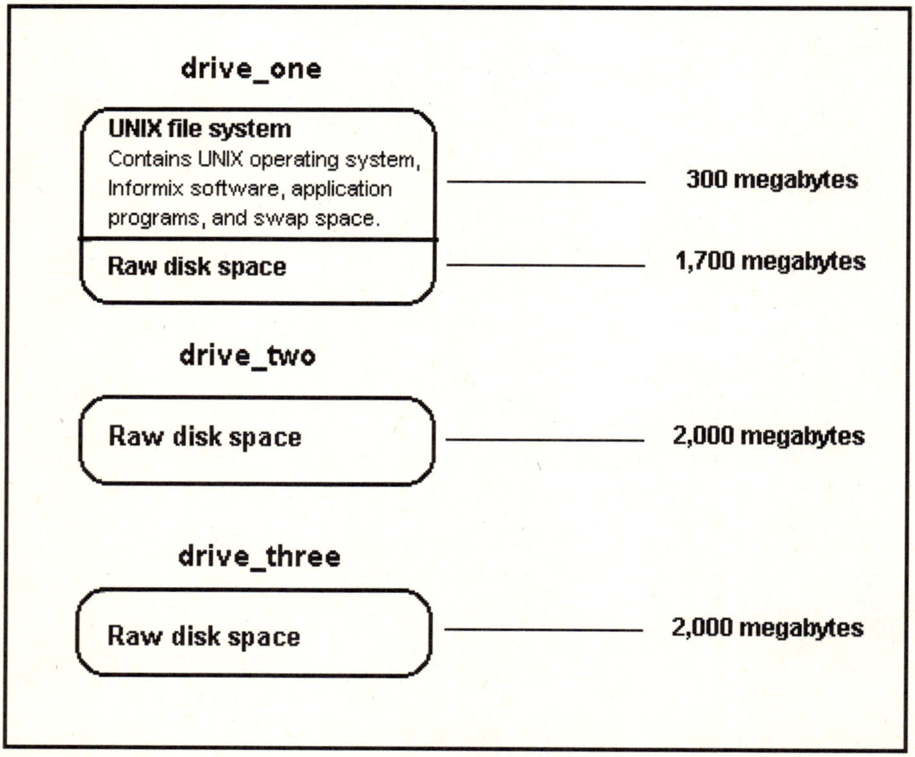

How can you determine how to distribute the six biggest tables listed above among these drives? Try following these steps:

1. Rank the tables by their size:

shipments	605 mb
inventory	500 mb
machinery_status	425 mb
product_tracking	400 mb
suppliers	335 mb
customer_requests	200 mb

2. Try to create three sets (one per disk drive) of tables. It's best if each set is approximately the same size as the other sets. Using the six tables listed above yields these three sets:

set 1:

shipments	605 mb
customer_requests	200 mb
total:	805 mb

set 2:

inventory	500 mb
suppliers	335 mb
total:	835 mb

set 3:

machinery_status	425 mb
product_tracking	400 mb
total:	825 mb

3. Create (at least) three dbspaces, one per disk drive.

4. Modify the table creation scripts for these tables to place them in the appropriate dbspace. For example, you would append the dbspace name to the script that creates the "shipments" table as shown:

```
CREATE TABLE SHIPMENTS
(
    . . .
    . . .
) IN data_set1 ;
```

By dividing these six large tables into three tables and approximately 800-megabyte sets, and then placing these sets in their own dbspaces on separate devices, you help improve performance by balancing the workload for your drives.

If you're using OnLine 7.00 or newer, you have the added power and flexibility of data fragmentation. For more information about this subject, see the "Data fragmentation & PDQ" section later in this chapter.

Temporary space

In OnLine version 5.0x and earlier, the engine built all temporary tables in the root dbspace, which could cause problems in some cases. For example, if there was only a little space left in the root dbspace, a large temporary table could potentially fill up the remaining space. This could easily block other processes from creating their own temporary tables. Furthermore, if the original process couldn't get enough space for its temporary table, the server would return an error message to the front-end process.

With OnLine 6.00 and newer, you can set up special dbspaces to hold transitory information. OnLine uses these dbspaces whenever it needs to create objects that aren't meant to last. This includes implicit temporary tables (e.g., scroll cursors, un-indexed ORDER BY and GROUP BY statements) and sort files. No matter what kind of transaction logging is in effect, OnLine doesn't log any activities relating to these types of objects. This helps improve system performance, as well as reducing the amount of data put into the logical logs. You can also create explicit temporary tables in a temporary dbspace.

If your processing environment has multiple disk drives, consider setting up several temporary dbspaces. You can then, at the application level, assign temporary dbspaces to maximize throughput.

For example, suppose that you have a four-disk system. Each disk contains a data dbspace, along with a temporary dbspace, as shown in Figure 4.3:

Figure 4.3

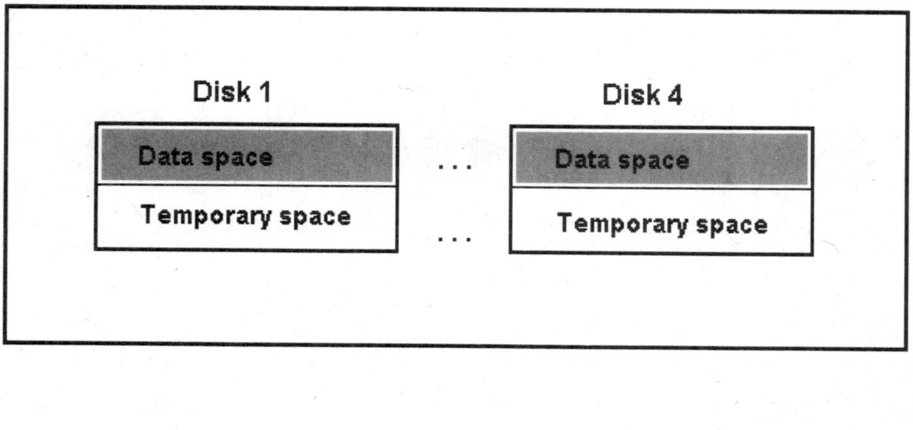

To spread the load of explicitly created temporary tables, you could instruct the developers of different classes of applications to create their temporary tables in particular dbspaces:

```
(For payroll application)

CREATE TEMP TABLE EMP_LIST
(
    ...
) IN tempdbs_1;

(For GL application)

CREATE TEMP TABLE ACCT_LIST
(
    ...
) IN tempdbs_4;
```

This helps minimize contention for valuable temporary dbspace storage.

Monitoring disk drive activity

If you have several disk drives, it's always a good idea to balance the processing load among all of the disk drives. How can you tell how much work each disk drive is performing? The answer depends on which version of OnLine you're running.

OnLine 5.0x and earlier

The easiest way to determine disk drive activity in these versions of OnLine is to use the "iostat" or "sar" utilities. These utilities tell you the current and historical loads on each of your disk drives. You can then use this information, along with the output of "tbstat -d", to determine if any of your disk drives are overloaded.

OnLine 6.00 and newer

With OnLine 6.00, you can still use "iostat" or "sar" to investigate disk usage. However, you now have a more precise tool, the "onstat" utility with the "-g iof" flag:

```
RSAM Version 6.00.UC2   -- On-Line -- Up 3 days 06:54:16 -- 10048 Kbytes

    AIO global files:
    gfd pathname           totalops  dskread dskwrite  io/s
      3 rootdbs               24730    17045     7685   0.1
      4 chunk2                    1        0        1   0.0
      5 srt00104771_1
      6 chunk2                  110        5      105   0.0
```

You can also review the sysmaster database to determine chunk activity:

```
SELECT  CHUNKNUM,
        FNAME,
        READS,
        PAGESREAD,
        WRITES,
        PAGESWRITTEN
FROM    SYSCHKIO  C,
        SYSCHUNKS K
WHERE   C.CHUNKNUM = K.CHKNUM;
```

```
chunknum       1
fname          /dev/informixlinks/chunk1
reads          1294
pagesread      6656
writes         7490
pageswritten   10305

chunknum       2
fname          /dev/informixlinks/chunk2
reads          95
pagesread      182
writes         258
pageswritten   749
    .            .
    .            .
```

You can also track table access, by running "onstat -g ppf":

```
RSAM Version 6.00.UC2    -- On-Line -- Up 3 days 06:56:58 -- 10048
    Kbytes

Partition profiles
partnum  lkrqs lkwts dlks  touts isrd  iswrt isrwt isdel bfrd  bfwrt seqsc
1048577  0      0     0     0     0      0      0      0  0      0      0
2097153  0      0     0     0     0      0      0      0  0      0      0
1048604  333817 0     0     0     131660  115513 0    43320 213778 163495 2
1048603  1      0     0     0     0      6295   0      0  6431   6468   0
1048632  397439 0     0     0     1129422 0     102632  0  153469 102674 29
1048608  124436 0     0     0     62192  1      0      1  150784 15     0
2097154  24252  0     0     0     0      23819  0      0  121012 48913  0
```

This output can become difficult to read; query from the "sysptprof" table in the "sysmaster" database to receive more readable output:

```
SELECT *
FROM   SYSPTPROF;
    .           .
    .           .
```

```
dbsname       sales_admin
tabname       systables
partnum       2097154
lockreqs      712
lockwts       0
deadlks       0
lktouts       0
isreads       116
iswrites      0
isrewrites    0
isdeletes     0
bufreads      300
bufwrites     0
seqscans      0
   .           .
   .           .
```

If you learn that one disk drive is underutilized, you can improve I/O performance by moving one or more tables (and indexes in 7.00 or newer) to the inactive drive. If you're using 7.00 or newer, you have the added power of data fragmentation. See the "Data fragmentation and PDQ" section for more information.

EXTENT MANAGEMENT

Extents are pre-allocated portions of disks set aside for tables to store data and indexes. When you first create a table, you have the option of specifying the initial extent size, along with the size of any additional extents. If you don't specify a size, OnLine defaults to an initial extent size of eight pages, with each additional extent taking eight pages as well. On a machine with a 2K page size, this works out to 16K for the initial extent, and 16K for subsequent extents. OnLine maintains extent sizing information in the "systables" system table, in the "fextsize" and "nextsize" columns.

When a table's data and indexes are spread out over numerous small extents rather than consolidated in a few, larger extents, performance is bound to suffer. To determine the number of extents in your database, run the "tbcheck -pe" report, which creates a map of your database.

Let's look at an example of some badly fragmented tables. In this example, you're maintaining a point-of-sale system. This system makes heavy use of two tables: "transactions" and "inventory". When you created these tables, you didn't specify an initial or subsequent extent size, so OnLine chose eight pages for each. As the tables grew, OnLine continually added eight page extents to each table. What resulted was an interleaving of the two tables, with each table having dozens of small extents:

```
WARNING:TBLSpace demo_db:db_user.transactions has more than 8 extents.
WARNING:TBLSpace demo_db:db_user.inventory has more than 8 extents.

DBSpace Usage Report:  rootdbs  Owner:  db_user  Created: 02/03/94

 Chunk: 1    /dev/online_disk1                 Size      Used      Free
                                              10000      4822      5178

         Disk usage for Chunk 1                          Start     Length

         .             .            .                     .           .
         .             .            .                     .           .

         demo_db:db_user.transactions                    4646          8
         demo_db:db_user.inventory                       4654          8
         demo_db:db_user.transactions                    4662          8
         demo_db:db_user.inventory                       4670          8
         demo_db:db_user.transactions                    4678          8
         demo_db:db_user.inventory                       4686          8
         demo_db:db_user.transactions                    4694          8
         demo_db:db_user.inventory                       4702          8
         demo_db:db_user.transactions                    4710          8
         demo_db:db_user.inventory                       4718          8
         demo_db:db_user.transactions                    4726          8
         demo_db:db_user.inventory                       4734          8
         demo_db:db_user.transactions                    4742          8
         demo_db:db_user.inventory                       4814          8

         .             .            .                     .           .
         .             .            .                     .           .

         FREE                                            4822       5178
```

With OnLine 6.00 and newer, you can also query the "sysextents" table to learn about table fragmentation:

```
SELECT *
FROM   SYSEXTENTS;

 .               .                  .                .
 .               .                  .                .
demo_db         sysprocbody        2097397           8
demo_db         inventory          2097405           8
demo_db         transactions       2097413           8
demo_db         inventory          2097421          32
demo_db         transactions       2097453           8
 .               .                  .                .
 .               .                  .                .
```

How can you prevent a situation like this from occurring? The best way is to carefully analyze the table before you create it, so you can specify an adequate initial extent size. You should also try to ascertain how big the table will be in one year, to help you determine a growth rate for the table. With this information, you can then specify what the initial and next extent sizes should be. For an existing table, you can get current sizing information for a table by running "tbcheck -pt" for the table:

```
TBLSpace Report for sales_admin:db_user.accounts

Physical Address                 20001e
Creation date                    09/19/95 20:57:15
TBLSpace Flags                   1             Page Locking
Maximum row size                 4
Number of special columns        0
Number of keys                   1
Number of extents                16
Current serial value             28294
First extent size                8
Next extent size                 30
Number of pages allocated        345
Number of pages used             322
Number of data pages             113
Number of rows                   28293

Extents
     Logical Page  Physical Page         Size
                0         200105            8
                8         20012d            8
               16         20016d            8
               24         2001b5            8
               32         2001f5            8
               40         20023d            8
               48         20027d            8
               56         2002cd            8
               64         20030d            8
               72         20034d            8
               80         200395            8
               88         2003d5            8
               96         200415            8
              104         20045d            8
              112         2004ad            8
              120         200655          225
```

This table is quite fragmented. To determine how large an extent the table would currently require, multiply the number of pages used by your system's page size. In this case, that produces this formula:

```
2048 * 322 = 659456 bytes

659456 bytes / 1000 = 659 kb extent size
```

Keep in mind that if your sizing estimates aren't correct, you can always tune the next extent size over time. For example, you might instruct the engine to allocate one megabyte for a particular table's next extent size. After a few extents are added, you realize that you need a bigger next extent size. All you need to do is issue the following SQL command:

```
ALTER TABLE <table name> NEXT SIZE nnn;
```

Here, nnn is the amount, in kilobytes, of the next extent. From that point forward, all new extents for that table will be the size that you requested. Remember that you can also alter the extent sizes of your system tables, if necessary. It's possible for the "syscolumns" table, for example, to fill many extents if you have a large number of tables.

What should you do if you "inherit" a system that has badly fragmented tables? There are a number of ways to reorganize your data. These include:

- Exporting the data, and rebuilding the table.
- Using a clustered index on the table.
- Using "dbaccess" to rebuild the table.

Each of these methods is described below.

Exporting

Follow these steps to export and rebuild your tables:

1. Unload the table to an ASCII file.
2. Save the schema of the table, using the "dbschema" utility.
3. Drop the table.
4. Modify the table creation script to contain the proper extent sizing parameters.
5. Recreate the table.
6. Reload the data.

At this point, you'll have a much less fragmented table. Remember that if many tables are interleaved, you may need to unload and then drop all of them before you can begin reloading.

You can also use the "dbexport/dbimport" and "tbunload/tbload" utilities to export, defragment, and then rebuild a table.

Clustered indexes

When you place a clustered index on a table, OnLine physically orders the pages within the table to match the order of the index. Therefore, when you add a clustered index (or refresh an existing clustered index), OnLine defragments the table (assuming that you have enough contiguous free space). For more information on clustered indexes, see the "Indexing strategies" section.

Rebuilding the table through "dbaccess"

You can use the "dbaccess" utility to rebuild (and defragment) your tables:

1. Alter the table, and add a "dummy" column.
2. Choose the "build-new-table" option.
3. Once the new table has been built, alter it again, and drop the dummy column.

Clearly, it's better not to have to perform any of the procedures listed above. As is usually the case, a little analysis and planning can save a lot of work in the future.

BLOB STORAGE

In addition to traditional data types (e.g., char, integer, decimal, etc.) OnLine supports binary large objects, or BLOBs. You define a BLOB column as TEXT, or BYTE. Typically, TEXT columns contain large character-only objects, such as text files, forms, and word-processing files. BYTE columns hold more esoteric types of information, including sound, video, and animation. You can even store program executables in BYTE columns.

OnLine provides a special storage area, known as blobspaces, to more efficiently store these special data types. In this section, we investigate several important factors to consider when you use blobspaces.

Should you use blobspaces?

When you create a table that holds BLOBs, OnLine gives you the option of either storing the BLOB data along with the regular data in the dbspace, or storing the BLOBs in a special area called a blobspace. Blobspaces are sections of disk that you define interactively using "tbmonitor" or from the command line using "tbspaces". Once you create a blobspace, you can instruct OnLine to store BLOBs in the space. Let's look at an example:

Suppose you are designing a system that stores check images. You create a dbspace called "datadbs" to hold regular, non-image data, and you also create a blobspace, called "blobdbs" to hold the actual pictures of the check. Your SQL looks like this:

```
CREATE TABLE CHECK_IMAGES
(
   CHECK_NUMBER   INTEGER,
   ACCOUNT_NUMBER INTEGER,
   CHECK_IMAGE    BYTE IN BLOBDBS
) IN DATADBS;
```

There are several reasons why you should consider using blobspaces to hold text or byte information:

- **Shared memory bypass.** OnLine achieves much of its high efficiency by using a shared memory pool to hold commonly used data. If user A is examining some information (a lookup table, for example), and user B needs to see this information as well, there's a good chance that user B's process will find it in shared memory. This minimizes costly disk access.

  If you use blobspaces to hold your byte or text information, OnLine bypasses the shared memory pool and writes the information directly to disk. If you don't use blobspaces, OnLine uses the regular shared memory pool to store this data. Since BLOB information is usually quite large (e.g., pictures, sound, program executables), it's quite possible that just a few BLOBs passing through shared memory would "force out" data that a large number of users could otherwise share. This can significantly degrade system throughput, and is an important reason to use blobspaces to hold text or byte information.

- **Improved I/O.** When you create a blobspace, you specify the page size. You don't have this ability with regular dbspaces; the number is fixed and can't be changed. When OnLine reads data from, or writes data to, a blobspace, it uses the page size for that blobspace to determine how much information to process. This can improve throughput by reducing the number of reads or writes that OnLine performs.

  For more information on accurately setting the blobspace page size, see the "Setting BLOB page size" section of this chapter.

- **Logging efficiency.** Normally, OnLine writes all data changes into the logical logs. OnLine uses the logical logs to help maintain transaction-level integrity. If you store your BLOBs in regular dbspaces, OnLine writes the entire BLOB into the logical log, just like any other data type. If you're storing pictures or sound or program executables in your database, it's easy to see how quickly the logical logs can fill up.

  If, in contrast, you store your BLOB information in a blobspace, OnLine doesn't write the entire BLOB in the logical log. Instead, it only writes a record of the BLOB into the logical log. This record consists only of the blobspace free-map and bitmap pages. This significantly minimizes the amount of data written to the logical logs. When you back up the logical log, OnLine uses the logged free-map and bitmap information to retrieve the correct BLOB pages and write them to the logical log tape. The result of this process is that you use up logical logs much more slowly.

Setting BLOB page size

When you create a blobspace using "tbmonitor" or "tbspaces", you can either set the BLOB page size or accept the default of 1 kilobyte per BLOB. If you set the BLOB page size, remember that it must be a multiple of the OnLine page size, which you can find in the "tbconfig.std" file. Try to set the size as accurately as possible, because only one BLOB can reside on a BLOB page. If you don't size your BLOB pages accurately, you can waste a large amount of disk storage. For example, if you've defined your blobspace page size to be 32 kilobytes, and the average BLOB in your system is only 16 kilobytes, OnLine doesn't store two BLOBs per page. Instead, OnLine stores only one 16-kilobyte BLOB on the 32-kilobyte BLOB page. The remaining 16 kilobytes on the page are empty. This effectively doubles the amount of disk storage you need for BLOBs.

Determining optimal BLOB page size

As with many other aspects of OnLine administration, it's best to plan ahead. In the case of setting blobspace page size, try to decide what the average BLOB size will be. Once you have calculated this number, choose a blobspace page size that divides fairly evenly into the average BLOB size. This helps to reduce the amount of wasted blobspace. If program speed is a bigger concern than optimizing data storage, set a blobspace page size that's big enough to hold even the largest BLOB. This reduces the amount of I/O that OnLine must perform to return BLOBs.

Remember that if you're storing BLOBs in more than one table or more than one column within the same table, you can set up separate blobspaces if necessary. For example, suppose that you're designing a personnel system. One of your most important tables holds employee information, including a picture of the employee and the employee's job application. How can you store this information as efficiently as possible? One way is to create two blobspaces, one for the pictures and one for the applications. You can then specify an optimal page size for each blobspace. You can even instruct OnLine to store the rest of the table in a standard dbspace. Your SQL looks like this:

```
CREATE TABLE EMPLOYEE_INFO
(
   EMPLOYEE_NUM  INTEGER,
      .    .    .    .
   EMPLOYEE_PIC  BYTE IN PICTURE_DBS,
      .    .    .    .
   EMPLOYEE_APP  TEXT IN APP_DBS,
      .    .    .    .
) IN DATADBS;
```

Archiving and blobs

There are two important issues to consider regarding archiving and BLOBs. First, OnLine doesn't free up BLOB page space immediately after you delete a BLOB. Instead, OnLine waits until you back up the logical log containing the transaction before freeing the affected pages. This could have an adverse effect on your applications. Programs that insert or update BLOBs could potentially fail if there is no remaining space in the blobspace. To reduce this potential for failure, back up the logical logs as soon as they fill, using the "tbtape -c" command. Or, if you're using the OnLine 6.0 "onarchive" utility, you can use the "continuous logical log backup" feature.

In addition, if you're using "tbtape" (or "ontape" / "onarchive" in versions 6.00 and newer), note that during an archive, OnLine treats blobspaces differently than regular dbspaces. While you can add or change the data contained on the pages in a regular dbspace during an archive, OnLine blocks any modifications to a blobspace during an archive, until that blobspace has been archived. This means that any applications that depend on being able to modify data in a blobspace could potentially fail during an archive.

To diminish the number of times that this can happen, create your blobspaces first, since OnLine archives chunks in the sequence that they were created. In any case, you should design your applications and procedures to gracefully handle this situation.

RAW DEVICES VERSUS COOKED FILES

What do we mean when we say a device is "raw"? What is a cooked file? How do you decide which type of device to use? These are all important questions as you set up and maintain your OnLine system. First, let's answer the questions about raw devices and cooked files.

A raw device is a character device that does not contain a UNIX file system. From the operating system's perspective, it is an unallocated disk drive, or sector of a disk drive. This lets Informix bypass the standard UNIX file reading and writing mechanisms, which results in better performance. We'll describe these performance benefits later in this section.

A cooked file is simply a UNIX filesystem file. When you use a cooked file, OnLine creates a file on the filesystem. The size of the file is whatever you specified. For example, suppose you create a cooked file called "datadbs", and that you specify a size of 20 megabytes. Your filesystem entry looks like this:

```
-rw-rw--- informix informix  20480000 Jan 30 21:50  datadbs
```

As soon as the amount of actual data in this file grows to the full 20 megabytes, OnLine fails if it tries to allocate any more space. This is because OnLine doesn't "grab" filesystem space when it needs it. If you run out of cooked file space, you would need to create another cooked file. Ideally, your second cooked file would be big enough to hold your data for the foreseeable future.

There are a number of reasons to choose raw devices over cooked files:

- **Speed.** When you use a raw device, OnLine performs data reads and writes by bypassing the relatively slow UNIX kernel. This can yield substantial performance gains. When you read from a cooked file, the data first passes through the UNIX buffer pool, and then enters the OnLine shared memory buffer pool. When you read from a raw device, OnLine bypasses the UNIX buffer pool, and reads directly into its shared memory buffer pool. This results in substantial time savings. Raw devices also let OnLine bypass the operating system's potentially slow inode management.
- **Disk space consolidation.** The disk space contained within a raw device is, by definition, contiguous. With an operating system cooked file, you have no guarantee that the file is contiguous. In fact, it may be spread all over the disk, which results in lowered performance.
- **Reliability.** When you issue a write command that goes through the UNIX kernel, you can't be absolutely sure when the write is actually performed. This is because UNIX doesn't perform disk writes in a real-time mode. Instead, it buffers up a number of writes before physically writing them to disk. When it writes to raw disk, OnLine provides a much better guarantee that data is actually getting written to disk immediately. The only exception to this rule is when you use buffered logging. For more information about buffered logging, see the "Logging" section of this chapter.
- **Security.** A cooked file resides on the UNIX filesystem for all the world to see. If a user with the right permission level deletes the cooked file, you've lost all or part of your database. Raw devices are much harder to "find" for the average user. Consequently, they're harder to damage. Be aware, however, that one way to wreck the raw devices that your OnLine system uses is to issue a "make filesystem" (mkfs) command for the raw device. UNIX doesn't check to see if the information contained on the device is important.

Despite these benefits, there are some reasons to consider using cooked files:

- **Ease of setup.** Cooked files are easy to set up; all you need to know is the name of the filesystem where you want to create the cooked file. In this case, assume that you're going to use the "/usr/db_admin/cooked_files" directory, and that you're calling your cooked file "rootdbs_chunk". Then follow these steps:

  1. Create the file name. One way is to use the "touch" command:

     ```
     touch /usr/db_admin/cooked_files/rootdbs_chunk
     ```

2. Change the group setting on the file to "informix":

```
chgrp informix rootdbs_chunk
```

3. Change the ownership of the file to "informix":

```
chown informix rootdbs_chunk
```

4. Set the permissions for the file:

```
chmod 660 rootdbs_chunk
```

Note that steps two through four are the same whether you're setting up a cooked file or a raw device.

- **Speed of setup.** It's usually faster to set up a cooked file than a raw device. If you want to get your system up and running as quickly as possible, you might consider starting with cooked files. Once you get your raw devices set up, you can use "dbexport" and "dbimport" to move the data from the cooked file instance to the raw device instance. If you want to set up a small development system, you might even decide to simplify your environment by using a cooked file OnLine instance.
- **Permissions.** To create an OnLine instance, you need either the root password or the informix password. However, if you're setting up a raw device-based OnLine system, you must have the root password to create the raw devices at the operating system level. If you have the informix password, but you don't have the root password, you still can set up a cooked file instance of OnLine.

USING LINKS INSTEAD OF DRIVE NAMES

As part of setting up an OnLine system, you provide the server with the names of the devices that hold your data. This happens when you first bring up the system (rootdbs), when you add a dbspace, and when you add a chunk to an existing dbspace. While it's easiest to just tell OnLine the actual device name, there's a good reason to use links instead.

Links are simply file system-based pointers that help provide a more meaningful name for a particular file or device. For example, if your root dbspace resides on the raw device /dev/rdsk/c0d3s0, you would normally enter the full device name into the database parameter initialization screen. Unfortunately, this approach has several drawbacks:

- **Lack of meaning.** /dev/rdsk/c0d3s0 is not a very meaningful name; it's hard to know what its purpose is just by looking at its name.

- **Lack of uniqueness.** There could be numerous other drives with very similar names (e.g., /dev/rdsk/c0d4s0, /dev/dsk/c0d3s0) This can present a problem when you're trying to decipher the roles and tasks of each device.
- **Difficult to replace.** This last disadvantage is the most significant. Let's look at an example to see what we mean. Suppose that you have a two-disk system. Disk one (/dev/rdsk/c1ds1) holds all the data on your system. Disk two (/dev/rdsk/c1ds2) acts as a mirror to disk one. One day, disk one fails. Because you had the foresight to mirroring your disk drive, your system keeps running.

  In the meantime, you frantically contact your hardware vendor, who installs a new disk. The new disk is identical to the old one in terms of size and layout. The only difference is that the new disk name is /dev/rdsk/c1ds5. How can you restore your system to its original state if the root device name has changed? Without links, it's very difficult to proceed. With links, it's a very simple task, as described below.

Let's look at how the above scenario changes if you used links. Your two devices are still known as /dev/rdsk/c1ds1 and /dev/rdsk/c1ds2. However, before you originally initialized OnLine, you created two links, one per device, using these commands:

```
ln -s /dev/rdsk/c1ds1 /dev/online_disk1
ln -s /dev/rdsk/c1ds2 /dev/online_disk1_mirror
```

Once you had your links in place, you then used the link names, rather than the actual device names to reference those disk drives. Consequently, when /dev/rdsk/c1ds1 failed and was replaced by /dev/rdsk/c1ds5, all you had to do was remove the old link, and make a new link:

```
rm /dev/online_disk1
ln -s /dev/rdsk/c1ds5 /dev/online_disk1
```

After this, OnLine can begin recovering the original data disk, which now points at the new disk drive.

Remember to use links wherever you can; they can greatly simplify your job as an administrator.

MIRRORING

Benefits and costs of mirroring

It's hard to overemphasize the importance of mirroring in maintaining a high-availability database system. The most common problem that plagues database servers is disk reliability. If, during operation, OnLine determines that your data has become corrupted, it may take the disk drive(s) off-line. At that point, you can run the "tbcheck" utility, and attempt to fix the problem. In many cases, however, your disk may be unrecoverable. It's bad enough if the disk contains data. If the damaged disk happens to contain all or part of the root dbspace, you have a real problem, because OnLine cannot operate without a good root dbspace. Neither of your options at this juncture is particularly palatable. The more acceptable option is to restore your most recent archive. If, however, you haven't been doing archives, or your archives are out of data, you have no choice but to re-initialize your system.

To prevent this kind of situation, use mirroring if you have the disk drives to spare. If nothing else, mirror your root dbspace (along with the physical and logical logs). Without these key components, OnLine cannot be brought up.

Mirroring does have some effect on performance. As we'll see, however, this effect is primarily confined to OnLine servers version 5.0x and earlier. With OnLine 6.0 and newer, the costs of mirroring are much lower. In fact, mirroring may even improve performance of these new database servers.

Mirroring with OnLine 5.0x and older

The primary cost of mirroring with OnLine versions 5.0x and older is the extra time it takes to write to the mirrored chunk. When OnLine writes data to the disk, it uses the low-level "write()" function. If the chunk that you're writing to is mirrored, OnLine calls this function twice: once for the primary chunk, and once for the mirrored chunk.

While the second "write()" call does slow data writing somewhat, don't be too concerned about it: from your users' perspectives, the most commonly used gauge of system speed is query response time, which isn't directly affected by mirroring.

Mirroring with OnLine 6.0 and newer

Beginning with OnLine 6.0, mirroring doesn't suffer from the same potential performance limitations as before. In fact, the enhancements contained in the database server may actually enable mirrored systems to be faster than non-mirrored systems. This is due to two major features: asynchronous writes and split reads.

- **Asynchronous writes.** The most time-consuming part of mirroring is always the write operation, because the database server must write to both the primary and the mirror locations. OnLine 6.0 utilizes asynchronous data writes, whereby the two write requests (primary and mirror) are submitted to the AIO virtual processors. If there happen to be two idle AIO VPs at the time of the request, they both can perform their writes at the same time, instead of serially. Once it issues the write requests, the thread that requested the writes is free to move on to other work. In earlier versions of OnLine, the entire process would happen serially.
- **Split reads.** When you request data from a mirrored chunk, OnLine makes use of both the primary and the mirrored storage location to speed retrieval.

During a query, OnLine determines which disk (primary or mirror) is positioned closer to the requested data. It then reads from the appropriate disk drive.

Should you use hardware or software mirroring?

Many hardware vendors now offer sophisticated mirroring built into the disk drive itself. This presents a dilemma for database administrators: Should you let the hardware handle mirroring for you, or should you rely on OnLine to perform the mirroring tasks?

In version 5.0x and earlier, there is no difference between methods. With version 6.0 and newer, however, OnLine mirroring is the better choice. This is because of the two major enhancements added to this version of the engine: asynchronous writes and split reads. If you choose hardware mirroring, OnLine has no way of knowing that the mirrored devices exist. Consequently, it can't use the new mirroring features to speed performance.

Shared memory configuration

INTRODUCTION

OnLine's shared memory is highly tunable; you can greatly affect performance by changing shared memory parameters. In this section, we discuss a number of these parameters. We examine what each parameter controls, along with how to determine whether you should alter the parameter's settings. We begin with shared memory buffers. These include the physical, logical, and data pool buffers.

Database and system administrators frequently ask questions related to shared memory, such as:

- How much of the available memory on my system should be used for OnLine shared memory?
- What happens if I don't allocate enough shared memory?
- What happens if I allocate too much shared memory?

In this section, we'll answer these questions and provide some general guidelines. One problem in setting concrete rules is that each application and environment is different. Occasionally, one particular environment has different needs depending on the operation. For example, you may be administering a system that for 24 days a month functions as a large-scale OLTP system. During the last week of the month, however, the system is used primarily for decision support. It's very difficult to identify the exact role of this system, since it changes throughout the month. In cases like this, be prepared to change certain shared memory parameters to fit the needs of your users.

Although there is no set rule regarding the optimal amount of shared memory, you can follow this guideline: Try to limit the amount of memory you allocate for OnLine's shared memory segment to no more than 25 percent of the total memory on your system.

For example, if your main memory is 256 megabytes, use no more than 64 megabytes for OnLine. If your system has 32 megabytes of memory, use no more than eight megabytes for OnLine. This recommendation applies regardless of the type of processing that your system performs. In fact, there are many cases where the optimal amount of shared memory is even lower than 25 percent.

This rule-of-thumb changes somewhat with OnLine versions 6.00 and newer, because OnLine's new multi-threaded architecture reduces individual process memory requirements while increasing engine shared memory usage. On the whole, however, this new architecture reduces the total amount of memory that you need to perform your processing.

Before we begin discussing specific shared memory parameters, let's first address the consequences of having too little shared memory versus too much shared memory.

What happens if there is too little shared memory?

Poor performance is the most common indicator of an OnLine system that doesn't have enough shared memory. OnLine uses shared memory caching to achieve much of its fast performance; consequently, if there isn't enough shared memory, OnLine is forced to directly use the disk drives for a greater proportion of I/O.

You can use the output of the "tbstat" utility as the best indicator of your system's memory utilization. Specifically, use the "-p" option to determine the current caching rate. For more information on configuring shared memory to maximize data caching, see the "Data buffers" section of this chapter.

What happens if there is too much shared memory?

It's not easy to tell if you've allocated too much shared memory to your OnLine system. Your database applications may run efficiently; your users may have no complaints. Despite the difficulty in diagnosing this type of problem, there are a number of symptoms to watch out for:

- **Excess swapping/paging.** When the operating system needs more memory than is currently available, it can use the disk-based swap space as a memory reserve. This is known as swapping, or paging. Your goal should be to minimize the number of times that the operating system is forced to swap, because disk drives are much slower than memory.

  One of the easiest ways to guarantee excess swapping is to allocate too much memory to OnLine. In addition, if you prevent UNIX from swapping out OnLine's shared memory (by setting the RESIDENT parameter in the TBCONFIG file to 1, for forced residency), you further reduce the amount of swappable memory. This means that the operating system swaps even more frequently.

Use the UNIX "vmstat" command to determine the amount of swapping that the operating system is performing. The following is an example of the utility's output:

```
       procs            memory                    page faults       cpu
 r       b      w      avm     free   re    at    pi    po     fr    de
sr      in     sy      cs   us sy id

 1       0      0    13480    56074    2     4     7     0      0     0
0      49   1326    159   13   2 85
 1       0      0    17442    56051    3     3     7     0      0     0
0     169   1116    300   10   4 86
 2       0      0    17449    56046    0     0     1     0      0     0
0     115    733    176    4   3 93
 2       0      0    17449    56046    2     9    12     0      0     0
0     272   1381    381   20   7 73
 4       0      0    12526    56046    0     2     3     0      0     0
0     291   1383    389   20   7 73
```

The "pi" and "po" columns are of interest to us here. The first column refers to the number of pages that the operating system swaps into memory; the second column is the number of pages that UNIX swaps out. The numbers in these columns in the above example aren't excessive.

- **High system usage of CPU resources.** If the operating system is continually swapping memory pages to disk, a large percentage of the CPU's work is dedicated to managing the swapping operation. This is reflected in the ratio of user to system to idle CPU percentages. Use the "vmstat" utility to learn what these ratios are. In the above "vmstat" output, the "us" column refers to the percentage of CPU time spent in user processing; the "sy" column is the percent spent in system processing, and the "id" column is the idle CPU percentage.

  If you consistently observe nearly equivalent amounts of CPU time spent between user and system processing, you should suspect that your system is devoting too much time to overhead tasks. One of the most common overhead tasks is memory management. Try reducing the amount of dedicated OnLine shared memory, and re-run the "vmstat" utility.

- **Database performance.** If you reduce the amount of shared memory allocated to OnLine (generally by reducing the number of buffers), and your database applications still run efficiently, you probably were wasting shared memory. Conversely, if you increase the amount of OnLine shared memory, and your programs still don't perform any better, it's safe to assume that the extra shared memory wasn't necessary.

The best tool that you can use to make these determinations is the "tbstat" utility. Use the "-p" option, and let the read and write cache rates serve as indicators of your system's performance. For more information on configuring shared memory to maximize data caching, see the "Data buffers" section of this chapter.

BUFFERS

Physical log buffer

When you change the data contained on a page (through INSERT, UPDATE, or DELETE), OnLine first stores a copy of the page in a section of memory known as the physical log buffer. This copy is known as a "before image". To improve system performance and concurrency, OnLine actually uses two physical log buffers.

Periodically, OnLine flushes the memory-based physical log buffer to the disk-based physical log. Any of the following events initiate a physical log buffer flush:

- OnLine performs a checkpoint.
- One of the two physical log buffers fills up. OnLine actually prepares to flush the buffer once it reaches 75 percent of capacity.
- OnLine needs to clear a (modified) shared-memory pool buffer page at the same time the original, unmodified page is in the physical log buffer.

OnLine uses the disk-based physical log to ensure database reliability and consistency during the "fast-recovery" operation.

As an administrator, you can tune the size of the physical log buffer to help improve performance. You can change this value by modifying the PHYSBUFF parameter in the TBCONFIG file, or you can use the "tbmonitor" interactive utility. The default value is 32 kilobytes, and is sufficient for many types of applications and environments.

The goal in tuning the physical log buffer size is to maximize performance without wasting shared memory. If you make the physical log buffer too small, you run the risk of needing checkpoints too frequently. If you make the buffer too large, you've wasted shared memory that could be better utilized. To determine what size your physical log buffer should be, use the "tbstat -l" command. For the best results, try to use this command with as realistic a system load as possible.

Here are examples of three configurations, each with a different physical log buffer size:

The first example uses the default PHYSBUFF setting of 32 kilobytes. The statistics tell us that each time OnLine flushes the buffer to disk, it writes, on average,

15.82 pages. This works out to a "pages/io" to "bufsize" ratio of nearly 99 percent. To improve performance, consider raising the size of the buffer so that it can hold more data before OnLine flushes it.

```
RSAM Version 6.00.UD1P9 -- On-Line -- Up 1 days 02:06:12 -- 30888 Kbytes

Physical Logging
Buffer bufused  bufsize  numerates numwrits pages/io
  P-2  15       16       249859    15796    15.82
   phybegin physize  phypos   phyused  %used
   200035   10053    6859     127      1.26
```

For the second example, we purposely set up a tiny physical log buffer of just two kilobytes. Notice how OnLine had to use 72 writes to flush 72 pages? This works out to only one page per write, and yields a "pages/io" to "bufsize" ratio of 100 percent. This is very inefficient; OnLine is working much harder during flushes than is necessary. If your numbers look like this, try raising PHYSBUFF until the "pages/io" to "bufsize" ratio is closer to 75 percent.

```
RSAM Version 5.01.UD1   -- On-Line -- Up 00:00:56 -- 2676
Kbytes

Physical Logging
Buffer bufused  bufsize  numpages numwrits pages/io
  P-2  0        1        72       72       1.00
  phybegin physize  phypos   phyused  %used
  1000da   1000     778      72       7.20
```

For the third example, we set up a very large physical log buffer of 256 kilobytes. Notice the low percentage of the "pages/io" to "bufsize" ratio. This means that this large physical log buffer wastes shared memory that could be utilized more efficiently elsewhere. In this case, reduce the physical log buffer size until the "pages/io" to "bufsize" ratio is closer to 75 percent.

```
RSAM Version 5.01.UD1   -- On-Line -- Up 00:03:12 -- 3264
Kbytes

Physical Logging
Buffer bufused  bufsize  numpages numwrits pages/io
P-2    0        128      28       2        14.00
   phybegin physize  phypos   phyused  %used
   1000da   1000     87       0        0.00
```

One final note regarding the physical log buffer: If you make the physical log buffer too big, and you're using buffered logging, you might lose some already-committed transactions if your system fails before the buffer gets flushed to disk. This can happen because OnLine can only restore transactions that were written to the disk-based logical log before the system went down. Since OnLine may not have had the chance to write buffered transactions from memory to disk prior to system failure, there is a possibility that you could lose this information. Keep this in mind before you increase the physical log buffer. If you cannot afford to lose any transactions, consider using unbuffered logging instead. Note that you can have different logging levels (e.g., buffered, unbuffered) for different databases within the same OnLine instance.

For more information about logging modes, see the "Logging" section of this chapter.

Logical log buffer

Just as the physical log buffer is a temporary, memory-based storage area for physical log information, the logical log buffer is also a temporary, memory-based storage area for logical log information.

Any of the following events initiates a logical log buffer flush:

- OnLine performs a checkpoint.
- One of the three logical log buffers fills up.
- A user prepares or commits a transaction within a database that is set up to use unbuffered logging.
- A session terminates that is connected to a non-logging database.

As an administrator, you can tune the size of the logical log buffer to help improve performance. You can change this value by modifying the LOGBUFF parameter in the TBCONFIG file, or you can use the "tbmonitor" interactive utility. The default value is 32 kilobytes, and is sufficient for many types of applications and environments.

Your goal in tuning the logical log buffer size is to maximize performance without wasting shared memory. If you make the logical log buffer too small, you can degrade system performance by forcing OnLine to continually flush the buffer. If you make the buffer too large, you've wasted shared memory that could be better utilized. To help determine what size your logical log buffer should be, use the "tbstat -l" command. For the best results, try to use this command with as realistic a system load as possible.

Here are examples of two configurations, each with a different logical log buffer size:

In the first example, we've defined a very large logical buffer size of 256 kilobytes. Notice how low the "pages/io" to "bufsize" ratio is. This means that OnLine isn't writing many pages each time it performs an I/O operation. If you see this type of low ratio, consider lowering the logical log buffer size. However, be aware that you can't reduce the buffer size below 32 kilobytes; OnLine won't accept anything lower than 32 kilobytes.

```
RSAM Version 5.01.UD1    -- On-Line -- Up 00:03:12 -- 3264 Kbytes

Logical Logging
Buffer bufused  bufsize  numrecs  numpages numwrits recs/pages pages/io
  L-1  0        128      107      8        3        13.4       2.7
```

The second example uses the default logical log buffer size of 32 kilobytes. Observe that in this case, our database uses unbuffered logging, which generally decreases the "pages/io" to "bufsize" ratio. If the database used buffered logging, OnLine would be able to process more pages per I/O operation.

```
RSAM Version 6.00.UD1P9 -- On-Line -- Up 1 days 02:06:12 -- 30888
Kbytes

Logical Logging
Buffer bufused  bufsize  numrecs  numpages numwrits recs/pages pages/io
  L-2  0        16       10954180 564340   55441    19.4       10.2
```

As is the case with a large physical log buffer, a large logical log buffer could lead to trouble if your system goes down before OnLine writes the memory-based transactions to disk.

Data buffers

Data buffers are the heart of OnLine's shared memory. Each buffer page is the size of one OnLine data page, usually 2048 or 4096 bytes. The BUFFERS parameter in your TBCONFIG file controls the number of data buffers for your OnLine system.

This shared memory parameter has, by far, the most impact on your system's performance. It also uses the most shared memory. For example, if you add 1000 additional buffers to the shared memory pool, and your system's data page size is 2048 bytes, you'll use an additional two megabytes of shared memory (2048 bytes x 1000 buffers). Consequently, be careful not to over-allocate data buffers. How can you tell if and when you need to add buffers? The easiest way is by examining the output of the "tbstat -p" command. Let's look at a few examples.

Our first example illustrates one of the widespread causes of sluggish OnLine systems: a low read cache rate. As we discussed earlier, if OnLine doesn't have enough shared memory data buffers, it is forced to read from the disk drive, which is a much slower operation. The read cache rate refers to the percentage of the time that OnLine finds the buffer it needs in memory, versus having to retrieve the data from disk. A cache rate of 75 percent means that, on average, OnLine finds the data that it needs 75 percent of the time in the shared memory buffer pool. In the sample output below, observe that the read cache rate is only a little more than 78 percent. Generally, your OnLine systems work best with a read cache rate above 95 percent.

```
RSAM Version 6.00.UD1P9 -- On-Line -- Up 12:08:57 -- 20454 Kbytes

Profile
dskreads pagreads bufreads %cached dskwrits pagwrits bufwrits %cached
23676    11150    108767   78.23   .............
  .        .        .        .       .        .        .
  .        .        .        .       .        .        .
```

If you add more shared memory buffers, "tbstat -p" should produce better output:

```
RSAM Version 6.00.UD1P9 -- On-Line -- Up 04:47:38 -- 22696 Kbytes

Profile
dskreads pagreads bufreads %cached dskwrits pagwrits bufwrits %cached
11112    11150    276989   95.99   .............
  .        .        .        .       .        .        .
  .        .        .        .       .        .        .
```

If you add more shared memory data buffers, and your read cache rate still doesn't improve, try lowering the LRU_MAX_DIRTY and LRU_MIN_DIRTY parameters. This effectively increases the number of available free pages in the shared memory pool. Since there are more free pages to use, OnLine can achieve better read caching performance.

Next, we examine what happens when OnLine's write cache rate is too low. Generally, OnLine works best when it can cache writes at a rate of at least 85 percent. This means that when OnLine writes data, it writes data into the shared memory buffer pool at least 85 percent of the time. In this example, note how low the write cache rate is:

```
RSAM Version 5.01.UD1   -- On-Line -- Up 5 days 00:01:16 -- 1200 Kbytes

Profile
dskreads pagreads bufreads %cached dskwrits pagwrits bufwrits %cached
................................. 103043   258154   407505   74.71
  .        .        .        .       .        .        .
  .        .        .        .       .        .        .
```

By adding more shared memory buffers, you increase the probability of OnLine being able to write into memory instead of onto the disk.

```
RSAM Version 5.01.UD1   -- On-Line -- Up 3 days 10:54:09 -- 1464 Kbytes

Profile
dskreads pagreads bufreads %cached dskwrits pagwrits bufwrits %cached
................................. 58245    117025   596504   90.24
 .        .        .        .        .        .        .
 .        .        .        .        .        .        .
```

If you increase the number of buffers, and the write cache rate still doesn't improve, try raising the values of the LRU_MIN_DIRTY and LRU_MAX_DIRTY parameters. If you raise these values, OnLine lets more dirty pages collect in the modified LRU queue. These pages are then more likely to be used more than once before they're written to disk.

Generally, it's more important to have a good read cache rate than a good write cache rate, because most users associate rapid query response with an efficient system. Users aren't quite so concerned about the system's response during an INSERT, an UPDATE, or a DELETE operation.

In summary, remember that shared memory tuning is an iterative process: you can expect to modify your parameters several times before you reach an optimal configuration. In addition, your system's activity profile might change over time, requiring a new analysis of your OnLine shared memory configuration.

LOCKS

The LOCKS parameter sets the maximum number of locks available to each user on your OnLine system. If a particular user runs out of locks, the "ovlock" counter is incremented. You can monitor this counter by examining the output of "tbstat -p":

```
RSAM Version 5.01.UD1   -- On-Line -- Up 5 days 00:01:16 -- 1200 Kbytes

Profile
 .        .        .        .        .        .        .
 .        .        .        .        .        .        .
ovtbls   ovlock   ovuser   ovbuff   usercpu  syscpu   numckpts flushes
0        63838    0        0        28.23    5.78     5        2700
         ^^^^^
 .        .        .        .        .        .        .
 .        .        .        .        .        .        .
```

Because the "ovlock" counter increments each time a user exceeds the LOCKS parameter, it's easy for this number to get very large.

You can also use the output of "tbstat -u" to locate any users who have exceeded the LOCKS limit:

```
RSAM Version 5.01.UD1   -- On-Line -- Up 4 days 23:59:39 -- 1200 Kbytes

Users
address  flags    pid    user      tty       wait tout locks nreads   nwrites
c005a120 ------D 5322   f         pty/ttyq 0    0    0     196      4
c005a194 ------D 0      f         pty/ttyq 0    0    0     0        0
c005a208 ------F 5323   informix           0    0    0     0        0
c005a27c --B-X-- 26714  db_user   pty/ttyr 0    0    1000  3        8

 4 active, 20 total
```

If you're using 6.00 or newer, you can also check the "syslocks" table in the "sysmaster" database to monitor user consumption of locks. See the "User monitoring" section of this chapter for more detail.

In the above output, the "db_user" is running a transaction that requires more than 1000 locks, which is the amount specified in this installation's LOCKS parameter. OnLine halts the user's transaction, and begins a rollback.

You can monitor the contents of your OnLine message log with the "tbstat -m" command. If a user's process exceeds the lock limit, you'll see a message like this in the message log:

```
11:43:04  Lock table overflow - user id 151, process id   26714
```

Since setting this parameter higher has a minimal impact on shared memory, don't be afraid to specify a large number. Note that there are certain types of situations where no matter how many locks you define, you'll still run out. For more information on how to handle these types of problems, see the "Concurrency" sub-section of the "General tips" section.

USERS

This parameter controls the number of users that OnLine allows to connect to the database. In version 5.0x and earlier, you set this value via the USERS parameter in the TBCONFIG file. In version 6.00 and newer, the concept of users has changed. Users are now counted as user threads, instead of actual operating system-level users.

If you exceed the available number of users, you'll see this type of message in your OnLine message log:

```
11:51:10  User table overflow - user id 151, process id 26884
```

You can track this kind of error using "tbstat -t" as well:

```
RSAM Version 5.01.UD1   -- On-Line -- Up 00:35:51 -- 1200 Kbytes

Profile
```

```
   .          .          .          .          .          .          .
   .          .          .          .          .          .          .
ovtbls    ovlock    ovuser    ovbuff    usercpu   syscpu    numckpts
flushes
0         0         10        0         0.05      0.07      2         7
                    ^^^^^
   .          .          .          .          .          .          .
   .          .          .          .          .          .          .
```

From an optimization standpoint, setting a high USERS/USERTHREADS value doesn't consume much additional shared memory. Therefore, it's better to "waste" some shared memory to avoid a situation where a user (or user thread) attempts to connect to the database and fails.

Also, remember when setting these parameters that certain OnLine overhead users/threads, such as page cleaners and the tbinit demon, also count as users/threads.

TABLESPACES

The TBLSPACES parameter in your TBCONFIG file sets the maximum number of OnLine tables that can be open at any one time. This includes system tables and temporary tables. Just as the USERS and LOCKS parameters don't have much of an impact on shared memory, there is little additional shared memory cost in setting a relatively high TBLSPACES value.

You can use the "tbstat -p" command to determine if you've exceeded the TBLSPACES value:

```
RSAM Version 5.01.UD1    -- On-Line -- Up 12 days 03:14:16 -- 1489 Kbytes

Profile
   .          .          .          .          .          .          .
   .          .          .          .          .          .          .
ovtbls    ovlock    ovuser    ovbuff    usercpu   syscpu    numckpts flushes
200         0       0         0         50.32     6.99      12         9809
^^^
   .          .          .          .          .          .          .
   .          .          .          .          .          .          .
```

PAGE CLEANERS

Page cleaners are responsible for an important job: flushing the shared memory buffer pool to disk. This action is part of the process of permanently saving modified data. It also frees up space in the buffer pool so OnLine can place new pages of information into shared memory. In this section, we examine several page cleaner issues, including configuring and tuning page cleaners and LRU queues. We also discuss how to handle page cleaner time-outs.

Number of page cleaners

OnLine always uses at least one page cleaner. For one disk drive environment, this is fine. If you have multiple disk drives, however, consider allocating one page cleaner per disk controller. Remember that some hardware configurations can have more than one disk per controller. In that case, don't set the number of page cleaners to be exactly equal to the number of disk drives supported by all your controllers. Instead, allocate a maximum of only two page cleaners per controller. Let's look at an example to further explain this concept. Suppose that you're administering a large database system. You have six disk drives that are managed by two controllers, as illustrated in Figure 4.4:

Figure 4.4

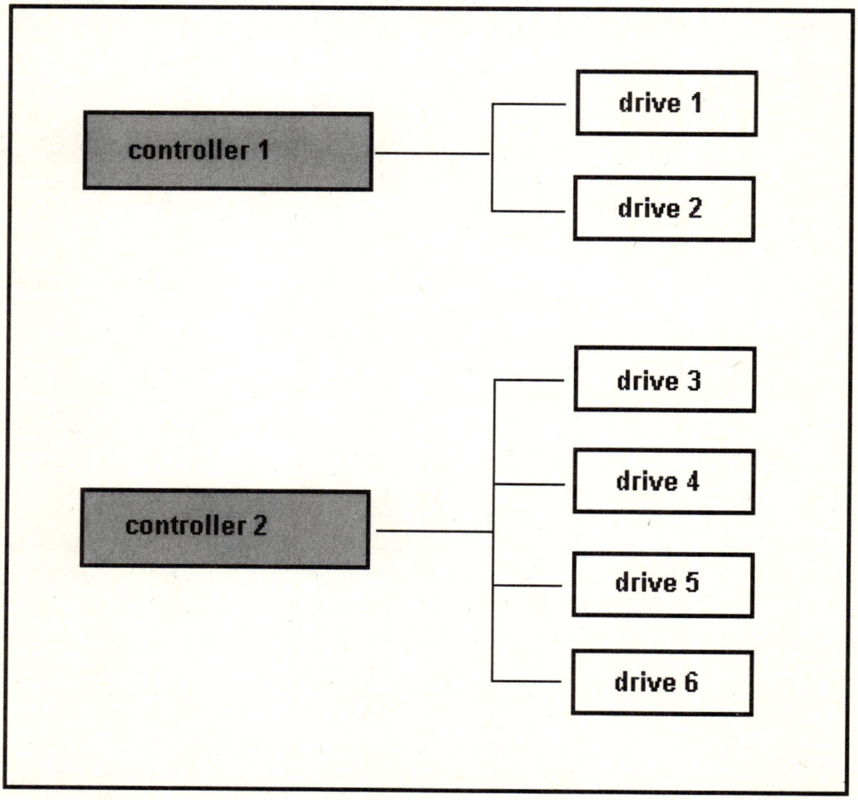

In the above example, you'd set the CLEANERS parameter in the TBCONFIG file to be five. The reason that you choose five is that your system has six disk drives, but controller 2 manages four drives. Generally, you can expect performance to degrade if you assign more than three page cleaners per controller. Therefore, the formula to set the number of page cleaners looks like this:

```
controller 1:    2 cleaners
     +
controller 2:    3 cleaners
                ----
       Total:    5 cleaners
```

Remember that the maximum number of page cleaners that you can choose is 32.

LRU queues

LRU queues are linked lists of buffers. Each LRU queue is actually two linked lists: one list of modified buffers (MLRU) and one list of free or unmodified buffers (FLRU). OnLine uses these queues to determine which pages should be flushed to disk, and when. The number of LRU queues is determined by the LRUS parameter from your TBCONFIG file. OnLine apportions the buffers between LRU queues by dividing the number of shared memory pool buffers (specified by the BUFFERS parameter) by the LRUS parameter. This yields an equal amount of buffers for each queue. With regard to page cleaners, if there is more than one page cleaner, OnLine divides the LRU queues among all of the page cleaners.

As an administrator, you're limited to an LRUS setting between 3 and 32. Generally, you can accept the default as specified in your TBCONFIG file. Like many other OnLine parameters, however, feel free to experiment with different values. Remember to change only one OnLine parameter at a time; otherwise, you have no way to know exactly which change affected performance (for better or worse).

Page cleaner parameters

Two important page cleaner parameters are LRU_MAX_DIRTY and LRU_MIN_DIRTY. These parameters instruct the page cleaners at what point to start (LRU_MAX_DIRTY) page cleaning, and at what point to finish (LRU_MIN_DIRTY) page cleaning. For example, if you set LRU_MAX_DIRTY to 30, and LRU_MIN_DIRTY to 20, this instructs the page cleaners to "wake up" whenever the percentage of "dirty" buffers is 30 or more. The cleaners continue to work, flushing buffers until the percentage of dirty buffers is 20 or less. At that point, the cleaners halt execution until the next time that they're needed.

OnLine defaults to an LRU_MAX_DIRTY of 60, and an LRU_MIN_DIRTY of 50. There are many cases, however, where you should change these numbers to improve performance. You can use the results of "tbstat -F" to help you set these parameters. Let's use an example to demonstrate this concept.

Page cleaner time-outs

You may notice, from time to time, the following message in your OnLine system log:

```
11:34:22 Page cleaner 0x2 timed out
```

This indicates that a page cleaner has not been able to finish its work in time. OnLine allocates 120 seconds (two minutes) for a page cleaner to do its work. If more than 120 seconds passes, the page cleaner times out. This is one of the best indications that your page cleaners need to perform frequent, but relatively small amounts of work, rather than infrequent, large amounts of work. The best way to achieve this result is to set the LRU_MAX_DIRTY and LRU_MIN_DIRTY parameters low enough so that the page cleaners are frequently active. Lower settings for these parameters also help keep checkpoint time down. See the next section of this chapter for more detail about checkpoint control.

CHECKPOINTS

Checkpoints are the mechanisms that OnLine uses to synchronize memory and disks. During a checkpoint, OnLine takes these steps:

1. User processes "halt", for example, they cannot enter any critical sections of shared memory.
2. The physical log shared memory buffer is written to the physical log on disk.
3. A chunk write flushes pages from shared memory onto disk.
4. A record of this checkpoint is written into the logical log buffer.
5. The disk-based physical log is cleared.
6. The memory-based logical log buffer is written to the current logical log.
7. The page cleaner updates the OnLine reserved pages with a record of this checkpoint.

OnLine initiates a checkpoint if any of the following conditions occur:

- The physical log reaches 75 percent of capacity.
- The number of seconds specified by the tbconfig CKPTINTVL parameter elapses.
- You request a checkpoint by issuing a "tbmode -c" command.
- The next logical log contains the last checkpoint record.
- A new chunk or dbspace is added.
- You perform an archive.

Note that checkpoints only occur if there is system activity. Even if you request a checkpoint every five minutes (CKPTINTVL = 300), OnLine won't perform a checkpoint if there are no data modifications.

From a user's perspective, a checkpoint can be a frustrating event, because the user's process appears to "freeze." Recall that during a checkpoint, OnLine blocks user processes from entering critical sections of shared memory. Only after the checkpoint completes can the user processes continue. It's a good idea to try to speed up the checkpoint process, especially if your system is interactive in nature (e.g., not heavily batch-oriented). There are a number of steps that you can take to achieve this goal:

- **Make sure that checkpoints occur frequently enough.** If a great deal of time elapses between checkpoints, there's a good chance that each checkpoint will be slow. Generally, you shouldn't let more than 10 minutes elapse (600 seconds). Most OnLine sites use the default value of 5 minutes (300 seconds).
- **Reduce the amount of work that the checkpoint needs to perform.** Before OnLine 6.00, it wasn't easy to tell how long a checkpoint took. With version 6.00, OnLine now logs the length of checkpoints in the message file: 15:11:14 Checkpoint Completed: duration was 5 seconds

  If you notice that checkpoints are taking more than 10 to 20 seconds to complete, you'll probably benefit from reducing the amount of work that the checkpoint performs.

  Since most of the labor entailed in a checkpoint involves flushing the shared memory buffer pool to disk, try to reduce the number of pages that need to be flushed to disk. The best way to achieve this is by letting the page cleaners work harder between checkpoints. See the "Page cleaners" section of this chapter for more information.

  One caveat regarding reducing the amount of work during checkpoints: Checkpoint disk writes are more efficient because OnLine writes consecutive, sorted pages to disk. This reduces the amount of I/O, which does have a positive impact on performance. Outside of a checkpoint, on the other hand, OnLine doesn't sort and write pages, which leads to somewhat higher levels of I/O.

PARALLEL SORTING

On multiprocessor machines, OnLine uses a parallel sorting package to greatly improve sorting performance. OnLine uses the parallel sorting package if any of the following conditions exist:

- Sort/merge join
- SELECT DISTINCT or SELECT UNIQUE queries
- ORDER BY

OnLine version 6.0 and later uses parallel sorting for these additional conditions:

- Index building
- UPDATE STATISTICS MEDIUM or HIGH

If you are sorting a small number of rows, or if you already have an index in place for an ORDER BY, OnLine won't use the parallel sorting package, since it probably wouldn't improve performance very much.

There are two environment variables that you should set to guide the parallel sorting utility: PSORT_NPROCS and PSORT_DBTEMP. If you set these environment variables on a uniprocessor machine, OnLine will simply ignore them.

PSORT_NPROCS tells the parallel sorting package how many processes to use during a sort. If you don't set this variable, the default value is three. The maximum value for PSORT_NPROCS is 10. Regardless of how high you set this value, OnLine may still use fewer processes if the sorting task is relatively small. This is because OnLine only dedicates a process for a minimum of 50 data pages.

For OnLine version 6.0 and later, the PSORT_NPROCS parameter refers to the number of threads, not the number of processes.

The PSORT_DBTEMP environment variable specifies where OnLine is to write intermediate files during the sorting process. You can use multiple directories by separating them with a colon:

```
setenv PSORT_DBTEMP /tmp:/usr/tmp
```

You can improve performance by setting PSORT_DBTEMP to use the fastest disk drives on your system. If you have a device that is actually in memory instead of on disk, try using it as the PSORT_DBTEMP directory. If you don't set PSORT_DBTEMP, OnLine uses the dbspaces and directories set by the DBSPACETEMP environment variable.

There is another sorting environment variable that applies to both uni- and multiprocessor machines. The PSORT_MAXALLOC variable sets the maximum amount of memory that a user can have during a sort. See the "SQL tips" section for more information about this variable.

Spinning

On uniprocessor machines, OnLine uses a "test-and-set" algorithm to determine if a resource is available. If the resource is available, the process sets a latch. If it is not available, the requesting process sleeps, and periodically awakens to retry the test-and-set operation.

For single processor machines, this is the most efficient way to handle shared resource requests. On multiprocessors, however, a requesting process could be resident in a different CPU. Instead of context switching, sleeping, and then retrying, it is more efficient for the process to remain resident in the CPU. The requesting process could then keep retrying: chances are that the requested resource will be available momentarily.

Many versions of UNIX support this concept; it is called "spinning." When a process "spins", it does not switch out of the CPU. Instead, it continually loops and retries its request. The number of times that it loops can be controlled by the SPINCNT parameter.

The SPINCNT parameter is found in your "tbconfig" file. You can only modify this value by editing the file; you cannot use the "tbmonitor" utility. The default value is 300. This means that OnLine will spin and test 300 times before giving up and switching out of the CPU. As with any other parameters, feel free to experiment with different settings.

If you have a uniprocessor machine, OnLine ignores this parameter, even though SPINCNT is present in the "tbconfig" file.

Virtual processor configuration

Before OnLine 6.00, Informix used a two-process architecture to communicate between front-end applications and the database. This meant that for every user that accessed the database, the "tbinit" demon started a "sqlturbo" process. The "sqlturbo" process then directly accessed the internal database structures.

With OnLine 6.00, Informix de-coupled the front-end and back-end processes. There is no longer a one-to-one correlation between front-end processes and "sqlturbo" processes. In fact, there are no longer any "sqlturbo" processes. OnLine now uses a variety of specialized processes to service database engine operations. These processes are called virtual processors (VP). Each type of virtual processor services a number of database users or tasks, just as the operating system services user sessions. Each of these database tasks is known as a "thread". OnLine is a multi-threaded engine, since it runs multiple threads at one time. You can think of threads as being divided into two major types:

- **Internal threads.** OnLine uses internal threads to perform a number of important tasks, including:

  A. Physical log I/O

  B. Logical log I/O

  C. Network communication

  D. Page flushing

  E. Administration

- **User threads.** When a user connects to OnLine, the engine starts a user thread. The most common user threads are called session threads. Session threads are labeled "sqlexec". User threads also encompass threads to service "onmode" and "onmonitor". While most user applications are serviced by only one user thread, there are some instances where OnLine runs multiple parallel session threads, including:

  – Joining

  – Sorting

- Grouping
- Indexing
- Data recovery

This new architecture results in faster OnLine performance for several reasons, including:

- **Reduced number of UNIX processes.** Overall, OnLine can now perform well with fewer UNIX processes, since there is no longer a one-to-one correlation between front-end and back-end processes. This means that UNIX no longer needs to juggle all those "sqlturbo" processes: they have been replaced by only a few VP processes.
- **Better process control.** OnLine is a much better judge of which threads need priority than the UNIX kernel. There is now much less operating system-level context switching; OnLine handles its own process control by switching between threads when appropriate. Only the VPs themselves are subject to system-level context switching, unless you've specified processor affinity (see below).
- **Parallel operations.** Since OnLine can start parallel threads for certain operations, these operations take significantly less time to complete. This is especially evident on multi-processor computers.
- **Dynamic load management.** You can start or stop additional VPs as your system's load increases or decreases. You don't need to shut the database down to make these changes.
- **Processor affinity.** If you're running on certain multi-processor computers, you can request that CPU VPs be bound to system CPUs. This means that the system CPU spends 100% of its time servicing the VP, often leading to substantial performance gains.

To track current thread utilization, run "onstat -g tpf":

RSAM Version 6.00.UC2 -- On-Line -- Up 3 days 06:56:14 -- 10048 Kbytes

Thread profiles

tid	lkreqs	lkw	dl	to	lgrs	isrd	iswr	isrw	isdl	isct	isrb	lx	bfr	bfw	lsus	lsmx	seq
0	0	0	0	0	15	0	0	0	0	0	0	0	175	131	1584	0	0
0	0	0	0	0	0	0	0	0	0	0	0	0	0	0	0	0	0
0	17	0	0	0	0	0	0	0	0	0	0	0	13	5	0	0	0
0	0	0	0	0	0	0	0	0	0	0	0	0	0	0	0	0	0
2833	8275	0	0	0	0	6098	0	2077	0	0	0	0	2384	2077	0	0	1
2702	61	0	0	0	0	27600	0	0	0	0	0	0	1082	0	0	0	1
1488	1991	0	0	0	14	1889	1859	0	0	0	0	0	9660	3810	420	0	1
2899	0	0	0	0	0	0	0	0	0	0	0	0	0	0	0	0	0

2799	7854	0	0	0	0	7815	7776	0	0	0	0	0	8543	7957	0	0	2
2800	64	0	0	0	9	10228	2916	0	0	0	0	0	3436	3003	360	0	1
2896	178	0	0	0	0	139	100	0	0	0	0	0	240	103	0	0	2
897	4384	0	0	0	40	4186	4156	0	0	0	0	0	21538	8646	1200	0	1
2898	65	0	0	0	0	30	0	1	0	0	0	0	84	1	0	0	0
612	17457	0	0	0	16	17227	17186	0	0	0	0	0	87781	35175	480	0	2

Let's look at each type of VP, including how you can tune each one most efficiently. If you're interested in more detail about multi-threading, VPs, or OnLine's internal architecture, see the *Informix OnLine DSA Administrators Guide*.

CPU VP

CPU VPs are responsible for user interaction with the database. They can also perform disk I/O operations, except in the case of physical or logical logging, which are handled by the PIO and LIO classes of VP, respectively. The only exception to this rule occurs on machines that have kernel asynchronous I/O capabilities. On these machines, the CPU VP handles all I/O, including physical and logical logging. You can tell if your machine has kernel asynchronous I/O by checking the release notes in the "$INFORMIXDIR/release" directory.

If your computer has only one CPU, you only need one CPU VP. Once you have multiple system CPUs, you can add more CPU VPs. Generally, your goal on multi-CPU machines should be to define one less CPU VP than system CPU. You can monitor OnLine's CPU VP usage by running the "onstat" command, with a parameter of "-g glo":

```
RSAM Version 6.00.UC2   -- On-Line -- Up 3 days 06:52:55 -- 10048 Kbytes

MT global info:
sessions threads  vps      lngspins
9        25       10       0

Virtual processor summary:
class    vps      usercpu        syscpu        total
 cpu       1       360.37          3.79        364.16
 aio       2         7.51         14.99         22.50
 pio       1         0.07          1.32          1.39
 lio       1         0.03          0.17          0.20
 soc       3         3.28          3.53          6.81
 tli       0         0.00          0.00          0.00
 shm       0         0.00          0.00          0.00
 adm       1         0.00          0.00          0.00
 opt       0         0.00          0.00          0.00
 msc       1         0.00          0.02          0.02
 adt       0         0.00          0.00          0.00
 total    10       371.26         23.82        395.08

Individual virtual processors:
vp       pid         class    usercpu       syscpu        total
 1       11188        cpu     360.37         3.79        364.16
 2       11189        adm       0.00         0.00          0.00
```

```
3      11190     lio      0.03     0.17     0.20
4      11191     pio      0.07     1.32     1.39
5      11192     aio      3.99     7.61    11.60
6      11193     msc      0.00     0.02     0.02
7      11194     aio      3.52     7.38    10.90
8      11195     soc      1.21     1.57     2.78
9      11196     soc      1.41     1.29     2.70
10     11197     soc      0.66     0.67     1.33
                 tot    371.26    23.82   395.08
```

You can get the same information from the "sysmaster" database, by querying the "sysvpprof" table.

Remember that you can always add and remove CPU VPs, even while your system is running, so don't be afraid to experiment.

AIO VPs

AIO VPs handle asynchronous I/O on those machines that don't have kernel asynchronous I/O, or in OnLine instances using cooked files. It's the job of the AIO VPs to ensure that the I/O queues for each chunk are being serviced efficiently.

How many AIO VPs should you set up? The answer depends on whether your machine supports kernel asynchronous I/O, along with whether or not you're using cooked files. You can use this method to arrive at a number:

```
Does your machine support asynchronous kernel I/O?
if yes then
   are you using any cooked files?
   if yes then
      set up two AIO VPs for each dbspace that is composed
          of cooked files.
   else
      you only need one AIO VP.
   end if
else
   allocate two AIO VPs for each disk.
end if
```

Keep in mind that it's not a major problem if you define too many AIO VPs. You can always reduce the number the next time you bring OnLine down.

PIO VPs (Physical log I/O)

PIO VPs handle all of the physical log's I/O if the system doesn't use kernel asynchronous I/O, or if the physical log resides in a cooked file. If your physical log is mirrored, OnLine runs two PIO VPs; otherwise, it runs one.

LIO VPs (Logical log I/O)

Just as PIO VPs handle all physical log I/O, LIOs handle all logical log I/O on systems that don't use kernel asynchronous I/O, or have their logical logs in a cooked file. Again, OnLine runs two LIO VPs if the logs are mirrored, and one if they are not.

You can track the cumulative activity of all of the AIO class VPs by running "onstat -g ioq":

```
RSAM Version 6.00.UC2   -- On-Line -- Up 3 days 06:51:56 -- 10048 Kbytes

AIO I/O queues:
class/hvp-id len maxlen totalops  dskread dskwrite  dskcopy
  msc    0     0      1       10        0        0        0
  aio    0     0    137    21556    16687     4869        0
  aio    1     0    137    19105    15110     3995        0
  pio    0     0      1      299        0      299        0
  lio    0     0      1      148        0      148        0
```

Networking VPs

In earlier versions of OnLine, the "sqlexecd" process was responsible for listening for client connections, and then starting "sqlturbo" back-end processes. With OnLine 6.00, networking virtual processors handle these tasks, instead. You can connect to OnLine using one of the following protocols:

- **TCP/IP using sockets.** The SOC VP handles this protocol.
- **TCP/IP using Transport Level Interface (TLI).** The TLI VP services this protocol.
- **Sequenced Packet Exchange (SPX) using TLI.** The TLI VP services this protocol as well.
- **Directly, via shared memory (for local clients only).** The SHM VP services these types of connections.

OnLine starts poll threads for each network protocol that you have enabled on your computer. You can use these VPs to run the poll threads, or you can let the CPU VP do this work. The CPU VP is the default VP; this is fine for most single processor computers. If you're running on a multiprocessor machine, especially if there's heavy network traffic, request that OnLine start up an appropriate network VP.

The "onstat" utility provides many important statistics regarding networking threads. For example, the following sample output is from "onstat -g ntu", which shows network user thread profile information:

```
RSAM Version 6.00.UC2    -- On-Line -- Up 16:56:55 -- 10048 Kbytes

global network information:
  #netscb connects      read     write     q-free  q-limits  q-exceed
  10/  16    45498  1111342  1111364      0/   0   10/  10     0/   0

Individual thread network information (basic):
  netscb type    thread name  sid    fd poll      reads    writes q-nrm q-exp
```

```
c230f860 ipcshm sqlexec      46182    0    0      20       20 -19/ 0   0/ 0
c230b860 ipcshm sqlexec      46181    0    0      22       21 -21/ 0   0/ 0
c2301860 ipcshm sqlexec      46178    0    0      27       27 -26/ 0   0/ 0
c1bee0d8 soctcp soctcplst        8    1    5       0        0   0/ 0   0/ 0
c1be20d8 ipcshm sm_discon        7    0    0       0        0   0/ 0   0/ 0
c05680d8 ipcshm sm_listen        5    0    0   45498        0   0/ 0   0/ 0
c055c0d8 soctcp soctcppoll       4    0    7       0        0   0/ 0   0/ 0
c054e0d8 soctcp soctcppoll       3    0    6       0        0   0/ 0   0/ 0
c05420d8 soctcp soctcppoll       2    0    5       0        0   0/ 0   0/ 0
c05360d8 ipcshm sm_poll          1    0    0   44693        0   0/ 0   0/ 0
```

If you want to track how long each network thread has been active, run the "onstat -g ntt" command:

```
RSAM Version 6.00.UC2    -- On-Line -- Up 17:00:23 -- 10048 Kbytes

global network information:
  #netscb connects      read     write    q-free  q-limits  q-exceed
  10/  16    46613  1141429  1141451     0/   0   10/  10     0/   0

Individual thread network information (times):
  netscb thread name     sid      open      read     write address

c1e47860 sqlexec      47297 13:55:03 13:55:04 13:55:04

c1e43860 sqlexec      47296 13:55:03 13:55:04 13:55:04

c1e27860 sqlexec      47295 13:55:03 13:55:04 13:55:04
  .       .             .      .        .        .
  .       .             .      .        .        .
```

If you're interested in overall network thread dispatch statistics, run "onstat -g ntd":

```
RSAM Version 6.00.UC2    -- On-Line -- Up 17:03:16 -- 10048 Kbytes

global network information:
  #netscb connects      read     write    q-free  q-limits  q-exceed
  13/  16    47591  1167797  1167816     0/   0   10/  10     0/   0

Client Type      Calls    Accepted   Rejected       Read       Write
sqlexec          yes         47578       1333    1117732     1165345
srvinfx          yes             0          0          0           0
onspace          yes             0          0          0           0
onlog            yes             0          0          0           0
onparam          yes             0          0          0           0
oncheck          yes             0          0          0           0
onload           yes             0          0          0           0
onunload         yes             0          0          0           0
onmonitor        yes             1          0         27          27
dr_accept        yes             0          0          0           0
ontape           yes             6          0       1767        1773
srvstat          yes             6          0          6          12
asfecho          yes             0          0          0           0
listener         yes             0          0      48265         659
Totals                       47591       1333    1167797     1167816
```

Logging

When you place a database into service, you need to decide whether or not to use transaction logging. Transaction logging is a substantial ingredient in OnLine's data integrity strategy. Regardless of the method you choose for transaction logging (and even if you don't use transaction logging at all), OnLine always records any of the following types of events into the logical log:

- **Archives.** When you create an archive, or restore from an archive, OnLine tracks this event in the logical log.
- **Logging status change for a database.** When you change the logging mode for a database (from buffered logging to unbuffered logging, for example), OnLine makes an entry into the logical log.
- **Checkpoints.** Whenever OnLine performs a checkpoint, it writes a record into the logical log.
- **Configuration changes.** If you add a chunk, dbspace, or blobspace, OnLine notes it in the logical log.
- **SQL data definition language.** OnLine makes an entry in the log whenever you issue any DDL statements. These types of statements include CREATE, ALTER, DROP, and RENAME.

For more information on the benefits of transaction logging, see the "Transaction logging" sub-section of the "General tips" section. When you use transaction logging, OnLine also records SQL data manipulation language (DML). Once you decide to use transaction logging for an OnLine database, your next decision is what type of logging to use.

BUFFERED LOGGING

When you use buffered logging for a database, OnLine retains the logical log statements in the logical log buffer until one of a series of events forces the engine to flush them to disk. For more information on which events force a logical log buffer flush, see the "Logical log buffer size" section of this chapter.

Buffered logging's best feature is its rapid performance. By buffering the logical log records in memory, OnLine can avoid a certain amount of relatively expensive disk I/O. The main drawback to buffered logging is the chance that you might lose some already-committed transactions if OnLine goes down before it flushes the logical log buffer.

We can illustrate how OnLine uses I/O more efficiently with buffered logging. In this example, a simple ESQL/C program inserts rows into a table. After every 100 rows, the program issues a COMMIT WORK command, and begins a new transaction.

For the database that uses buffered logging, the results of "tbstat -l" look like this:

```
RSAM Version 5.01.UD1   -- On-Line -- Up 00:10:13 -- 2736 Kbytes

Logical Logging
Buffer bufused  bufsize  numrecs  numpages numwrits recs/pages pages/io
  L-1  8        16       33821    2557     2229     13.2       1.1
```

Notice how OnLine is able to write 13.2 log records per page. Compare this with the number of log records per page that OnLine is able to achieve in the unbuffered logging example.

UNBUFFERED LOGGING

When you instruct OnLine to use unbuffered logging for a database, it writes the contents of the logical log buffer to disk as soon as you issue a COMMIT WORK statement. This supplies you with a higher level of data integrity, at the cost of slightly degraded performance, and increased logical log consumption. The performance degradation mainly arises from OnLine's continual flushing of the logical log buffer, even if some pages are only partially filled. Since OnLine is flushing the log buffer more frequently, you'll also notice that your logical logs fill up faster. This can have some impact on your operational environment.

Using the example from the buffered logging section, look at the output of "tbstat -l":

```
RSAM Version 5.01.UD1   -- On-Line -- Up 00:09:44 -- 2736 Kbytes


Logical Logging
Buffer bufused  bufsize  numrecs  numpages numwrits recs/pages pages/io
  L-2  0        16       6062     1990     1989     3.0        1.0
```

For the identical program, OnLine is only able to place three records on each log page. This is the most significant cost of unbuffered logging.

In the end, it's your decision whether to use buffered or unbuffered logging. If you cannot tolerate any data loss if the server goes down and are willing to pay a slight performance price, use unbuffered logging. If speed is more important than potentially losing a few transactions (as in a decision support system, for example), then use buffered logging to squeeze as much speed as possible from the server. Note that if you designate a database to conform to mode-ANSI, it automatically uses unbuffered logging.

Finally, if you're using distributed database processing, be aware that all the databases within an operation need to have the same logging mode. This means that you can't work with a database that uses buffered logging at the same time you're working with a database that uses unbuffered logging.

Key-only reads

If you request data that is already stored in an index, OnLine returns your information directly from the index, instead of using the index to locate the data within the table. This reduces the amount of I/O that the engine needs to perform, and can be useful to you in certain situations.

For example, suppose you're writing a query to read information from the "sales_calls" table. In this case, you only want to retrieve the "city" column, which is one of the columns in an index. The results of the SET EXPLAIN command are as follows:

```
QUERY:
------
select city from sales_calls

Estimated Cost: 2
Estimated # of Rows Returned: 10

   1) db_user.sales_calls: INDEX PATH

      (1) Index Keys: city appt_date (Key-Only)
```

The "Key-Only" message in the output tells you that OnLine only went as far as the index to return your data. Also note that "city" was only one of two columns in the index, yet OnLine still used the index to return the information.

Regardless of which engine you use, it's always a good idea to select only the columns that you need. If you're using OnLine, key-only reads are an added benefit of this type of strategy. For more details on why you should keep your SELECT statements as focused as possible, see the "Reducing pipe traffic" sub-section of the "General tips" section.

Setting sqlturbo priority

Recall that prior to version 6.00, OnLine used a two-process architecture, consisting of a front-end process that communicated via named pipes to a back-end sqlturbo process. Generally, the sqlturbo process is the most resource-consuming process in an Informix database application. The sqlturbo process is no different than any other UNIX process; this means that you can use the "nice" command to alter the priority of a particular sqlturbo. For more information about this command, see the documentation for your UNIX operating system.

Be aware that this feature isn't present in OnLine 6.00 or newer, since the newer database servers no longer use the two-process architecture.

Parallel archiving and restoring

One of the most time-consuming tasks that database administrators perform is data archiving and retrieval.

If you're using OnLine 6.00 or newer, you can use the "onarchive" utility to archive and restore dbspaces in parallel. This often greatly reduces the amount of time that you must spend backing up or restoring data, whether or not you have a multiprocessor machine. "onarchive" is a powerful, complex utility that requires careful planning to use most efficiently. If you want more detailed information about this utility, see the *Informix OnLine DSA Archive and Backup Guide*. Let's look at a simple example that shows how you can use this utility to help streamline the data-archiving process.

Suppose that you have eight disk drives that you've divided into sixteen dbspaces:

```
drive one       drive two       drive three     drive four

rootdbs         physdbs         logdbs          datadbs4
datadbs1        datadbs2        datadbs3        datadbs5


drive five      drive six       drive seven     drive eight

datadbs6        datadbs7        datadbs8        datadbs9
tempdbs1        tempdbs2        tempdbs3        datadbs10
```

You also have two tape drives that you can dedicate to concurrent data backup. Before we discuss how to back up data in parallel, let's first define some important terms:

- **Volume set (VSET).** A volume set is composed of individual volumes that are usually linked to one tape drive.
- **Volume.** A volume is a unit of media that you plan to use to store data. While you can define both magnetic tapes and disk drives as volumes, for the purposes of our discussion, assume that it is a tape.
- **Dbspaceset.** Dbspacesets are groups of dbspaces that "onarchive" processes together.

In this example, you would perform these steps to back up data in parallel:

1. Create two volume sets, and assign one volume set to each tape drive.
2. Define two volumes, and assign one volume per volume set.
3. Create two dbspacesets. Assign an equal number of dbspaces to each dbspaceset. To speed up the archive, you can omit any temporary dbspaces from the dbspacesets, since you would never need to restore a temporary dbspace.
4. Submit two archive requests. Assign one dbspaceset for each volume set.

You can now execute both requests at the same time, using the "onarchive" virtual operator (autovop). This is much faster than executing the requests serially.

If you need to restore data, you can also perform this task in parallel. Since minimizing data restoration time is usually critical, this can be very helpful.

If you're using OnLine 7.00 or newer, remember that you don't need to back up dbspaces that contain only indexes; you can always rebuild indexes after restoring data.

Advanced user monitoring

Prior to OnLine 6.00, administrators faced a difficult challenge when trying to determine the exact database operations occurring at any one time. With OnLine 6.00, you can now monitor individual user sessions and track their SQL statements. To do this, use the “onstat” command. Let's look at how you can employ this utility to track user activity.

In this case, suppose that you're receiving complaints from several users that the system is running very slowly. How do you proceed?

First, get an overall picture of OnLine's performance by running the “onstat” utility, with the “-p” option:

```
RSAM Version 6.00.UC2    -- On-Line -- Up 4 days 04:44:47 -- 10048 Kbytes

Profile
dskreads pagreads bufreads %cached dskwrits pagwrits bufwrits %cached
31928    32450    792698   95.97   4391     6373     481771   99.09

isamtot  open     start    read     write    rewrite  delete   commit   rollbk
6267160  13726    53397    2646459  444969   13117    686      535      0

ovtbls   ovlock   ovuserthread ovbuff   usercpu  syscpu   numckptsflushes
0        0        0            0        667.89   25.48    18       2407

bufwaits lokwaits lockreqs deadlks  dltouts  ckpwaits compress seqscans
44       0        242706   0        0        12       504      486

ixda-RA  idx-RA   da-RA    RA-pgsused lchreqs  lchwaits
179      0        28943    28532      2744857  58
```

These numbers don't show any particular problems. The next step is to get a list of current user sessions, by running “onstat - u”:

```
RSAM Version 6.00.UC2    -- On-Line -- Up 4 days 05:07:24 -- 10048 Kbytes

Userthreads
address  flags   sessid   user     tty      wait     tout locks nreads   nwrites

c03ab0c8 ---P--D 0        informix -        0        0    0     92       65
c03ab430 ---P--F 0        informix -        0        0    0     0        0
c03ab798 ---P--B 10       informix -        0        0    0     17       11
c03abb00 ---P--D 0        informix -        0        0    0     0        0
c03ac1d0 ---P--- 5260     soupdog  -        0        0    1     454      0
c03ad640 ---P--- 5508     dktrdre  -        0        0    0     0        0
c03add10 ---P--- 5273     manni    -        0        0    2     382      124
c03ae078 ---P--- 5509     mojak    -        0        0    0     0        0
c03ae748 B--PX-- 5291     warung   -        c03e12d8 0    3     232      144
c03aeab0 B--PX-- 4778     sidneyv  -        c03e12d8 0    3     2951     2583
c03aee18 --BP--- 5285     sammy    -        0        0    2     330      290
c03af180 --BPR-- 5259     howards  -        0        0    2     461      100
 12 active, 20 total
```

You can use all of the preceding commands for earlier versions of OnLine as well. With OnLine 6.00 and newer, you have much more diagnostic power at your disposal, because you can now monitor individual sessions. Let's look at some sample output from the “onstat -g ses” command, which displays information about current sessions:

```
RSAM Version 6.00.UC2    -- On-Line -- Up 4 days 05:11:16 -- 10048 Kbytes

session                                      #RSAM    total       used
id        user     tty       pid   hostname threads  memory      memory
6499      informix -         0     -        0        8192        6040
6498      jeromes  -         21311 newyork  1        16384       12152
6497      florencs -         21310 newyork  1        16384       12152
6398      melanieb -         21210 newyork  1        155648      141344
6372      kenz     -         21180 newyork  1        32768       25960
6286      sharonz  -         21092 newyork  1        32768       25920
9         informix -         0     -        0        8192        6040
```

```
8         informix -         0    -     0          8192         6904
7         informix -         0    -     0          8192         4848
5         informix -         0    -     0          8192         6832
4         informix -         0    -     0          8192         4848
3         informix -         0    -     0          8192         4848
2         informix -         0    -     0          8192         4848
1         informix -         0    -     0          8192         4848
```

We can get more detailed statistics for an individual session by providing a session ID with the "onstat -g ses" command:

```
session                                   #RSAM    total      used
id       user     tty      pid   hostname threads  memory     memory
6372     kenz     -        21180 newyork  1        32768      25960

tid      name     rstcb    flags    curstk   status
276      sqlexec  c03ac1d0 --BPX--  33936    running

Memory pools    count 1
name          class addr     totalsize freesize #allocfrag #freefrag
260           V     c099e010 32768     6848     82         5

name           free       used          name           free       used
overhead       0          128           scb            0          40
opentable      0          3160          filetable      0          584
ru             0          224           misc           0          24
log            0          2120          temprec        840        1608
ralloc         600        4160          gentcb         0          136
ostcb          0          1552          net            0          2968
sqscb          72         6256          sql            240        0
rdahead        5096       0             hashfiletab    0          56
osenv          0          832           buft_buffer    0          2072

Sess  SQL            Current             Iso Lock        SQL  ISAM F.E.
Id    Stmt type      Database            Lvl Mode        ERR  ERR  Vers
6372  SELECT INTO    sample              NL  Not Wait    0    0    6.00

Current SQL statement :
  select * from transactions where trans_amount between 100 and 500 into
 temp daily_log

Last parsed SQL statement :
  select * from transactions where trans_amount between 100 and 500 into
 temp daily_log
```

Another approach that you can take to learn more about user sessions is to run "onstat -g sql", which lists all current SQL statements:

```
RSAM Version 6.00.UC2   -- On-Line -- Up 4 days 05:01:39 -- 10048 Kbytes

Sess  SQL            Current             Iso Lock        SQL  ISAM F.E.
Id    Stmt type      Database            Lvl Mode        ERR  ERR  Vers
4778  INSERT         traffic             NL  Wait 20     0    0    6.00
4755  SELECT         complaints          NL  Not Wait    0    0    6.00
4594  UPDATE         sample              NL  Wait 20     0    0    6.00
4560  SELECT INTO    admin               NL  Not Wait    0    0    6.00
4272  DELETE         sample              NL  Wait 20     0    0    6.00
```

Just as providing a session number to the "onstat -g ses" command gives more detail about the session, specifying a session number when running "onstat -g sql" shows you more detail about the session's current SQL:

```
RSAM Version 6.00.UC2    -- On-Line -- Up 4 days 05:17:15 -- 10048 Kbytes

Sess  SQL             Current             Iso Lock       SQL  ISAM F.E.
Id    Stmt type       Database            Lvl Mode       ERR  ERR  Vers
4594  UPDATE          sample              NL  Wait 20    0    0    6.00

Current SQL statement :
  update transactions set trans_amount = trans_amount + (trans_amount * .02)
 where trans_id between 500 and 6500

Last parsed SQL statement :
  update transactions set trans_amount = trans_amount + (trans_amount * .02)
 where trans_id between 500 and 6500
```

Armed with this information, you can now determine which SQL statements are causing your system's delays. For example, you could run SET EXPLAIN on the preceding SQL statement to see what kind of query plan the optimizer produces for this operation. You could then use the query plan as a guide to speed up the query.

You can also run many useful queries against the "sysmaster" database. Let's look at one query that can help determine which users are holding locks.

In this example, your users are complaining that their transactions are failing with locked record error messages. You can use the following query to see which users are currently holding locks:

```
SELECT TABNAME,
       ROWIDLK,
       TYPE,
       OWNER,
       USERNAME
FROM   SYSLOCKS L,
       SYSSESSIONS S
WHERE  L.OWNER = S.SID
ORDER BY TABNAME, OWNER;
```

```
tabname                rowidlk type       owner username

_temptable                   0 X          18534 mtaub
accounts                 10496 X          19086 jtusa
accounts                     0 IX         19088 szlot
accounts                 11008 X          19089 jmigdal
accounts                     0 IX         19090 stseng
sales_calls                  0 IX         19088 szlot
sales_calls              79360 X          19090 stseng
sysdatabases               513 S          18534 mtaub
sysdatabases               514 S          19086 jtusa
sysdatabases               514 S          19088 szlot
sysdatabases               514 S          19089 jmigdal
sysdatabases               514 S          19090 stseng
    .                        . .              .    .
    .                        . .              .    .
```

You can construct a library of dozens of different administrative queries that use the "sysmaster" database to locate information. Be sure to take advantage of the power of SQL to return only those records that meet a certain criteria. This reduces the amount of data that you must wade through to find what you're looking for. Let's look at some examples:

Suppose you want to identify those users holding more than a certain number of locks. You can run this query against the "sysmaster" database to locate appropriate records:

```
SELECT DBSNAME,
       TABNAME,
       COUNT(*) NUMBER_OF_LOCKS,
       OWNER,
       USERNAME
FROM   SYSLOCKS,
       SYSSESSIONS
WHERE  OWNER = SID
GROUP BY DBSNAME,TABNAME,OWNER,USERNAME
HAVING COUNT(*) > 5
ORDER BY NUMBER_OF_LOCKS;
```

```
dbsname      tabname       number_of_locks      owner      username

marketing    promotions        2125             54904      alexe
payroll      staff              908              3321      coctz
marketing    inquiries          330             40443      mbailey
    .            .               .                .           .
    .            .               .                .           .
```

Use this query to get a helpful summary report on your system's extent status:

```
SELECT DBSNAME,
       TABNAME,
       COUNT(*) NUMBER_OF_EXTENTS,
       SUM (SIZE) TOTAL_PAGES
FROM   SYSEXTENTS
GROUP BY DBSNAME, TABNAME
ORDER BY DBSNAME, TOTAL_PAGES, TABNAME;
```

```
dbsname      tabname           number_of_extents      total_pages

marketing    inquiries                11                405004
payroll      employee_hours            8                200446
    .             .                    .                   .
    .             .                    .                   .
```

This next query displays all sessions that have a higher "bufreads" value than average:

```
SELECT S.SID,
       USERNAME,
       BUFREADS
FROM   SYSSESPROF P,
       SYSSESSIONS S
WHERE  P.SID = S.SID
AND BUFREADS >
   (SELECT AVG(BUFREADS)
    FROM   SYSSESPROF);
```

```
sid     username        bufreads

4004    hankw           70079
1136    ldueer          66553
  .       .               .
  .       .               .
```

These are just a small sample of the variety of queries that you can build.

DATA FRAGMENTATION AND PDQ

Introduction

Fragmentation and parallel data query (PDQ) are two important new features introduced in OnLine 7.00 that can greatly increase database application performance. In this section, we discuss each of these new features, along with how you can combine them to realize improved system response.

Since PDQ relies heavily on fragmentation, we devote the beginning of this section to that topic. Once we've reviewed fragmentation, it's on to PDQ. Finally, we conclude this section with some tips you can use to best take advantage of these new features.

Fragmentation

What is fragmentation? Fragmentation is a feature that lets database and system administrators spread data and indexes across multiple disk drives. Fragmenting these structures among a number of drives provides several important benefits:

- **More control over data archiving and restoration.** Since OnLine lets you archive and restore at the dbspace level, you now have the added option of archiving and restoring portions of fragmented tables, as well as entire tables or the entire system.

- **Added disk failure options.** You can use the SET DATASKIP command to request that OnLine continue processing after encountering an unavailable disk drive.
- **Faster query response.** Fragmentation helps to distribute and balance the I/O requests among the disk drives. Since I/O is the most expensive part of data access, improving I/O speed leads to faster query response.

Let's look at each of these benefits in more detail.

MORE CONTROL OVER DATA ARCHIVING AND RESTORATION

Since data fragmentation lets you separate data and indexes, you can reduce the amount of time that your backups require by not archiving index dbspaces. You can always re-create indexes after you perform a data restore; the main goal during restore is to retrieve all table data.

For example, suppose that you have a 100-gigabyte OnLine instance, spread over 50 two-gigabyte drives. You've created one dbspace for each disk drive, yielding 50 dbspaces. You can design your tables so that you store the system catalogs, physical and logical logs, and data in dbspaces 1 through 35. The rest of the spaces can hold indexes (and temporary dbspaces). When you archive your OnLine instance, you can explicitly instruct the "onarchive" utility to back up only dbspaces 1 through 35. This saves OnLine from processing 30 gigabytes worth of information, thereby cutting archive time. If you ever had to completely restore data, this savings would be especially valuable.

ADDED DISK FAILURE OPTIONS

If you're maintaining an application that must stay up at all costs, you can instruct OnLine to keep processing, if possible, when it encounters an unavailable disk drive. The SET DATASKIP command controls this behavior. Dataskip can be invoked in any of these ways:

- **In the ONCONFIG file.** You can specify a default dataskip behavior for the entire OnLine instance by setting the DATASKIP parameter in the ONCONFIG file.
- **Through an SQL statement.** You can turn dataskip on and off by entering:

```
SET DATASKIP ON
SET DATASKIP OFF
```

- **Embedded in a 3GL or 4GL program.** You can select a dataskip option programmatically:

```
EXEC SQL SET DATASKIP ON;
```

Let's look at an example that shows how you can use SET DATASKIP in conjunction with fragmenting. Suppose that you're maintaining a decision support system that tracks purchase orders. Your most important table is the "po_issued" table, which has the following layout:

```
po_issued

po_number      po_date       po_amount      po_vendor_no...
-------------------------------------------------------------
 239929    | 03/29/96    |   506.00     |     304
 239930    | 03/29/96    |  1020.96     |    1108
 239931    | 03/29/96    |    43.00     |      17
    .            .             .                .
    .            .             .                .
```

You've decided to fragment this table on the "po_vendor_no" column (we'll discuss more about exactly how to fragment data later in this section):

```
.   .   .

.   .   .
) FRAGMENT BY EXPRESSION
   PO_VENDOR_NO <  1000 IN DATASPACE1,
   PO_VENDOR_NO >= 1000 AND
   PO_VENDOR_NO <  2000 IN DATASPACE2
   REMAINDER IN DATASPACE3;
```

What happens if the dataspace1 dbspace goes down? If you request information from this table, and you haven't enabled dataskip, you get an error message similar to this:

```
243: Could not position within a table (db_user.po_issued).
155: ISAM error: Primary and Mirror chunks are bad
```

If, in contrast, you've requested that OnLine use the dataskip feature, the engine attempts to continue processing despite the missing dbspace. If OnLine encounters a down dbspace with dataskip enabled, the database server lets you know by setting the "sqlwarn.sqlwarn7" variable to "W".

Be careful when using dataskip: your queries might return a set of information that is incomplete. Consequently, it's a good idea to monitor the "sqlwarn.sqlwarn7" variable to determine if OnLine has used dataskip. If it has, consider alerting your users that the query results might not be complete.

Remember that if OnLine is attempting any of the following operations and encounters an unavailable disk drive, it fails, regardless of whether you've used the SET DATASKIP command:

- **Serial columns insert.** If your table contains a serial column, OnLine needs to be able to access the first fragment, since the current serial value is stored there. If OnLine can't access this fragment, it returns an error.
- **INSERT/DELETE statement.** If OnLine tries to INSERT or DELETE a record in a particular fragment, the engine returns an error.
- **UPDATE statement.** If, during an update, OnLine tries to relocate a record from an accessible fragment to a non-accessible fragment, the engine returns an error.
- **Index access.** If OnLine needs to modify an index during an INSERT, UPDATE, or DELETE statement, and the index is in an unavailable fragment, the operation fails.
- **Referential integrity check.** Both child and parent record fragments must be available for OnLine to complete a transaction.

FASTER QUERY RESPONSE

Fragmentation is the framework on which OnLine implements PDQ to produce faster queries. Without fragmentation, PDQ is not very effective. We'll discuss exactly how you can use PDQ later in this chapter; for now, keep in mind that a good fragmentation strategy is a key building block of your PDQ strategy.

How is fragmentation implemented?

To support fragmentation, Informix added a new system table, known as "sysfragments". This table contains one row per index or table fragment, as shown:

Table 4.2 sysfragments

column name	type	purpose
fragtype	char(1)	Type of fragment: I : Index T : Table
tabid	integer	The table number (corresponds to the "systables" table).
indexname	char(18)	The index name.
colno	smallint	The BLOB's column identifier.
partn	integer	Identifier of physical location.
strategy	char(1)	Method used for distribution: E : Expression R : Round robin T : Table-based
location	char(1)	Not used at this time.
servername	char(18)	Not used at this time.
evalpos	integer	Fragment's position in fragment list.
exprtext	text	Fragmenting expression represented in text form.
exprbin	byte	Fragmenting expression represented in binary form.
exprarr	byte	Used to optimize fragmentation expression.
flags	integer	Internal use only.
dbspace	char(18)	The fragment's dbspace name.
levels	smallint	Number of levels in the index B+ tree.
npused	integer	Number of data pages if entry is for a table fragment, or number of leaf pages if entry is for an index fragment.
nrows	integer	Number of rows if entry is for a table fragment, or number of unique values if entry is for an index fragment.
clust	integer	Measure of index fragmentation; the lower the number, the greater the clustering.

When fragmenting a table or index, you must choose between two different methods of fragmentation: round robin fragmentation, and expression-based fragmentation. Let's look at these two techniques in more detail.

ROUND ROBIN FRAGMENTATION

This method of fragmentation requires the least amount of planning. You simply request the database server to evenly divide inserted data among a list of dbspaces. For example, suppose that you are developing a cellular phone call tracking system. You expect very large amounts of data to be inserted into the "calls_made" table each minute. You have four disk drives that you want to hold the data. You can request round robin fragmentation when you create the table:

```
CREATE TABLE CALLS_MADE
(
   CALL_ID            SERIAL PRIMARY KEY,
   ACCOUNT_NUM        CHAR(20),
   SOURCE_AREA        SMALLINT,
   SOURCE_NO          INTEGER,
   DESTINATION_AREA   SMALLINT,
   DESTINATION_NO     INTEGER,
   TIME_OF_CALL       DATETIME YEAR TO SECOND,
   LENGTH_OF_CALL     INTERVAL HOUR TO SECOND
) FRAGMENT BY ROUND ROBIN IN DATASPACE1, DATASPACE2,
  DATASPACE3, DATASPACE4 EXTENT SIZE 100000 NEXT SIZE
50000;
```

Once you've created the table, the database server automatically places newly-inserted rows into one of the four fragments. You can also fragment an existing table with the following SQL:

```
ALTER FRAGMENT ON TABLE CALLS_MADE INIT
   FRAGMENT BY ROUND ROBIN IN DATASPACE1, DATASPACE2
   DATASPACE3, DATASPACE4;
```

If you're using transaction logging, one potential problem that you might encounter when adding fragmentation is a long transaction. OnLine fragments a table within a single transaction; if the underlying table is large enough, the transaction might exceed existing logical log space. The easiest way to avoid this problem is to temporarily turn off logging until after the table is fragmented. You can also break up the ALTER FRAGMENT statement into several smaller statements, but this requires more planning.

You can also fragment indexes. For example, suppose that you place an index on the "calls_made" table's "source_no" column. If the underlying table is already fragmented, and you don't specify a separate fragmentation strategy for the index, the index is fragmented in the same way as the underlying table. If "calls_made" is fragmented by round robin, you only need to run the following SQL statement to achieve round robin distribution for the index:

```
CREATE INDEX CM_IDX1 ON CALLS_MADE(SOURCE_NO);
```

You can also create the index in a separate dbspace:

```
CREATE INDEX CM_IDX1 ON CALLS_MADE(SOURCE_NO) IN IDXSPACE;
```

Even if the underlying table is fragmented, the index won't follow the fragmentation strategy if it is created in a separate dbspace.

What are the advantages and drawbacks of round robin fragmentation?

Advantages

The main advantage of round robin fragmenting is simplicity: you don't need to spend much time analyzing your data to begin fragmenting. OnLine distributes the data evenly among all named disk drives. This means that you can rapidly initiate fragmentation, and be confident that your data will be relatively evenly balanced. Keep in mind that while the data may be evenly balanced, users might still spend a greater portion of time accessing data in one dbspace, if that data is more commonly needed. For this reason, it's a good idea to monitor the overall disk load situation. You can do this using the "onstat" command, or by reviewing the "sysmaster" database. For more information about monitoring disk load, see the "OnLine tips" section.

Drawbacks

The main drawbacks of round robin fragmentation are the lack of control over data placement, reduced archiving options, and diminished dataskip potential. Conversely, expression-based fragmentation addresses all of these features. See the next section of this chapter for more detail.

EXPRESSION-BASED FRAGMENTATION

With this method of fragmentation, it's up to the database or system administrator to provide the database server with criteria to use when fragmenting information. You can fragment by an arbitrary rule, hash rule, or range rule. Using the cellular phone tracking example from above, let's look at each type of expression-based fragmentation:

- **Arbitrary rule.** To use this method, you provide the database server with the criteria necessary to fragment the table:

```
CREATE TABLE CALLS_MADE
(
    CALL_ID              SERIAL PRIMARY KEY,
    ACCOUNT_NUM          CHAR(20),
```

```
    SOURCE_AREA         SMALLINT,
    SOURCE_NO           INTEGER,
    DESTINATION_AREA    SMALLINT,
    DESTINATION_NO      INTEGER,
    TIME_OF_CALL        DATETIME YEAR TO SECOND,
    LENGTH_OF_CALL      INTERVAL HOUR TO SECOND
) FRAGMENT BY EXPRESSION
  SOURCE_AREA = 415 OR SOURCE_AREA = 213 IN DATASPACE1,
  SOURCE_AREA = 510 OR SOURCE_AREA = 310 IN DATASPACE2,
  SOURCE_AREA = 408 OR SOURCE_AREA = 619 IN DATASPACE3,
  SOURCE_AREA = 818 OR SOURCE_AREA = 707 IN DATASPACE4
  REMAINDER IN DATASPACE5;
```

If you use this strategy, your job as administrator is to carefully analyze your data and arrive at a meaningful distribution plan.

- **Hash rule.** This method typically uses the MOD function to divide data among the dbspaces:

```
CREATE TABLE CALLS_MADE
(
    CALL_ID             SERIAL PRIMARY KEY,
    ACCOUNT_NUM         CHAR(20),
    SOURCE_AREA         SMALLINT,
    SOURCE_NO           INTEGER,
    DESTINATION_AREA    SMALLINT,
    DESTINATION_NO      INTEGER,
    TIME_OF_CALL        DATETIME YEAR TO SECOND,
    LENGTH_OF_CALL      INTERVAL HOUR TO SECOND
) FRAGMENT BY EXPRESSION
  MOD(CALL_ID, 4) = 0 IN DATASPACE1,
  MOD(CALL_ID, 4) = 1 IN DATASPACE2,
  MOD(CALL_ID, 4) = 2 IN DATASPACE3,
  MOD(CALL_ID, 4) = 3 IN DATASPACE4
```

Among the three expression-based fragmentation strategies, the hash rule method is the closest to the round robin fragmentation approach.

- **Range rule.** This fragmentation technique uses a range to help decide where to place data:

```
CREATE TABLE CALLS_MADE
(
    CALL_ID             SERIAL PRIMARY KEY,
```

```
      ACCOUNT_NUM          CHAR(20),
      SOURCE_AREA          SMALLINT,
      SOURCE_NO            INTEGER,
      DESTINATION_AREA     SMALLINT,
      DESTINATION_NO       INTEGER,
      TIME_OF_CALL         DATETIME YEAR TO SECOND,
      LENGTH_OF_CALL       INTERVAL HOUR TO SECOND
   ) FRAGMENT BY EXPRESSION
     ACCOUNT_NUM <  "F0000000000000000000" IN
       DATASPACE1,
     ACCOUNT_NUM >= "F0000000000000000000" AND
     ACCOUNT_NUM <  "H0000000000000000000" IN
       DATASPACE2,
     ACCOUNT_NUM >= "H0000000000000000000" AND
     ACCOUNT_NUM <  "S0000000000000000000" IN
       DATASPACE3,
     ACCOUNT_NUM >= "S0000000000000000000" IN
       DATASPACE4
```

Remember that you can fragment indexes on expression, just as you can with data. You can choose from the same three expression-based fragmentation techniques that you use for cxcddtables.

What are the advantages and drawbacks of expression-based fragmentation?

Advantages

These are some of the most common advantages in choosing expression-based fragmentation over round-robin fragmentation:

- **Data fragmented intelligently.** The expression-based fragmentation algorithm that you choose is usually based on your organization's actual data distribution. This is closer to reality than simply distributing data randomly, which essentially what happens when you use round-robin fragmentation.
- **Dataskip.** If you've fragmented your data based on an expression, you can choose dataskip with more confidence than if you fragmented by round robin. For example, suppose that you have an enormous transaction table that you want to fragment. You decide to fragment based on transaction date, placing each month's data on a separate drive. If the current month is November, and the drive containing June's data becomes unavailable, OnLine can use dataskip to keep servicing database requests. If a user wants to see information from July, he can keep working, since July's data is unaffected by the disk outage. In contrast, if you fragmented by round-robin, there's a good chance that some of July's data resides on the unavailable disk. You can still use dataskip (with the

exception of certain types of transactions as described in the "Dataskip" section of this chapter), but you'll probably miss important information.

- **Archiving.** When you fragment based on expression, you have a good idea where certain data resides. Using the transaction table example from above, you can decide only to archive the data from the most recent two months. This shortens both archive and restore time. If you used round-robin fragmentation, you would have to archive all the disks to make sure that you saved the data from the last two months.

Drawbacks

The main risk that you face when fragmenting data based on an expression is that you might not choose an evenly-balanced distribution strategy. This could lead to an uneven data balance among your disk drives. How can you avoid this situation? One way is to generate a data distribution for each table before you decide on a fragmentation technique.

Let's look at an example. Suppose that you have a large table that you want to divide among five new disk drives:

Table 4.3 trouble_calls

call_id	office_loc	call_timestamp
2144	15	1996-03-15 12:03:44
2145	203	1996-03-15 12:04:11
.	.	.
.	.	.

You've decided to fragment on the "office_loc" column. You want to obtain five even fragments, one fragment for each disk drive. You could run UPDATE STATISTICS HIGH on the "office_loc" column, to get an idea of how the data is distributed. You could then run "dbschema -d support_dbs -hd trouble_calls" to review the data distribution:

```
Distribution for db_user.trouble_calls.office_location

Constructed on 09/23/1995

High Mode, 10.000000 Resolution
```

```
--- DISTRIBUTION ---

   (                                0)
   1: (   77480,       98,        97)
   2: (   77480,       41,       138)
   3: (   77480,       33,       171)
   4: (   77480,       32,       204)
   5: (   77480,       31,       236)
   6: (   77480,       31,       268)
   7: (   77480,       31,       300)
   8: (   77480,       32,       332)
   9: (   77480,       41,       373)
  10: (   77220,       98,       471)
```

With this knowledge, you can create an accurate fragmentation strategy. Since you have five disk drives, you can divide the data into five approximately equal segments:

```
ALTER FRAGMENT ON TABLE TROUBLE_CALLS INIT
   FRAGMENT BY EXPRESSION
      OFFICE_LOCATION < 138 IN DATASPACE1,
      OFFICE_LOCATION >= 138
      AND < 204 IN DATASPACE2,
      OFFICE_LOCATION >= 268
      AND < 300 IN DATASPACE3,
      OFFICE_LOCATION >= 300
      AND < 332 IN DATASPACE4,
      REMAINDER IN DATASPACE5;
```

We chose these dividing points by creating a 10 percent resolution data distribution. This created 10 equally-sized bins. We then took every other high value as the break point between fragments.

Remember that if you learn that your existing fragmentation strategy isn't completely correct, you can always add new fragments, or modify or delete existing fragments. You can also completely de-fragment any fragmented table, as long as you have enough space to store the defragmented table. For example, if you wanted to de-fragment the “calls_made” table, and store the newly-defragmented table in the “dataspace6” dbspace, you would run this SQL:

```
ALTER FRAGMENT ON CALLS_MADE INIT IN DATASPACE6;
```

PDQ

OnLine uses parallel data query (PDQ) to maximize performance when reading fragmented data. To understand how OnLine implements PDQ, it helps to first understand the difference between the two most common types of database access:

- **Online transaction processing (OLTP).** OLTP is primarily composed of traditional interactive database access applications. These applications include order processing, banking, airline reservation, and similar systems that requires instant access to specific pieces of data. OLTP applications are often crucial components of an organization's operations. Therefore, your primary goal as an administrator or a developer is to maximize OLTP performance.
- **Decision support processing.** Decision support applications typically analyze large quantities of data. This data is often output to a report, which can be quite large. Many decision support applications run during off hours, in batch mode, although large numbers of users are beginning to demand instant access to this type of information as well.

While PDQ provides some benefit on uniprocessor machines with non-fragmented data, you'll really see noticeable throughput improvements if you're using a multiprocessor system in conjunction with data fragmentation.

Next, let's look at how OnLine uses PDQ when processing both OLTP and decision support processing.

OLTP

Typically, OLTP applications use indexes to access data. For example, a typical airline reservation query may use any of the following pieces of information as search criteria:

- Passenger name
- Flight number
- Flight date
- Origin city
- Destination city

In most cases, all of these fields are indexed, meaning that the database server can return the requested records extremely quickly, with a relatively low I/O cost. Since these types of queries don't usually benefit from parallel access, OnLine doesn't use PDQ to service OLTP requests.

DECISION SUPPORT

Since decision support applications typically process large volumes of data, this data access is often sequential in nature. This leads to heavy I/O costs, which can greatly slow down response time. If you've fragmented your data, and spread it across several dbspaces, OnLine can use PDQ to scan these dbspaces in parallel. This often leads to dramatic performance enhancements.

Be aware that there are a number of circumstances where OnLine won't use PDQ. These include:

- Cursors declared with the FOR UPDATE clause.
- Cursors declared with the WITH HOLD clause.
- Queries that call stored procedure language (SPL) functions.
- Queries that use an isolation level of CURSOR STABILITY.

If a query processes 10 separate fragments, it's possible that OnLine will spawn 10 separate scan threads. If many users are running these types of queries, OnLine might get bogged down servicing all of the scan threads.

HOW DOES PDQ WORK?

PDQ works on the basis of "divide-and-conquer." OnLine breaks up certain types of queries into much smaller subqueries. Each of these subqueries gets assigned to separate threads. Each thread works on its job in parallel, and the database engine then reassembles and processes the resulting data sets before presenting the answer to the user. If you've fragmented your data on an expression, OnLine can "rule out" certain fragments based on your query. See the PDQ examples later in this chapter for further explanation.

While it's best to use PDQ on a multiprocessor machine with data fragmentation, you can still take advantage of PDQ on a single processor machine. If you're using a multiprocessor, PDQ utilizes as many processors as possible. While this doesn't happen on a single processor, PDQ can still get better speed by handling multiple I/O requests at one time.

PDQ helps all of these types of database operations:

- Grouping
- Sorting
- Scanning
- Joining

CONFIGURING PDQ

One challenge that database administrators face when configuring PDQ is how to balance PDQ's requirements with those of other applications. For example, if one computer is supporting both OLTP and decision support systems concurrently, OLTP users might not appreciate it if the decision support users consume all available resources. Both user communities look to the database administrator for help; your job is to analyze your environment to determine exactly what configuration is most appropriate.

Let's look at how you can control some of PDQ's resource requirements:

- **Threads.** When OnLine uses PDQ to process a query, it launches a number of threads to handle the work. You can control the overall number of active scan threads by setting the DS_MAX_SCANS parameter in the ONCONFIG file.

  The DS_MAX_QUERIES parameter limits the total number of PDQ queries that OnLine can service at any one time.

- **Priority.** Set the PDQPRIORITY parameter to tell OnLine what priority it should assign to PDQ. You can use a numeric value between 0 and 100. A setting of 0 means that PDQ is turned off, while 100 means that PDQ has maximum priority. You can also use mnemonics, such as:

  - OFF: PDQ is completely disabled (same as 0)
  - LOW: PDQ only scans in parallel (same as 1)
  - HIGH: Maximum PDQ priority (same as 100)

  You can set PDQPRIORITY in one of three ways:

  - **In the ONCONFIG file.** If you set this parameter in the ONCONFIG file, all applications use this value unless otherwise specified.
  - **As an environment variable.** If you set PDQPRIORITY in the environment, OnLine lets the user's sessions override the ONCONFIG file's PDQPRIORITY value. Keep in mind that you can set an absolute maximum PDQPRIORITY value by setting the MAX_PDQPRIORITY parameter in the ONCONFIG file.
  - **Through SQL.** You can use the SET PDQPRIORITY statement to a session-specific value. Remember that you can never exceed the MAX_PDQPRIORITY value, no matter what value you supply through SQL.

- **Memory.** PDQ can consume copious amounts of memory, especially when many users are running concurrent queries. Fortunately, you can set a limit on the total amount of available PDQ memory by setting the DS_TOTAL_MEMORY parameter.

- **Join strategy.** When joining tables, the optimizer can choose among these techniques:

  - Nested loop joins
  - Hash joins
  - Sort-merge joins

We review these types of join techniques in the "Understanding the Informix optimizer" section.

Join Strategies

To tell the optimizer what kind of join strategy you want to use, set the OPTCOMPIND configuration and environment variable. Hash joins are generally faster. However, if you're using repeatable read isolation level, hash joins might cause your program to briefly lock thousands of rows, thereby reducing concurrency.

You can set OPTCOMPIND to any of the following values:

- **0** : Choose a nested loop join over both hash and sort-merge joins.
- **1** : If the transaction is using repeatable read isolation, follow the previous strategy. If the transaction is not using repeatable read isolation, follow the next strategy.
- **2** : Let the cost drive the join decision strategy no matter what isolation level is currently active.

For those programs that don't use repeatable read isolation, such as large reports, set OPTCOMPIND to 2. This method ensures that the optimizer chooses the fastest join method, without considering the isolation level.

If your program occasionally uses repeatable read isolation, try setting OPTCOMPIND to 1. This means that the optimizer chooses a nested join loop only when faced with an isolation level of repeatable read. This method is the best balance between performance and concurrency.

For example, look at the following two query plans. OPTCOMPIND is set to 1 in both cases. For the first case, we ran SET ISOLATION TO COMMITTED READ:

```
QUERY:
------
SELECT MACHINE_ID,
       ERROR_TIMESTAMP
FROM   MACHINE_STATUS M,
OUTER MACHINE_ERROR E
WHERE  M.MACHINE_ID = E.ERROR_MACHINE
AND    M.MACHINE_DATA < 1000

Estimated Cost: 97
Estimated # of Rows Returned: 375

1) db_user.m: INDEX PATH

     (1) Index Keys: machine_data   (Parallel, fragments: ALL)
         Upper Index Filter: db_user.m.machine_data < 1000.00

2) db_user.e: SEQUENTIAL SCAN


DYNAMIC HASH JOIN
    Dynamic Hash Filters: db_user.m.machine_id =
      db_user.e.error_machine

# of Secondary Threads = 4
```

Next, we ran SET ISOLATION TO REPEATABLE READ:

```
QUERY:
------
SELECT MACHINE_ID,
       ERROR_TIMESTAMP
FROM   MACHINE_STATUS M,
OUTER MACHINE_ERROR E
WHERE  M.MACHINE_ID = E.ERROR_MACHINE
AND    M.MACHINE_DATA < 1000

Estimated Cost: 848
Estimated # of Rows Returned: 375

1) db_user.m: INDEX PATH

     (1) Index Keys: machine_data   (Parallel, fragments: ALL)
         Upper Index Filter: db_user.m.machine_data < 1000.00

2) db_user.e: SEQUENTIAL SCAN


DYNAMIC HASH JOIN
    Dynamic Hash Filters: db_user.m.machine_id =
      db_user.e.error_machine

# of Secondary Threads = 3
```

Since OPTCOMPIND was set to 1, and REPEATABLE READ was the isolation mode, OnLine didn't use the hash join method to join the tables. Note the significantly higher query cost.

If you want the optimizer never to use a hash join, set OPTCOMPIND to 0. This is also the default value for this parameter.

Keep in mind that you can dynamically change this parameter at the instance, user, or session level, just as you can do with PDQPRIORITY.

USING THE MEMORY GRANT MANAGER (MGM)

To observe how OnLine is currently handling PDQ, you can use the "onstat -g mgm" command:

```
RSAM Version 7.00.UC4   -- On-Line -- Up 00:42:39 -- 29064 Kbytes
```

The first part of the MGM report displays the current settings of four PDQ configuration parameters:

```
Memory Grant Manager (MGM)
--------------------------


MAX_PDQ_PRIORITY:  100
DS_MAX_QUERIES:    10
DS_MAX_SCANS:      2000
DS_TOTAL_MEMORY:   20000 KB
```

Next, the MGM reports how many queries are currently running, how many are ready to run but currently on hold, and the total number of decision support queries that OnLine lets you run concurrently. This last value corresponds to the DS_MAX_QUERIES configuration parameter:

```
Queries:     Active        Ready    Maximum
                  2            5        10
```

The next part of the MGM report shows how PDQ uses memory. The "Total" field corresponds to the DS_TOTAL_MEMORY configuration parameter, and is the total amount of memory that OnLine can allocate for decision support queries. The "Free" column shows the actual current amount of available memory for these types of queries. "Quantum" displays the smallest amount of memory that OnLine provides to a decision support query; it corresponds to DS_TOTAL_MEMORY divided by DS_MAX_QUERIES:

```
Memory:        Total        Free    Quantum
(KB)           20000        1000       2000
```

The "Scans" portion shows the current state of PDQ scans. The "Total" field matches the DS_MAX_SCANS configuration parameter. The "Free" field signifies how many threads are currently ready for use. "Quantum" is the number of scan threads that OnLine starts if there are enough available fragments:

```
Scans:         Total        Free    Quantum
                2000        1999       2000
```

MGM next reports on PDQ load balancing. When a PDQ query needs access to a resource, the MGM first applies a number of tests to see if there are sufficient available resources. These tests are known as "gates," and queries that can't get enough resources will wait in queues for the appropriate gate. The number below each gate is the count of queries currently queued at the gate.

The MGM assigns a different gate type for each resource, such as memory, scans, priority, and maximum queries. You can use this information to learn more about potential PDQ bottlenecks. For example, if you observed many queries waiting in the "Memory" gate queue, you could conclude that DS_TOTAL_MEMORY is not sufficient to meet the current PDQ memory requirements. If you saw a large number of queries waiting in the "Scans" gate queue, you would know that DS_MAX_SCANS could be set too low. The "Priority" and "Max Queries" gates correspond to the PDQPRIORITY and DS_MAX_QUERIES configuration parameters, respectively:

```
Load Control:      (Memory)       (Scans)  (Priority)  (Max Queries)    (Reinit)
                    Gate 1         Gate 2    Gate 3      Gate 4          Gate 5
(Queue Length)         1              0         4           0               0
```

The next part of this report describes both active and waiting decision support queries. Pay special attention to the session id; you can learn more about what this session is actually doing by running "onstat -g ses <id>". Notice the "Priority" column: it shows each query's priority, which corresponds to the PDQPRIORITY parameter. The MGM also reports on the query's current memory usage, along with the total amount of reserved memory. These numbers are denominated in 8 kilobytes, meaning that query 16dcbd0 is currently using 10,000 kilobytes (1250 * 8k), and has a total of 20,000 kilobytes (2500 * 8k) reserved. The next values are the number of currently used scan threads, along with the total number of reserved scan threads. Finally, if a query is waiting at a gate, the MGM reports the gate number. Notice how there are a total of five ready queries. Compare these to the "Load Control" numbers listed above:

```
Active Queries:
---------------
Session   Query   Priority  Thread    Memory   Scans      Gate
  31 16dcbd0    100      192e23c 1250/2500   0/0         -
  31 172a818    100      1f06500    0/2500   0/1         -

Ready Queries:
--------------
Session   Query   Priority  Thread    Memory   Scans      Gate
  32 16e4bd0    100      1936a90    0/2500   0/0         1
  35 1786bd0    100      1936c20    0/2500   0/0         3
  33 16eebd0    100      195c67c    0/2500   0/0         3
  34 16f8bd0    100      1968574    0/2500   0/0         3
  36 17d2bd0    100      19963cc    0/2500   0/0         3
```

The last section of the report lists averages for PDQ memory usage and scans, along with averages and counts for both active and ready queries. Remember that these numbers are zeroed out when you reboot the engine, or run onmode -Q, onmode -S, or onmode -M:

```
Free Resource       Average #         Minimum #
--------------    ---------------     ---------
Memory             483.9 +- 1502.7      2500
Scans             9999.0 +- 0.5         9997

Queries             Average #         Maximum #    Total #
--------------    ---------------     ---------    -------
Active               1.3 +- 0.5           2          31
Ready                2.5 +- 1.3           5          11

Resource/Lock Cycle Prevention count:  0
```

SAMPLE QUERIES

Let's look at the query plans of some sample queries that take advantage of PDQ. In these examples, we're retrieving information from a factory floor automation system. The "machine_status" table stores information about the current state of 3,000 separate robotic controllers:

```
CREATE TABLE MACHINE_STATUS
(
    STATUS_ID           SERIAL,
    MACHINE_ID          INTEGER,
    MACHINE_TIMESTAMP   DATETIME YEAR TO FRACTION(5),
    MACHINE_DATA        DECIMAL(8,2)
);
CREATE UNIQUE INDEX MS1 ON MACHINE_STATUS (STATUS_ID);
CREATE INDEX MS2 ON MACHINE_STATUS(MACHINE_ID);
```

This table currently has 741,000 rows.

The "machines" table stores the identifier for the machine, as well as its description:

```
CREATE TABLE MACHINES
(
    MACHINE_ID          SERIAL,
    MACHINE_NAME        CHAR(80)
);
CREATE UNIQUE INDEX MA1 ON MACHINES(MACHINE_ID);
```

This table has 3,000 rows.

PRE-FRAGMENTATION

For the first set of queries, both tables reside in the same dbspace. This means that OnLine can't fully use PDQ and fragmentation to speed up response. Notice how OnLine does start secondary threads, even without data fragmentation:

```
Query 1 (Simple join)

QUERY:
------
SELECT MACHINE_NAME,
       MACHINE_DATA
FROM   MACHINES M,
       MACHINE_STATUS S
```

```
WHERE  M.MACHINE_ID = S.MACHINE_ID

Estimated Cost: 5505
Estimated # of Rows Returned: 5293

1) db_user.m: SEQUENTIAL SCAN

2) db_user.s: INDEX PATH

    (1) Index Keys: machine_id
        Lower Index Filter: db_user.s.machine_id =
          db_user.m.machine_id


# of Secondary Threads = 6

Query 2 (Single-table SELECT)

QUERY:
------
SELECT *
FROM  MACHINE_STATUS
WHERE MACHINE_ID BETWEEN 1500 AND 1700
ORDER BY MACHINE_TIMESTAMP DESC

Estimated Cost: 50956
Estimated # of Rows Returned: 49445
Temporary Files Required For: Order By

1) db_user.machine_status: SEQUENTIAL SCAN

   Filters: (db_user.machine_status.machine_id >= 1500
             AND db_user.machine_status.machine_
              id <= 1700 )


# of Secondary Threads = 1


Query 3 (Single-table SELECT with subquery)
```

```
QUERY:
------
SELECT MACHINE_ID,
       MACHINE_DATA,
       COUNT(*)
FROM   MACHINE_STATUS
GROUP BY 1,2
HAVING MACHINE_DATA <
(SELECT AVG(MACHINE_DATA) FROM MACHINE_STATUS)

Estimated Cost: 616861
Estimated # of Rows Returned: 229902
Temporary Files Required For: Group By

1) db_user.machine_status: SEQUENTIAL SCAN

   Filters: db_user.machine_status.machine_data <
      <subquery>

   Subquery:
   ---------
   Estimated Cost: 26981
   Estimated # of Rows Returned: 1

   1) db_user.machine_status: SEQUENTIAL SCAN


# of Secondary Threads = 6


Query 4 (Two-table join with subquery)

QUERY:
------
SELECT M.MACHINE_NAME,
       S.MACHINE_ID,
       COUNT(*) Number_of_records
FROM   MACHINES M,
       MACHINE_STATUS S
WHERE  S.MACHINE_ID = M.MACHINE_ID
AND    M.MACHINE_ID IN
(
   SELECT MACHINE_ID
```

```
      FROM MACHINES
     WHERE MACHINE_NAME = "High Voltage"
)
GROUP BY 1,2

Estimated Cost: 188578
Estimated # of Rows Returned: 107
Temporary Files Required For: Group By

1) db_user.s: INDEX PATH

    (1) Index Keys: machine_id   (Key-Only)
        Lower Index Filter: db_user.s.machine_id = ANY
           <subquery>

2) db_user.m: INDEX PATH

    (1) Index Keys: machine_id
        Lower Index Filter: db_user.m.machine_id = ANY
           <subquery>

DYNAMIC HASH JOIN
   Dynamic Hash Filters: db_user.s.machine_id =
  db_user.m.machine_id

   Subquery:
   ---------
   Estimated Cost: 157
   Estimated # of Rows Returned: 1000

   1) db_user.machines: SEQUENTIAL SCAN

        Filters: db_user.machines.machine_name = 'High
          Voltage'

# of Secondary Threads = 7
```

Post-Fragmentation

Next, we partition the "machine_status" table among three dbspaces:

```
ALTER FRAGMENT ON TABLE MACHINE_STATS INIT
   FRAGMENT BY EXPRESSION
      MACHINE_ID < 2000 IN DATADBS1,
```

```
        MACHINE_ID >= 2000 AND MACHINE_ID < 3000 IN DATADBS2,
        MACHINE_ID >= 3000 IN DATADBS3
```

Let's look at the query plans for the same queries:

```
Query 1 (Simple join: committed read isolation)

QUERY:
------
SELECT MACHINE_NAME,
       MACHINE_DATA
FROM   MACHINES M,
       MACHINE_STATUS S
WHERE  M.MACHINE_ID = S.MACHINE_ID

Estimated Cost: 9062
Estimated # of Rows Returned: 726000

1) db_user.s: SEQUENTIAL SCAN  (Parallel, fragments: ALL)

2) db_user.m: SEQUENTIAL SCAN

DYNAMIC HASH JOIN
    Dynamic Hash Filters: db_user.s.machine_id =
      db_user.m.machine_id

# of Secondary Threads = 9
```

Notice how an isolation level of repeatable read produces a different query plan. This is because the OPTCOMPIND parameter is set to one. Remember that this happens when you use an isolation level of repeatable read and OPTCOMPIND is set to one. In these cases, OnLine chooses a nested loop join algorithm over dynamic hash join, because the former method uses fewer locks than the latter:

```
Query 1 (Simple join: repeatable read isolation)

QUERY:
------
SELECT MACHINE_NAME,
       MACHINE_DATA
FROM   MACHINES M,
       MACHINE_STATUS S
WHERE  M.MACHINE_ID = S.MACHINE_ID
```

```
Estimated Cost: 536067
Estimated # of Rows Returned: 726000

1) db_user.m: SEQUENTIAL SCAN

2) db_user.s: INDEX PATH

    (1) Index Keys: machine_id   (Parallel, fragments: ALL)
        Lower Index Filter: db_user.s.machine_id =
         db_user.m.machine_id

# of Secondary Threads = 6

Query 2 (Single-table SELECT: committed read isolation)

QUERY:
------
SELECT *
FROM  MACHINE_STATUS
WHERE MACHINE_ID BETWEEN 1500 AND 1700
ORDER BY MACHINE_TIMESTAMP DESC

Estimated Cost: 32350
Estimated # of Rows Returned: 48497
Temporary Files Required For: Order By

1) db_user.machine_status: SEQUENTIAL SCAN  (Parallel,
    fragments:0)

   Filters: (db_user.machine_status.machine_id >= 1500
             AND db_user.machine_status.machine_id <= 1700)

# of Secondary Threads = 1


Query 2 (Single-table SELECT: with repeatable read isolation)

QUERY:
------
SELECT *
FROM  MACHINE_STATUS
WHERE MACHINE_ID BETWEEN 1500 AND 1700
ORDER BY MACHINE_TIMESTAMP DESC
```

```
Estimated Cost: 41227
Estimated # of Rows Returned: 48497
Temporary Files Required For: Order By

1) db_user.machine_status: INDEX PATH

    (1) Index Keys: machine_id   (Parallel, fragments: 0)
        Lower Index Filter: db_user.machine_
           status.machine_id >= 1500
        Upper Index Filter: db_user.machine_
           status.machine_id <= 1700

# of Secondary Threads = 1

Query 3 (Single-table SELECT with subquery: all isolation levels)

QUERY:
------
SELECT MACHINE_ID,
       MACHINE_DATA,
       COUNT(*)
FROM   MACHINE_STATUS
GROUP BY 1,2
HAVING MACHINE_DATA <
(SELECT AVG(MACHINE_DATA) FROM MACHINE_STATUS)

Estimated Cost: 569605
Estimated # of Rows Returned: 121000
Temporary Files Required For: Group By

1) db_user.machine_status: SEQUENTIAL SCAN  (Parallel,
    fragments: ALL)

   Filters: db_user.machine_status.machine_data < <subquery>

   Subquery:
   ---------
   Estimated Cost: 8813
   Estimated # of Rows Returned: 1

   1) db_user.machine_status: SEQUENTIAL SCAN
     (Parallel,fragments: ALL)

# of Secondary Threads = 8
```

```
Query 4 (Two-table join with subquery: all isolation levels)

QUERY:
------
SELECT M.MACHINE_NAME,
       S.MACHINE_ID,
       COUNT(*) Number_of_records
FROM   MACHINES M,
       MACHINE_STATUS S
WHERE  S.MACHINE_ID = M.MACHINE_ID
AND    M.MACHINE_ID IN
(
   SELECT MACHINE_ID
    FROM  MACHINES
   WHERE  MACHINE_NAME = "High Voltage"
)
GROUP BY 1,2

Estimated Cost: 367
Estimated # of Rows Returned: 1
Temporary Files Required For: Group By

1) db_user.m: INDEX PATH

   (1) Index Keys: machine_id
        Lower Index Filter: db_user.m.machine_id = ANY <subquery>

2) db_user.s: INDEX PATH

   (1) Index Keys: machine_id   (Key-Only)  (Parallel,
    fragments: ALL)
       Lower Index Filter: db_user.s.machine_id =
    db_user.m.machine_id

   Subquery:
   ---------
   Estimated Cost: 157
   Estimated # of Rows Returned: 1

   1) db_user.machines: SEQUENTIAL SCAN

      Filters: db_user.machines.machine_name = 'High Voltage'

# of Secondary Threads = 6
```

Chapter 5
Case Studies

INTRODUCTION

Real-world performance problems rarely happen in isolation. Typically, administrators and developers face a multitude of intertwined problems and obstacles. In this chapter, we present a number of case studies, each featuring multi-faceted performance impediments. After we describe the problems, we propose a variety of solutions, with references to the sections in this book that provide additional information.

Although this chapter does not cover every potential bottleneck that you might encounter, we've tried to realistically combine a number of problems in each case. See if all or part of these cases resemble the challenges that you face in your daily responsibilities. If they do, try testing some of the solutions described here to see if they help alleviate your performance problems.

Case study 1

Our first case study begins with a memo from a user:

To: Nicole Taylor
From: Florence Berson
Date: 12/30/95
Subject: User complaints

Nicole -

Thanks for asking about some of the problems we've been experiencing. Here's what some of the people in our department have been telling me:

Screen freeze
Sometimes when there are a lot of users entering data on the system, everyone's screen freezes up for about 15 seconds. This seems to happen several times an hour. We can't figure out why, because no one is running any big jobs or queries.

Slow reports
We're also having problems with the sales call summary and account detail reports. These reports have always been pretty slow, but as our database has grown, they've gotten much worse.

"Can't connect" error message
Every day, around 3 p.m. or so, we start getting complaints from users that they can't start the application. The first screen comes up, but then it displays an error message, and aborts. What's really strange is that there's no pattern to who experiences the

problem. What makes it even harder to understand is that if those users keep trying to start the program, they usually get it to work.

HOW TO PROCEED?

Armed with this information, you set out to solve these problems. The users ask you to solve the screen freeze mystery first, because this is having the most impact on their work. Remember always to get input from your users before you begin optimizing an application or system. Their priorities may be different than yours. See the "Setting up an optimization test environment" section for more information about how to start your inquiries.

First, you decide to view the OnLine message log during the late afternoon, when most of the screen freezes start to happen. The "onstat -m" command provides some interesting information:

```
.    .    .    .    .    .
.    .    .    .    .    .
15:03:25  Checkpoint Completed:  duration was 34 seconds
15:06:44  User table overflow - user id 331, process id 20919
15:08:04  User table overflow - user id 236, process id 20923
15:08:27  Checkpoint Completed:  duration was 22 seconds
15:12:18  ERROR: page cleaner # 2 has timed out
15:12:18  ERROR: page cleaner # 1 has timed out
15:12:55  User table overflow - user id 71, process id 20957
15:13:30  Checkpoint Completed:  duration was 37 seconds
15:15:02  User table overflow - user id 331, process id 20959
15:28:36  Checkpoint Completed:  duration was 8 seconds
15:30:29  Logical Log 76 Complete
15:33:39  Checkpoint Completed:  duration was 12 seconds
15:38:41  Checkpoint Completed:  duration was 18 seconds
.    .    .    .    .    .
.    .    .    .    .    .
```

This log highlights a number of problems:

- **Checkpoint duration.** During a checkpoint, OnLine suspends all user processes until it finishes the checkpoint. To a user, it would appear that the system has "frozen" if the checkpoint takes more than a second or two. Your goal is to better balance the work load by increasing the page cleaner work outside of checkpoints, and reducing the amount of work during checkpoints. You suspect that the cause of the "freeze" problem is tied to the relationship between page cleaners and checkpoints, particularly when you consider the next problem that you found in the log.
- **Page cleaner timeouts.** Generally, page cleaners should not time out. If they're timing out, it means that they probably have too much work to do during checkpoints. To investigate this lead, you run "onstat -R" between checkpoints, to view the LRU queues:

```
8 buffer LRU queue pairs
# f/m   length   % of   pair total
 0 f        45   18.0%        250
 1 m       205   79.0%
 2 f        51   20.4%        250
 3 m       199   79.6%
 4 f        70   28.0%        250
 5 m       180   72.0%
 6 f        49   19.6%        250
 7 m       201   80.4%
 8 f        37   14.8%        250
 9 m       213   85.2%
10 F        52   20.8%        250
11 m       198   79.2%
12 f        68   27.2%        250
13 m       182   72.8%
14 f        57   22.8%        250
15 m       193   77.2%
1571 dirty, 2000 queued, 2000 total, 256 hash buckets, 2048 buffer
size start clean at 60% (of pair total) dirty, or 150 buffs dirty,
stop at 50%
```

From the above output, it appears that the page cleaners can't flush all of the buffers to disk during checkpoints.

See the "OnLine tips" section for more information on choosing the right page cleaner parameters.

- **User table overflow.** It appears that you may have found the source of the mysterious "Can't connect" error messages. If you attempt to exceed the USERS/USERTHREADS parameter, OnLine cannot accommodate additional users, and sends error messages to those users' applications. To those users, this error appears random; there's no way for them to easily predict when the failure will occur.

  Fortunately, it's easy to test your hypotheses. All you need to do is increase the USERTHREADS parameter in your OnLine configuration file. If the user complaints cease, you've fixed this problem. It's also a good idea to ask the programmers to provide more information to users in case of a serious database error. For more information about the USERS/USERTHREADS parameter, see the "OnLine tips" section.

Next, you turn your attention to the sluggish reports. Working with each programmer, you put some timing messages into the code, which helps you isolate those portions of the programs that take the longest time. The account detail report seems to have big problems with the following segments of code:

```
Segment 1
---------

.    .    .    .    .
.    .    .    .    .
DECLARE ACCOUNT_CUR SCROLL CURSOR FOR
   SELECT H.ACCOUNT_NUM,
          H.ACCOUNT_NAME,
          D.SALES_DATE,
          D.SALES_AMOUNT
     FROM ACCOUNT_HEADER H,
          ACCOUNT_DETAIL D
    WHERE H.ACCOUNT_NUM = D.ACCOUNT_NUM
 ORDER BY H.ACCOUNT_NUM

START REPORT ACCOUNT_SUMMARY
FOREACH ACCOUNT_CUR INTO G_ACCOUNT_INFO.*
   OUTPUT TO REPORT ACCOUNT_SUMMARY(G_ACCOUNT_INFO.*)
END FOREACH
FINISH REPORT ACCOUNT_SUMMARY
.    .    .    .    .
.    .    .    .    .

Segment 2
---------

REPORT ACCOUNT_SUMMARY(ACCOUNT_REC)

   DEFINE ACCOUNT_REC RECORD ....

   ORDER BY ACCOUNT_REC.ACCOUNT_NUM

.    .    .    .    .
.    .    .    .    .

END REPORT
```

When you review these segments of code, you realize that you're creating at least two unnecessary temporary tables. You also discover that since the underlying tables (account_header, account_detail) are very large, the temporary tables that the engine generates are also very large.

The first temporary table arises from the scroll cursor. Remember that a scroll cursor generates a temporary table, regardless of whether you move backwards through the cursor. Since you're only moving forward through the cursor, there's no need to use a scroll cursor in this case. See the "General tips" section for more advice about scroll cursors.

The second temporary table gets created by the report itself, since it's told to sort the incoming data by the "account_num" column. Unfortunately, all this extra work is superfluous: the data is already sorted outside the report. To eliminate the temporary table, you only need to add one word to the ORDER BY clause:

```
ORDER EXTERNAL BY ACCOUNT_REC.ACCOUNT_NUM
```

See the "4GL tips" section for more information about increasing report velocity.

Unlike the account detail report, it's not easy to find the actual location of the delay in the sales summary report. However, after running the program a few times, you begin to suspect the section of code responsible for fetching records into host variables:

```
DECLARE SALES_REP_CUR CURSOR FOR
   SELECT LAST_NAME,
          FIRST_NAME,
          EMPLOYEE_ID
     FROM EMPLOYEES
 ORDER BY LAST_NAME

FOREACH SALES_REP_CUR INTO SALES_REP_REC.*
   DECLARE SALES_CALL_CUR CURSOR FOR
      SELECT CLIENT_ID,
             CALL_DATE,
             CALL_RESULT
        FROM SALES_CALLS
       WHERE SALES_CALLS.SALES_ID = SALES_REP_REC.EMPLOYEE_ID
   FOREACH SALES_CALL_CUR INTO SALES_CALL_REC.*
      DECLARE CLIENT_CUR CURSOR FOR
         SELECT CLIENT_COMPANY,
                ACCOUNT_BALANCE
           FROM CLIENTS
          WHERE CLIENTS.CLIENT_ID = SALES_CALL_REC.CLIENT_ID
      FOREACH CLIENT_CUR INTO CLIENT_CUR_REC.*
         OUTPUT TO REPORT SALES_SUMMARY(CLIENT_CUR_REC.*)
      END FOREACH
   END FOREACH
END FOREACH
```

When you examine this code more closely, you realize that you're repeatedly declaring the SALES_CALL_CUR and CLIENT_CUR cursors. This is quite expensive, especially when you recognize that your company has 3,000 sales representatives, each of whom makes 20 sales calls each month and visits 10 clients. This adds up to tens of thousands of extra SQL parsing and optimizing calls. Luckily, it's simple to alter the code to greatly reduce the amount of engine work:

```
DECLARE SALES_REP_CUR CURSOR FOR
   SELECT LAST_NAME,
          FIRST_NAME,
          EMPLOYEE_ID
     FROM EMPLOYEES
 ORDER BY LAST_NAME

LET SALES_CALL_STMT = "SELECT CLIENT_ID,CALL_DATE,CALL_RESULT
   FROM SALES_CALLS WHERE SALES_CALLS.SALES_ID = ?"

PREPARE SALES_CALL_PREP FROM SALES_CALL_STMT

DECLARE SALES_CALL_CUR CURSOR FOR SALES_CALL_PREP

LET CLIENT_STMT = "SELECT CLIENT_COMPANY,ACCOUNT_BALANCE FROM CLIENTS
                   WHERE CLIENTS.CLIENT_ID = ?"

PREPARE CLIENT_PREP FROM CLIENT_STMT

DECLARE CLIENT_CUR CURSOR FOR CLIENT_PREP

FOREACH SALES_REP_CUR INTO SALES_REP_REC.*
   OPEN SALES_CALL_CUR USING SALES_REP_REC.EMPLOYEE_ID
   WHILE (1)
      FETCH SALES_CALL_CUR INTO SALES_CALL_REC.*
      IF (SQLCA.SQLCODE != 0) THEN
         EXIT WHILE
      END IF
      OPEN CLIENT_CUR USING SALES_CALL_REC.CLIENT_ID
      WHILE (SQLCA.SQLCODE = 0)
         FETCH CLIENT_CUR INTO CLIENT_CUR_REC.*
         OUTPUT TO REPORT SALES_SUMMARY(CLIENT_CUR_REC.*)
      END WHILE
   END WHILE
END FOREACH
```

For more information about how to properly use the PREPARE and DECLARE statements see the "General tips" section.

Another way to streamline the above code is to use joins between the tables. This lets you declare fewer cursors, and retrieve more information from fewer database calls. For more details on the benefits of joins versus single SELECTs, see the "General tips" section.

Case study 2

You've been receiving confusing and contradictory messages from a number of users over the past few months. You've decided to put together a plan to address all of the complaints at one time, since you speculate that these problems might somehow all be related:

BATCH JOB FAILURE

One of the night operators tells you that she's been having trouble running some of the month-end posting programs. Sometimes the programs run to completion, but other times, they stop running, and eventually fail. The operators then have to restart the jobs, which inconveniences many users, and delays the entire month-end procedure.

IMAGING APPLICATION CRASH

Several users in the accounts receivable department point out that their check scanning program (which was written by an outside company) periodically crashes. There's no way to predict what will cause the crash, but it only happens between 8 and 9 p.m.

SLOW UNIX SYSTEM PERFORMANCE

There are other applications that run on your system that don't use the database. The UNIX administrator has been hearing criticism from the users of these other applications that their programs are running very slowly. This is quite puzzling, because the applications that use OnLine seem to run very well.

HOW TO PROCEED?

Your first priority is to solve the month-end program problems, since those programs are a very important part of the company's business operation. They're also having the biggest negative impact on the most number of users.

The month-end posting process involves one large ESQL/COBOL batch program. You can't continually test this program on the production machine: it would wreak havoc on the database's integrity. To avoid this problem, you decide to set up a test environment that faithfully replicates your production environment, from a hardware, software, and database perspective. You can then test the program as much as you'd like.

Once you set up the test environment, you try running the batch program. Sure enough, the program has a number of problems, and can't finish its work. The OnLine log reflects these failures:

```
16:07:40  Lock table overflow - user id 151, process id 29184
16:07:40  Lock table overflow - user id 151, process id 29184
16:07:40  Lock table overflow - user id 151, process id 29184
16:07:40  Lock table overflow - user id 151, process id 29184
16:07:40  Lock table overflow - user id 151, process id 29184
16:07:40  Lock table overflow - user id 151, process id 29184
16:07:40  Logical Log 228 Complete
16:09:44  Logical Log 229 Complete
16:09:44  Checkpoint Completed
16:09:51  Logical Log 230 Complete
16:09:53  Checkpoint Completed
16:09:53  Aborting Long Transaction: tx 0xc0433570 0
16:09:59  Logical Log 231 Complete
16:10:06  Logical Log 232 Complete
16:10:12  Logical Log 233 Complete
16:10:12  Checkpoint Completed
```

Here's one part of the update segment from the program:

```
Program 1
.       .       .       .       .
.       .       .       .       .
PROCEDURE DIVISION.

.       .       .       .       .
PERFORM C-1000-CREATE-CURSOR.
PERFORM T-4000-START-TRANSACTION.
PERFORM X-1000-OPEN-CURSOR.
PERFORM X-2000-PROCESS-CURSOR.
.       .       .       .       .
.       .       .       .       .
PERFORM T-5000-END-TRANSACTION.

C-1000-CREATE CURSOR.
   EXEC SQL.
      DECLARE BALANCE_UPD_CUR CURSOR FOR
         SELECT ACCT_NUM, ACCT_BALANCE
           FROM CLIENT_PROFILE
            FOR UPDATE.
   END EXEC.

T-4000-START-TRANSACTION.
   EXEC SQL.
      BEGIN WORK.
   END EXEC.

T-5000-END-TRANSACTION.
   IF :WS-OK-TO-COMMIT EQUALS 1
      EXEC SQL.
         COMMIT WORK.
      END EXEC.
   ELSE
      EXEC SQL.
         ROLLBACK WORK.
      END EXEC.

X-1000-OPEN-CURSOR.
   EXEC SQL.
      OPEN BALANCE_UPD_CUR.
   END EXEC.

X-2000-PROCESS-CURSOR.
   EXEC SQL.
      FETCH BALANCE_UPD_CUR INTO :WS-ACCT-NUM, :WS-ACCT-BALANCE.
   END EXEC.

   EXEC SQL.
      SELECT SUM(TRANSACTION_AMOUNT)
        INTO :WS-MONTH-TOTAL
        FROM TRANSACTION_DETAIL T
       WHERE T.ACCOUNT_NUM = :WS-ACCT-NUM
         AND T.TRANSACTION_DATE BETWEEN :WS-START-DATE AND :WS-END-DATE.
   END EXEC.

   EXEC SQL.
      UPDATE CLIENT_PROFILE
         SET ACCT_BALANCE = ACCT_BALANCE + :WS-MONTH-TOTAL
       WHERE CURRENT OF BALANCE_UPD_CUR.
   END EXEC.

   IF SQLERROR
      MOVE -1 TO :WS-OK-TO-COMMIT.
```

```
.      .      .      .      .
:      :      :      :      :
```

Right before the program failed, you ran "tbstat -l" to see what the logical logs looked like at the time:

```
RSAM Version 5.02.UC1    -- On-Line -- Up  4 days 4:31:01 -- 30048 Kbytes

Physical Logging
Buffer bufused   bufsize  numpages numwrits pages/io
  P-2  0         16       38       4         9.50
   phybegin physize  phypos    phyused  %used
   1000da   1000     876       0        0.00

Logical Logging
Buffer bufused   bufsize  numrecs   numpages numwrits recs/pages pages/io
  L-2  0         16       222       28       28         7.9       1.0

address   number    flags     uniqid   begin        size     used    %used
c00367d8 1          F------   228      1004c2        500        0   100.00
c00367f4 2          F------   229      1006b6        500        0   100.00
c0036810 3          F------   230      1008aa        500        0   100.00
c003682c 4          U---C-L   231      100a9e        500      433    86.60
```

You decide to review the "systables" entry for the "client_profile" table:

```
tabname      client_profile
owner        db_user
partnum      16777718
tabid        100
rowsize      258
ncols        12
nindexes     4
nrows        203404
created      07/12/1994
version      6553602
tabtype      T
locklevel    R
npused       31044
fextsize     40000
nextsize     4000
flags        0
site
dbname
```

The output from "tbstat" and "dbaccess", along with the source code, indicate a number of reasons why you're experiencing these problems:

- Number of requested locks exceeds number of available locks. The "lock table overflow" message from the OnLine log means that a process tried to allocate more locks than were available at the time.

- Transaction is longer than the available logical log space. The "Aborting Long Transaction" message from the OnLine log means that the engine didn't have enough space in the logical logs to service your request.

You can choose one or more of these solutions to resolve these problems:

- **Locking deficiency**
  - Increase the number of locks. If you're running out of locks, try increasing the value of the LOCKS parameter in your TBCONFIG/ONCONFIG file. The "OnLine tips" section discusses this topic in more detail.
  - Change the lock level for the table. This table currently has row level locking. This improves concurrency, but requires many more locks. If you're running a batch job that consistently runs out of locks, consider temporarily changing the table's lock level to page. Once the job finishes, you can change the lock level back to its original value. See the "OnLine tips" section for more about this subject.
  - Lock the table before running the job. If none of the above suggestions eliminate the problem, try locking the table in either exclusive or shared mode before you begin the batch job. For very large transactions, this may be the only way to avoid running out of locks.
- **Long transaction**
  - Shorten the transaction. You can minimize the likelihood of a long transaction by breaking up the number of rows that you must process into several, shorter transactions. See the "General tips" section for more detail about the benefits of more compact transactions.
  - Increase the number and/or size of logical logs. If you believe that your transaction is barely exceeding the available logical log space, you might be able to make the transaction succeed by adding more logical logs or increasing the size of your existing logical logs (6.00 and newer). However, while this approach may work in the short term, it doesn't mean that you'll never experience any other long transactions in the future. It's a good idea to review your programs and eliminate long transactions at the source code level. See the "General tips" section for additional suggestions about long transactions.
  - Change the long transaction high water mark. Recall that OnLine uses the LTXHWM parameter to decide when to roll back a long transaction. If you have LTXHWM set too low, OnLine may rollback a transaction that might have otherwise finished successfully. See the "OnLine tips" section for more information.

Next on your agenda is the mystery of a fast OnLine engine running under a seemingly slow UNIX system. As you begin your investigation, you run "tbstat -p" to make sure that OnLine is truly running quickly:

```
RSAM Version 5.01.UD1    -- On-Line -- Up 9 days 19:31:15 -- 12576 Kbytes

Profile
dskreads pagreads bufreads %cached dskwrits pagwrits bufwrits %cached
11120    11300    838770   98.67   15810    25540    190880   91.72

isamtot  open     start    read     write    rewrite  delete   commit   rollbk
603980   69996    72473    211054   5499     7212     1795     528      0

ovtbls   ovlock   ovuser     ovbuff   usercpu  syscpu   numckpts flushes
0        0        0             0       729.83   248.61   1193      6164

bufwaits lokwaits lockreqs deadlks  dltouts  lchwaits ckpwaits compress
44       0        673372   0        0        21169    5        208
```

These numbers look good; you also run several typical large, complex queries to see how they perform. They seem to run very well, but you observe other, non-database programs that have serious delays. This only adds to your confusion about how the database can run so quickly while other applications creep along.

Once you run the "vmstat" utility, however, you start to realize what's causing the problem:

```
      procs            memory                      page                            faults       cpu
 r     b     w     avm    free   re   at   pi   po    fr   de    sr     in     sy    cs   us sy id
61     0     0   34388     471    0    0   17  135     5    0   161    212    147   191  54  42 0
61     0     0   34399     277    0    0    6  128     4    0   157    194    143   189  45  55 0
61     0     0   34399     219    0    0    3  153     3    0   180    233    127   204  44  56 0
61     0     0   34432     327    0    0    8  159     6    0   194    259    137   211  45  55 0
61     0     0   34482     236    9    0   16  157     9    0   188    220    126   173  40  60 0
61     0     0   34438     281   24    0   44  180     1    0   198    157    134   129  36  64 0
61     0     0   34591     117   12    0   68  219     0    0   230    156    142   130  38  62 0
```

These statistics show a system that's running out of memory. The "free" column's numbers are much lower than the "avm" column. In addition, the CPU is spending a larger percentage of its time handling system work than handling user requests. This also indicates a computer that is spending too much time administering, and not enough time actually working.

If OnLine's cache rates are good, but your UNIX performance is bad, try freeing up some memory for the operating system to use, by reducing the number of shared memory buffers. Remember that the shared memory buffers have the biggest impact on OnLine's response. The best approach is to lower, in small increments, the number of shared memory buffers that you've granted OnLine. After each change, see if your system is faster than before. If it is, continue to lower the number of shared memory buffers. You need only stop when additional changes stop helping (and begin hurting).

For more information about the relationship between OnLine shared memory buffers and UNIX performance, see the "OnLine tips" section.

Finally, you focus on the last problem. Solving this third party imaging application enigma won't be easy: you don't have the source code, and the vendor wants $2,000 a day (plus expenses) to send a consultant out to your site to research your problem. Before you go to your management and ask for a purchase order, you try to learn more about the symptoms of this puzzle.

The users have told you that the application crash only occurs between 8 and 9 p.m. Unfortunately, no other applications (e.g., order entry, sales tracking) have any problems during that time span. In addition, the OnLine log doesn't indicate any engine problems during that time:

```
Sun Jul 30 19:58:21 1995

20:02:25  Checkpoint Completed
20:09:10  Checkpoint Completed
20:15:09  Checkpoint Completed
20:22:01  Checkpoint Completed
20:25:00  Logical Log 45 Complete
20:28:54  Checkpoint Completed
20:35:18  Checkpoint Completed
20:42:33  Checkpoint Completed
20:50:12  Checkpoint Completed
20:59:44  Checkpoint Completed
```

You decide to first find out if any jobs that affect the database are regularly run between 8 and 9 p.m. You speak with all of the application project managers for your site to learn if their applications might be affecting yours. Remember that it's always a good idea to maintain good relationships with the other members of the IS department; you'll need their cooperation when you try to enhance your system's performance.

After you finish speaking to all of the other project managers, you conclude that there are only two jobs regularly running during the time in question. To see if either of these two jobs has an effect, you ask each project manager to abstain from running his application's job. To reduce the number of variables, and increase your chance of correctly identifying the trouble-causing program, you only remove one job per night.

Unfortunately, it doesn't seem to matter which job is or isn't running: the imaging crash still happens each night. Your next alternative is to talk to the operations staff to see what jobs they run between 8 and 9 p.m. The only jobs that the operations staff runs in the evenings are the daily system backup and the OnLine archive. You decide to go back and look at a wider range of the OnLine log:

```
Sun Jul 30 21:14:37 1995

18:45:11  Level 0 Archive Started
18:55:33  Checkpoint Completed
19:02:25  Checkpoint Completed
   .          .           .
   .          .           .
```

```
21:14:38  Checkpoint Completed
21:14:39  Level 0 Archive Completed
```

You didn't notice the archive when you first looked at the log because it started before, and finished after, the time period in which the application failures were occurring.

At this point, you remember that OnLine treats BLOBs stored in blobspaces differently than BLOBs stored in standard dbspaces. During an archive, OnLine prevents applications from inserting, updating, or deleting rows that have one or more columns kept in blobspaces until the blobspace has been archived. You run "tbstat -d" to look at your disk layout:

```
RSAM Version 5.01.UD1    -- On-Line -- Up 9 days 19:31:15 -- 12576 Kbytes

Dbspaces
address  number   flags    fchunk   nchunks  flags    owner    name
c001f698 1        1        1        1        N        informix rootdbs
c001f6c8 2        1        2        2        N        informix logdbs
c001f6f8 3        1        4        1        N        informix salesdbs
c001f728 4        1        5        1        N        informix orderdbs
c001f758 5        10       6        1        N B      informix blobdbs
 5 active, 10 total


Chunks
address  chk/dbs offset   size     free     bpages   flags pathname
c001f0a8 1   1   0        100000   13680             PO-   /usr/informix/rootchunk1
c001f140 2   2   0         50000    3000             PO-   /usr/informix/logchunk1
c001f1d8 3   3   0        250000   24080             PO-   /usr/informix/saleschunk1
c001f270 4   4   0        300000    2040             PO-   /usr/informix/orderchunk1
c001f308 5   2   0         50000   12000             PO-   /usr/informix/logchunk2
c001f3a0 6   5   0        400000  ~24890    400000   POB   /usr/informix/blobchunk1

 6 active, 10 total
```

The "blobdbs" blobspace is defined last. This means that during an archive, no one is able to modify any pages in the space until the archive has finished backing up the blobspace. This essentially locks the space for the duration of the entire archive. Your next task is to see if the imaging application actually uses this space. As it turns out, one important table does indeed store its byte column in the blobdbs blobspace. The application apparently wasn't coded to handle a locked blobspace. To confirm your theory, you ask operations to wait to run the archive until after all the imaging users have left. Sure enough, there are no application crashes that night.

You now have a number of alternatives from which to choose to correct this flaw:

- Reschedule the archive. If you can possibly change the archive time to a time period when users are less likely to be working with the imaging application, do so. This requires the least amount of work.
- Re-create the dbspaces, and define the blobspace sooner. Remember that OnLine archives in chunk order. Blobspaces are locked until their chunk(s) have been archived. If you define the blobspace right after the root dbspace, it

will be archived closer to the start of the operation, and freed sooner. Unfortunately, this requires a complete re-initialization of your system.

- Insist that the vendor gracefully handle blobspace lock conditions. You should always code your BLOB-handling programs to deal with this type of problem.

For more information about working more efficiently with BLOBs, see the "OnLine tips" section.

Case study 3

You're the database administrator for an executive information system (EIS). Senior management uses this system to track sales at each of your company's 350 restaurants. Each restaurant is open 24 hours a day, and generates hundreds of transactions per hour. Lately, you've been hearing some complaints from your users that the system isn't running as fast as they'd like. Specifically, they cite the amount of time it takes to get results from their reports.

As usual, when you ask the users to identify individual queries or reports, they respond by saying that all of the queries and reports are too slow. Still, you decide to move forward and focus on one heavily used report, figuring that if you can overcome its bottlenecks, you'll be able to do the same for the rest of the application.

HOW TO PROCEED?

The report that you chose to work on tracks daily sales at all of your company's restaurants. Once an hour, your central computer polls each restaurant, and uploads the transaction file. This file contains detailed information about each check, including what was ordered, when it was ordered, and how much it cost. Once the transaction file is uploaded, you post all the details into the "item_history", "ticket_history", and "item_ticket" tables:

Table 5.1 item_history

restaurant_id	item_id	item_cost	order_time
.	.	.	.
209	45	12.99	1996-01-30 12:09:19
209	2	1.99	1996-01-30 12:10:25
152	101	7.99	1996-01-30 12:10:30
.	.	.	.

Table 5.2 ticket_history

restaurant_id	ticket_id	ticket_total	ticket_time
.	.	.	.
175	130995	34.18	1996-01-30 13:17:44
175	130996	106.92	1996-01-30 13:19:08
298	207889	56.71	1996-01-30 13:20:55
.	.	.	.

Table 5.3 item_ticket

restaurant_id	ticket_id	item_id
.	.	.
95	103392	18
95	103392	6
304	909553	41
304	909553	33
304	909553	11
.	.	.

The hourly sales report sums up, by restaurant, all of the sales for the current day. As you review the program, you realize that it spends the majority of its processing time retrieving and summing up the individual sales detail records. What would happen if you simply kept a summary table, and acquired your daily sales information from it, rather than continually re-reading the "ticket_history" table and re-calculating the sales figures? You could update this new table as records came in from the field, thereby spreading the processing load more evenly over the day.

Your new summary table could have this format:

Table 5.4 daily_sales_total

restaurant_id	sales_date	sales_total
.	.	.
25	01/29/1996	12099.21
25	01/30/1996	6733.09
.	.	.
26	01/29/1996	9508.94
26	01/30/1996	8801.53
.	.	.

If you placed a unique composite index on the "restaurant_id" and "sales_date" columns, you could quickly locate the appropriate row to update as the latest hour's sales data came in. Once you found the right row, you would only need to update the "sales_total" column to reflect the most recent hour's added sales. When you ran summary reports, you could then read this (smaller) table, instead of churning through mountains of data. For more information about the benefits of storing historic data versus continually recalculating summaries, see the "Relational database design concepts" section.

When you first installed OnLine, you didn't explicitly create any dbspaces other than root. This means that your physical log, all of your logical logs, and all of your data are stored in the root dbspace.

When you run the UNIX "iostat" command, you notice that one of the disk drives is continually under a heavy load, while the other drive has much less work:

```
/dev/informixdb  /dev/rdsk/c0d0s2
bps  sps  msps  bps  sps  msps

 206  3.3  72.2   12  0.9  60.3
 123  1.8  80.5    6  0.3  11.1
  55  1.6  36.9   15  0.5  54.0
 107  2.8  48.1   31  1.1   7.0
  96  0.8 136.8    7  1.3  12.2
 138  1.0 183.4   21  0.9  24.8
  94  1.4  77.0   17  1.4  30.9
  54  1.0  67.3   43  2.3  38.1
 135  1.2 150.1   15  1.7  18.9
 163  2.8  85.6   42  0.8  23.3
```

```
 68  1.2  85.0    0  0.0   0.0
 44  0.2 338.1    0  0.0   0.0
 81  2.0  57.5    0  0.0   0.0
 83  1.6  66.5   55  1.2  27.7
115  2.2  75.0    6  1.4  19.8
193  1.8 146.9    0  0.0   0.0
 75  0.4 217.4   28  2.0  44.2
```

In the above output, "bps" stands for number of bytes per second, "sps" is the number of seeks per second, and "msps" is the number of milliseconds it took to satisfy the average seek.

You realize that if you did a better job of spreading the load between your disk drives, you should get better I/O performance.

In this case, that means placing your physical log and some heavily used tables on one drive, and placing your logical log and other heavily used tables on another drive. You can even set up two temporary dbspaces, one per drive. This should help balance the amount of I/O work that each drive has to do.

If you're using OnLine 7.1 or newer, you can use the new fragmentation feature to help spread your data among your disk drives.

For more information about the relationship between disk layout and OnLine engine performance, see the "OnLine tips" section. For more detail about fragmentation, see the "Fragmentation and PDQ" section.

Case study 4

This next case study begins with a frantic meeting among the users, software development team, and database administration team. You're part of the development team, which has spent the last year developing a student records system for a large university. You wrote the application in 4GL, and it uses the SE database engine.

The school year begins in two weeks, and the users are already beginning to notice some serious performance obstacles. What will happen when all the students start arriving and using the system? The users are especially worried about these obstacles:

PERFORMING INQUIRY PROBLEMS

One of the nicest features of this new system is the student inquiry screen, which provides authorized users with a free-form query screen to rapidly locate information from the database. Unfortunately, certain queries take too long because the database has grown.

SLOW REPORT

One of the larger monthly reports retrieves and sums up student tuition payment data. During production, you expect that this report will exceed 200 pages. The users are quite worried, because it currently takes 30 minutes just to produce a 10-page report.

They inform you that it won't be acceptable for the production report to take longer than one hour to print.

MYSTERIOUS POSTING FAILURES

Periodically, users have noticed that changes they made to the database were not posted, even though the update program reports that the changes were made. They're wondering why this is happening.

SLOWLY DEGRADING QUERY RESPONSE

The users have been testing the system over the last three months. They've been adding a lot of information to the database, and they've noticed that the system has gradually begun to lose speed. Queries that took three seconds to search the original small database now take 10 seconds to read the larger database, which itself is only one-tenth of the expected size of the production database. There haven't been any changes to the source code; the only difference is that there's now more data.

All of this is news to the software development and database administration teams. They had installed the software three months ago, and hadn't heard much from the users. In fact, no one from either of these teams has even logged onto the test machine in the last few weeks.

HOW TO PROCEED?

Your first priority is to fix the student inquiry screen: this is the most visible part of the new system. If it continues to run very slowly, the users may reject the application entirely.

The inquiry screen contains a number of fields, but the three most commonly searched fields are student_id, campus, and major. When you search on "student_number", the program returns information from the "student_profile" table almost instantly. If you search on the "student_number", "campus" and "major_code" fields together, performance is also very good. However, if you search only on the "campus" or "major_code" column, the response really suffers. Even though you can search on these fields individually, they're all combined in the "student_id" column, which is the primary key of the "student_profile" table. This is an 11-byte character field that can broken down as follows:

```
nnnnnnxxyyy
```

where "nnnnnn" is a six-digit student number, "xx" is a two-character campus identifier, and "yyy" is a three-character code that identifies the student's major.

You isolate certain segments of the actual SQL queries to see what kind of performance they encounter:

When you request information based on the initial six-digit student number, the query plan looks like this:

```
QUERY:
------
SELECT * FROM STUDENT_PROFILE WHERE STUDENT_ID MATCHES "174334*"

Estimated Cost: 103
Estimated # of Rows Returned: 2

1) db_user.student_profile: INDEX PATH

    (1) Index Keys: student_id
        Lower Index Filter: db_user.student_profile.student_id
        MATCHES '174334*'
```

If you make an inquiry, and provide the student number, campus identifier, and the major code, the query plan looks like this:

```
QUERY:
------
SELECT * FROM STUDENT_PROFILE WHERE STUDENT_ID = "109943NPSPA"

Estimated Cost: 76
Estimated # of Rows Returned: 1

1) db_user.student_profile: INDEX PATH

    (1) Index Keys: student_id
        Lower Index Filter: db_user.student_profile.student_id =
        '109943NPSPA'
```

When you search the database based on the major code, you get this query plan:

```
QUERY:
------
SELECT * FROM STUDENT_PROFILE WHERE STUDENT_ID[9,11] = "MED"

Estimated Cost: 2582
Estimated # of Rows Returned: 28

1) db_user.student_profile: SEQUENTIAL SCAN

    Filters: db_user.student_profile.student_id[9,11] = 'MED'
```

If you combine the campus identifier and major code in a query, you get a query plan that looks like this:

```
QUERY:
------
SELECT * FROM STUDENT_PROFILE
WHERE STUDENT_ID[7,8] = "AB" AND STUDENT_ID[9,11] = "MED"

Estimated Cost: 2099
Estimated # of Rows Returned: 10
```

```
1) db_user.student_profile: SEQUENTIAL SCAN

 Filters: (db_user.student_profile.student_id[7,8] = 'AB' AND
           db_user.student_profile.student_id[9,11] = 'MED' )
```

The problem with the inquiry screen is the database design. Specifically, the primary key of the "student_profile" table is not atomic (e.g., it can be broken down further). Consequently, users may want to search based on sub-components of the primary key. Remember that non-initial substring searches don't utilize any indexes: you must always start with the leftmost byte if you want to avoid a sequential scan.

For the short term, one way around this problem would be to append two new columns to the "student_profile" table. One column could store the campus identifier, while the other could store the student's major code. You could then each index of these columns, and even create composite indexes with these columns in the first field of the index. This would be helpful, for example, if you wanted to search for all students having a psychology major, and sort the results by campus and student number. For more information about creating good primary keys, see the "Creating a Well-Designed Database" chapter.

Next, you examine the posting failure problem. You pay special attention to the class request program, because it seems to have the most trouble with this issue. The class request program works with two tables: "class_status" and "wait_list". The "class_status" table stores information about the current state of each class, while the "wait_list" table contains a list of all students wanting to register for a particular class:

Table 5.5 class_status

class_id	**description**
.	.
C3945	Psychology 101
C3946	Theory of CP/M
.	.

Table 5.6 wait_list

student_id	class_id	date_requested...
.	.	.
174334ALPSY	C3945	08/28/1995
050333BUSOC	C1031	08/28/1995
.	.	.

To prevent orphaned "wait_list" records, you've referenced the "class_id" column in the "wait_list" table to the corresponding column in the "class_status" table.

Sometimes, classes are canceled because there aren't enough students interested in enrolling. This cancellation process begins when an authorized user selects a class to be dropped. The program then sends an electronic mail message to all the students who wanted to take the class, informing them that the class is no longer offered. Next, it removes all affected student records from the "wait_list" table, and deletes the "class_status" record. This is where the problem sometimes occurs. Other users occasionally report that they can still see the class, even though it should have been removed.

You review the segment of 4GL that processes the delete:

```
DEFINE CLASS_TO_DELETE    LIKE CLASS_STATUS.CLASS_ID
DEFINE STUDENT_MAIL_CODE LIKE WAIT_LIST.STUDENT_ID
.      .      .      .      .
.      .      .      .      .
WHENEVER ERROR CONTINUE

DECLARE MAIL_CURSOR CURSOR FOR
   SELECT STUDENT_ID
   FROM   WAIT_LIST
   WHERE  CLASS_ID = CLASS_TO_DELETE

FOREACH MAIL_CURSOR INTO STUDENT_MAIL_CODE
   CALL SEND_MAIL(STUDENT_MAIL_CODE, CLASS_TO_DELETE, "CLASS
     DROPPED")
END FOREACH

BEGIN WORK

DELETE FROM WAIT_LIST WHERE CLASS_ID = CLASS_TO_DELETE

DELETE FROM CLASS_STATUS WHERE CLASS_ID = CLASS_TO_DELETE

COMMIT WORK

MESSAGE "Class deleted"
.      .      .      .      .
.      .      .      .      .
```

There are at least two problems with this segment of code that would explain the posting failure:

- **WHENEVER ERROR CONTINUE.** When you issue this command, the program continues past any errors, even if the errors are serious. Unfortunately, this means that the program may proceed when it really should halt. In the above example, the program ran to completion, regardless of whether data in either table was locked. When WHENEVER ERROR CONTINUE was replaced by WHENEVER ERROR STOP, the program failed, and printed the following error message:

```
Program stopped at "del_class.4gl", line number 1310.
SQL statement error number -244.
Could not do a physical-order read to fetch next row.
SYSTEM error number -107.
ISAM error:  record is locked.
```

  During testing, it's a good idea to let programs fail when they encounter errors. Otherwise, how will you know if your code is truly running well? See the "General tips" section for more detail about using WHENEVER ERROR.

- **Error checking.** The program doesn't check for any errors after important SQL statements. What happens, for example, if a row that you want to delete from the "wait_list" table is locked by another user? It's always a good idea to make error checking an integral part of all your programs, especially around SQL statements.

Since you have an entire month before the slowly running end-of-month report is executed, you've saved this question for last. You print out the report's 4GL code, and focus on the SQL that retrieves the records to be printed:

```
DECLARE PAYMENT_CUR CURSOR FOR
   SELECT STUDENT_ID,
          STUDENT_LAST,
          STUDENT_FIRST,
          PAYMENT_DATE,
          PAYMENT_AMOUNT,
          LENDER_CODE,
          LENDER_NAME
     FROM STUDENT_PROFILE S,
          PAYMENTS P,
          LENDERS L
    WHERE S.STUDENT_ID   = P.STUDENT_ID
      AND P.LENDER_CODE = L.LENDER_CODE
    ORDER BY L.LENDER_CODE, S.STUDENT_ID, P.PAYMENT_DATE
```

The three tables in this query are laid out like this:

Table 5.7 student_profile

student_id	student_last	student_first....
.	.	.
174334ALPSY	Tseng	Steven
174335BUCSI	Gibb	Ellen
174356SBMED	Lankpoop	Franz
.	.	.

This table has a unique index on the "student_id" column, and a composite index on the "student_last" and "student_first" columns.

Table 5.8 payments

payment_id	lender_code	student_code	payment_date	payment_amount
.	.	.	.	.
30844	98	174334ALPSY	09/04/1995	200.00
30845	97	270910SCRCO	09/04/1995	088.45
.	.	.	.	.

This table has a unique index on the "payment_id" column, and a composite index on the student_code, payment_date, payment_amount, and lender_code columns.

Table 5.9 lenders

lender_code	lender_name
.	.
97	Bank of East San Carlos
98	Vinnie's Loans in a Hurry
99	Dai-Segundo Bank
.	.

This table has a unique index on the "lender_code" column.

There are several reasons why this report runs slowly:

- **Multi-table ORDER BY.** If you ORDER BY columns from different tables, the optimizer is forced to create a temporary table, even if each of the columns is indexed in its own table. See the "Indexing strategies" section for more detail about sorting from different tables.
- **Incorrect order in composite index.** Even if you ORDER BY the "lender_code", "student_id", and "payment_date" columns from the "payments" table, you'd still create a temporary table, because you wouldn't be using the composite index correctly. Remember that if you have a composite index on columns a,b, and c, for example, you can sort on the following columns and not create a temporary table:

```
ORDER BY A,B,C
ORDER BY A,B
ORDER BY A
```

  If you create a composite index on the "lender_code", "student_id", and "payment_date" columns from the "payments" table, you'll be able to avoid a large and potentially expensive temporary table. For more detail about composite indexes, see the "Indexing strategies" section.

Case study 5

You've just been hired to administer a large, distributed, hotel reservation system. Your environment consists of one big central server that services a few dozen local clients (some on terminals, and some on PCs), and hundreds of remote PC clients. The remote PCs communicate with the server via 9600 baud leased lines. Performance is generally good, but there are a few issues that the users want you to address:

SLUGGISH INSERT/UPDATE/DELETE STATEMENTS

Your employer has set response guidelines for your application: When a customer calls in to make or update a reservation, it should take no longer than two seconds for the database to acknowledge the request. When a customer calls in to inquire about an existing reservation, it should take no longer than one second for the database to return the customer's record.

At this point, the application is easily meeting the inquiry response goal, but barely inserting or updating reservations quickly enough. This is very puzzling to all involved, since everyone knows that it takes longer to retrieve data than to insert/update it.

SLOW REMOTE REPORTS

You get conflicting information from your users regarding report performance. Those users directly connected to the server are satisfied with their reports, while most PC-based users claim that it takes too long to produce their more commonly used reports.

HOW TO PROCEED?

Since good screen response is the most visible part of your application's performance (both to users and customers), you choose it as your first topic to study. Reservations are stored in the "property_reserv" table:

```
create table property_reserv
(
   reserv_id           serial primary key,
   property_id         smallint references property_header,
   customer_last       char(30),
   customer_first      char(15),
   customer_addr1      char(40),
   customer_addr2      char(40),
   customer_city       char(20),
   customer_state      char(2),
   customer_country    char(15),
   customer_phone      char(20),
   reserv_date         date,
   special_needs       char(1) check (special_needs in ('Y','N')),
   payment_method      char(2) check (payment_method in
     ('CC','CA','PO')),
   frequent_guest      char(1) check (frequent_guest in ('Y','N')),
   promotion_code      char(2) references promotions
);
```

In addition to the unique index on the "reserv_id" column (primary key) and the index on the "property_id" and "promotion_code" columns (foreign key), your predecessor created these indexes:

```
create index pr_idx1 on
property_reserv(reserv_id,property_id);
create index pr_idx2 on
    property_reserv(property_id,reserv_id);
create index pr_idx3 on property_reserv(customer_last);
create index pr_idx4 on
    property_reserv(customer_last,customer_first);
create index pr_idx5 on property_reserv(customer_city);
create index pr_idx6 on property_reserv(reserv_date,
    customer_last);
create index pr_idx7 on property_reserv(payment_method);
create index pr_idx8 on property_reserv(special_needs);
create index pr_idx9 on property_reserv(frequent_guest);
create index pr_idx10 on
    property_reserv(promotion_code,payment_method);
```

Note that this table holds all of the worldwide reservations for your company's hotels: the table has nearly 100,000 rows at any one time. Once you insert a row in this table, you also trigger a stored procedure that updates that specific hotel's database with data pertaining to the new reservation.

Can you see why inserting or updating data in this table might take much longer than simply reading information? Remember that the database engine needs to refresh all or some of this table's indexes each time you insert or update a row. If you're inserting, all indexes are affected; if you're updating, the engine only refreshes those indexes whose corresponding columns" values have changed. The "property_reserv" table has 13 indexes; this means that the engine must perform at least 13 additional write operations each time you add a row. The extra cost doesn't stop there, however: the engine also may need to rebalance the index b-tree for each index. Finally, some of the indexes on this table are highly duplicate (e.g., the indexes on the "special_needs", "frequent_guest", and "payment_type'), which places an even greater load on the engine as it attempts to find the right location to insert this new value into the index.

If you're ever faced with a situation like this, see if you can remove some of the extra indexes. Instead of taking a "top-down" approach to identifying which indexes to remove, try using a "bottom-up" technique: remove all the indexes from the table, and then add back only those indexes that you're sure that you need. See the "Indexing strategies" section for a more detailed discussion about the costs of excess indexing and highly-redundant indexes.

Aside from the indexes, the trigger might add a delay into the process, since it could take a few moments for the remote system to receive and acknowledge the reservation record. This time lag might not be a problem for most types of applications, but it can become an issue for OLTP systems that need sub-second response. In this example, a better procedure for notifying the hotels about their future guests would be to run an asynchronous process. This process would periodically (between every few minutes and every few hours) scan the "property_reserv" table, and update the remote databases with new records. This procedure would effectively de-couple the local database and remote database operations, and should help remove one of the barriers to good screen response.

With regard to the slow remote reports, rather than examine all reports at once, you decide to focus on one of the most requested reports. This report displays reservation information for all of your properties within a particular region. This report is run hundreds of times by dozens of operators and managers over the course of each day.

Here's the segment of code that obtains the data for the report:

```
EXEC SQL BEGIN DECLARE SECTION;

.    .    .    .
.    .    .    .
```

```
struct header_mask
{
   int property_id;
   char property_region[10];
   char property_name[30];
   char property_address1[40];
   char property_address2[40];
   .   .   .   .
   .   .   .   .
} header_struct;

struct reserv_mask
{
   int reserv_id;
   int property_id;
   char customer_last[30];
   .   .   .   .
   .   .   .   .
} reserv_struct;

EXEC SQL END DECLARE SECTION;
.   .   .   .   .
.   .   .   .   .

EXEC SQL prepare header_prep from
   "select * from property_header where property_region = ?";
EXEC SQL declare header_cur cursor for header_prep;

EXEC SQL prepare reserv_prep from
   "select * from property_reserv where property_id = ?";
EXEC SQL declare reserv_cur cursor for reserv_prep;

/* Get the region code from the user */
.   .   .   .   .
.   .   .   .   .
EXEC SQL open header_cur using :property_region;

while (1)
{
   EXEC SQL fetch header_cur into :header_struct;
   if (sqlca.sqlcode)
      break;
   EXEC SQL open reserv_cur using :header_struct.property_id;
   while (1)
   {
      EXEC SQL fetch reserv_cur into :reserv_struct;
      if (sqlca.sqlcode)
         break;
      print_record(header_struct.property_id,  \  /* Send
         data to report */
                    header_struct.property_name,\
                    reserv_struct);
   }
}

EXEC SQL commit work;
.   .   .   .   .
.   .   .   .   .
```

When you look at the code, you realize that there are a number of problems with it, especially when you consider that the report runs in a client/server environment:

- **Retrieving unnecessary columns.** In the above example, you really only need the "property_id" and "property_name" columns from the "property_header" table for the report, yet you're retrieving all of the "property_header" table's columns. Fetching these extra columns might not have much impact on local clients or terminals, yet remote clients or terminals would probably notice an improvement if you eliminated any superfluous columns from your queries. See the "General tips" section for other recommendations on reducing pipe traffic.
- **Sequential SELECTs instead of single joins.** Recall that successive, sequential SELECT statements usually result in more traffic between the front-end and the back-end processes than joins. This really adds up in a distributed processing environment, since the front-end and back-end processes may communicate over relatively poor data lines, and be separated by thousands of miles. If you're developing a client/server application, try to reduce the amount of data flowing between the client and server wherever possible. See the "General tips" and "Distributed processing tips" sections for further information.
- **Report within a transaction.** It's never a good idea to run reports inside transactions, whether the report is run locally or remotely. The only exception to this rule is when the report actually modifies data. Even in that case, however, remember to keep the transaction as short as possible. For additional transaction suggestions, see the "General tips" section.

Index

—D—

—E—

—F—

—H—

—I—

—S—

—T—

—U—

—V—

—W—